WITHDRAWN

Freud's Rules of Dream Interpretation

Freud's Rules
of
Dream Interpretation

Alexander Grinstein, M.D.

INTERNATIONAL UNIVERSITIES PRESS, INC.

Madison   Connecticut

Library of Congress Cataloging in Publication Data

Grinstein, Alexander.
    Freud's rules of dream interpretation.

    Bibliography: p.
    Includes index.
    1. Dreams. 2. Psychotherapy. 3. Freud, Sigmund, 1856-1939. I. Title. [DNLM: 1. Dreams. 2. Psychoanalytic interpretation. WM 460.5.D8 G868f]
RC489.D74074 1983   616.89'14   83-12952
ISBN 0-8236-2035-2

Fourth Printing, 1988

Grateful acknowledgment is made to the following publishers for permission to use material from:
    The Standard Edition of the Complete Psychological Works of Sigmund Freud, translated and edited by James Strachey, Sigmund Freud Copyrights Ltd., The Institute of Psycho-Analysis and The Hogarth Press ltd. *The Interpretation of Dreams*, by Sigmund Freud, translated from the German and edited by James Strachey, George Allen & Unwin Ltd., London. Published in the United States by Basic Books, Inc., New York, and in Canada by Avon Books Inc., New York, by arrangement with George Allen & Unwin Ltd. and The Hogarth Press. *On Dreams*, by Sigmund Freud, translated by James Strachey, copyright 1952 by W.W. Norton & Company, Inc., New York. *Introductory Lectures on Psycho-Analysis*, by Sigmund Freud, George Allen & Unwin Ltd., London. Published in the United States by W.W. Norton & Company, Inc., New York. *New Introductory Lectures on Psycho-Analysis*, by Sigmund Freud, The Hogarth Press, London. Published in the United States and Canada by W.W. Norton & Company, Inc., New York. *Delusions and Dreams in Jensen's "Gradiva"* by Sigmund Freud, George Allen & Unwin, Ltd., London. *Beyond the Pleasure Principle*, by Sigmund Freud, The Hogarth Press, London. Published in the United States by W.W. Norton & Co., New York. *Inhibitions, Symptoms and Anxiety*, by Sigmund Freud, The Hogarth Press, London. Published in the United States by W.W. Norton & Co., New York. *Group Psychology and the Analysis of the Ego*, by Sigmund Freud, The Hogarth Press, London. Published in the United States by W.W. Norton & Co., New York.
    Dreams in Folklore, by Sigmund Freud & D.E. Oppenheim, International Universities Press, Inc., New York.
    The Dream in Clinical Practice, edited by J.M. Natterson, Jason Aronson, Inc., New York.
    The Pychoanalytic Reader, edited by R. Fliess, International Universities Press, Inc.
    The Analysis of the Self: A Systematic Approach to the Psychoanalytic Treatment of Narcissistic Personality by H. Kohut, International Universities Press, Inc., New York.
    The Restoration of the Self, by H. Kohut, International Universities Press, Inc., New York.
    Dream Analysis, by E.F. Sharpe, The Hogarth Press, London. Published in the United States, its dependencies and the Philippine Islands by Brunner/Mazel, Inc., New York.
    Clinical Papers and Essays on Psycho-Analysis, by Karl Abraham, The Hogarth Press, London. Published in the United States, its dependencies and the Philippine Islands by Brunner/Mazel, Inc., New York.
    Collected Papers, Vol. 1, by Sigmund Freud, Authorized Translation under the supervision of Joan Riviere. Published by Basic Books, Inc. by arrangement with The Hogarth Press Ltd. and The Institute of Psycho-Analysis, London. Reprinted by Permission. *Collected Papers*, Vol. 2, by Sigmund Freud, Authorized Translation under the supervision of Joan Published by Basic Books, Inc. by arrangement with The Hogarth Press Ltd. and The Institute of Psycho-Analysis, London. Reprinted by permission. *Collected Papers*, Vol. 3, by Sigmund Freud, Authorized Translation by Alix and James Strachey. Published by Basic Books, Inc. by arrangement with The Hogarth Press Ltd. and The Institute of Psycho-Analysis, London. Reprinted by permission. *Collected Papers*, Vol. 4, by Sigmund Freud, Authorized Translation under the supervision of Joan Riviere. Published by Basic Books, Inc. by arrangement with The Hogarth Press Ltd. and The Institute of Psycho-Analysis, London. Reprinted by permission. *Collected Papers*, Vol. 5, by Sigmund Freud, Edited by James Strachey. Published by Basic Books, Inc. by arrangement with The Hogarth Press Ltd. and The Institute of Psycho-Analysis, London. Reprinted by permission.

Manufactured in the United States of America

We are such stuff
As dreams are made on . . . .
The Tempest, Act IV.

Contents

Preface

The understanding of a patient's dreams may be considered a touchstone of psychotherapy. Dreams provide an important vehicle of communication between the patient and the therapist revealing more than the patient can say directly, or may even be aware of. They give important information about the patient's current problems, his character structure, his mental and bodily state, his personal history and fantasy life. They reveal a great deal about his conflicts: real and internal, those of the present and those leading back to his early life. Dreams indicate a good deal about the relative strength of his ego, superego, and id and their relationship to each other. They provide valuable information about the nature of the transference and about the patient's defenses. In addition, they indicate to the therapist whether his interpretations or reconstructions are accurate or have missed the point, whether the therapy is progressing or whether the patient is in a state of resistance.

Yet despite the importance of understanding dreams, in well over thirty years of teaching and supervision I have found that students and even experienced clinicians are often baffled, sometimes to the point of panic, whenever dream material is presented by their patients. It is my impression, one confirmed by the opinion of others, that a systematic presentation of basic rules and suggestions regarding dream interpretation, collated from the Freudian corpus, would be of great value to therapists in their work with dreams.

The importance of providing such an instrument cannot be overestimated. Some psychotherapists have an uncanny or intuitive talent for understanding dreams, for being empathic with patients and their dream material, and have the ability to interpret some essentials of the dream content to their patients. Others, not knowing what to do with dreams, become frustrated when their patients present such material. They either ignore the dream altogether or utilize *ad hoc* interpretations based on their own ideas that carry them far afield from what the patient is trying to communicate. The resultant misunderstanding leads the therapist, in his genuine interest in helping his patient, to seek other, "quicker" methods of therapy that may dispense with the interpretation of dreams altogether or deal with them only partially. Often, as a result, some of the patient's basic problems are not dealt with because they are not sufficiently understood.

This book does not presume to supplant other excellent books on the subject of dream interpretation. Nor is it intended to be a compendium or review of the extensive literature on the subject of dream interpretation and collateral studies. The bibliography has been enlarged to include a number of books and articles that are relevant to the material contained in this work. It must be emphasized, however, that these references are by no means all-inclusive, nor are they judgmental in any way. This book does not deal with theories of dream formation, dream interpretation, the electrophysiology of dreams, or the relationship of dreams to various sleep states.

All dreams used for illustrative purposes here are deliberately presented in isolation from complete case presentations and from a full analysis of all their determinants and dynamics. They are used only to illustrate specific points. The author is fully aware that in each instance there are multiple significances and determinants. Some of these are discussed in connection with the various examples; at other times these have been purposefully omitted in order to focus on a specific point.

Acknowledgments

I am grateful to my patients and the candidates of the Michigan Psychoanalytic Institute for providing me the wealth of clinical material from which I have learned so much and which I have been able to utilize in this book. I also want to express my appreciation to my colleagues of the Michigan Psychoanalytic Society and the Michigan Association for Psychoanalysis, with whom I have shared many practical and technical discussions about dreams. In addition, I want to thank Mrs. Frances Shepherd, Administrative Director of the Michigan Psychoanalytic Institute, for making the facilities of the Ira Miller Memorial Library readily accessible to me. I want to acknowledge the help of Glenn E. Miller, Librarian, The Chicago Institute for Psychoanalysis; the professional staff at the New York Psychoanalytic Institute Library; and the libraries of Wayne State University, Detroit, Michigan. The reference librarians and staff members at Baldwin Public Library, Birmingham, Michigan, also deserve special acknowledgment. I want to thank Mark Paterson and John Charlton, whose advice and cooperation greatly facilitated the matter of obtaining permission from various publishers to quote from the writings of Sigmund Freud.

I especially want to thank Richard F. Sterba, M.D., for

Acknowledgments

encouraging me to write this book and for his kindness in taking the time to read and comment on a draft of the manuscript. I am grateful to Michael Farrin for his work in editing the manuscript in preparation for publication.

I am particularly grateful to Mrs. Jacqueline Olivanti for her conscientious diligence and unwavering dedication to the innumerable labors involved in connection with this project from its very inception to its ultimate completion.

And finally, I want to thank my wife, Adele, helpmate throughout the years, whose continued support and encouragement in this work, as in all the others, has been invaluable. My appreciation for her very generous help, her many personal sacrifices, her comments and suggestions about the material, as well as her devoted assistance in editing this manuscript, cannot be fully expressed.

Alexander Grinstein, M.D.
Birmingham, Michigan

Chapter One

Beginning Work with Dreams

This book is primarily concerned with the use of the dream in psychoanalytic practice or in dynamically oriented psychotherapy. It is important to emphasize that although dreams are a necessary and important adjunct in therapy, they should always be viewed in the context of the total therapeutic situation.

Dreams appear in the various stages of an analysis or in psychotherapy as associations within the general context or concatenation of other associations. As Freud points out, "It is only too easy to forget that a dream is as a rule merely a thought like any other, made possible by a relaxation of the censorship and by unconscious reinforcement, and distorted by the operation of the censorship and by unconscious revision" (1923a, p. 112). Yet because of their particular nature dreams must be handled in accordance with certain technical considerations which we will discuss in the course of this book. It must be emphasized, however, that in the consideration of any dream the requirements of the therapeutic situation at the time will determine not only the level of interpretation but also whether the dream is to be used at all. Freud clearly stressed that "dream-interpretation should not be pursued in analytic treatment as an art for its own sake, but that its handling should be subject to those technical rules that govern the conduct of the treatment as a whole" (1911, p. 94).

In dealing with dream material and associations, the general rules applicable to all material to which one listens are relevant. It is essential that the therapist keep his attention suspended, listening passively, and not attempt to concentrate on any particular element or association. The therapist does not put his "powers of reflection into action" (1933, p. 10). In this state of hovering attention, the therapist allows his own thoughts and associations to pass into his consciousness while he listens to what his patient is saying and observes his reactions. This is one of the most difficult tasks for many therapists, especially since at times they may feel guilty about their own thoughts or reactions to the patient's material.

Freud used his own associations to his patients' dreams to help him understand what the patient was saying (1900, pp. 285–289, 305, 326–327). Reik (1949) and others recommended that therapists use their own thoughts and associations as an aid to understanding patients' material. While I do not believe that as a general practice the therapist's own reactions and associations should be a substitute for those of the patient, I do, nonetheless, recommend that the therapist be aware of his own thoughts and feelings. The main reason for this suggestion is that the therapist's unconscious often picks up and reacts to the patient's conscious or unconscious attempt to elicit some countertransference response. Frequently the therapist's awareness of his own feelings and thoughts is tremendously valuable, as it helps him understand the underlying determinants of a patient's dream that might be lost if he were actively trying to follow the material directly. By focusing his attention on the details, the therapist may be unaware of or overlook his own reactions: antagonism, disgust, irritation, frustration, sexual arousal, etc. Actually, this may be the very material that is important, as it may reveal how the patient is repeating the dynamics of his early

2

experiences by evoking countertransference reactions in the therapist.

Freud summarized the general orientation of the therapist in listening to dream material as follows:

> 1. We must not concern ourselves with what the dream *appears* to tell us, whether it is intelligible or absurd, clear or confused, since it cannot possibly be the unconscious material we are in search of.
>
> 2. We must restrict our work to calling up the substitutive ideas for each element, we must not reflect about them, or consider whether they contain anything relevant, and we must not trouble ourselves with how far they diverge from the dream-element.
>
> 3. We must wait till the concealed unconscious material we are in search of emerges of its own accord. [1916–1917, p. 114]

Freud clearly distinguishes between the patient's associations and the latent dream thoughts. He indicates that

> the associations to the dream are not yet the latent dream-thoughts. The latter are contained in the associations like an alkali in the mother-liquor, but yet not quite completely contained in them. On the one hand, the associations give us far more than we need for formulating the latent dream-thoughts—namely all the explanations, transitions, and connections which the patient's intellect is bound to produce in the course of his approach to the dream-thoughts. On the other hand, an association often comes to a stop precisely before the genuine dream-thought: it has only come near to it and has only had contact with it through allusions. [1933, p. 12]

The therapist's task is to help the patient bring up associations to the various dream elements, to facilitate their flow by encouragement, by appropriate questions, and by dealing with the patient's resistances and transferences. From this body of material, the therapist seeks to understand the latent dream thoughts behind the associations, often by seeing

3

the thread or common denominator that links them into a cohesive unity. This orientation does not differ from the therapist's usual task of understanding the treatment situation at the time.

When a patient presents a dream for the first time, the therapist has the opportunity to inquire about the patient's knowledge about dreams. Obviously, whatever instructions, explanations, or interpretations are given to the patient will depend upon his degree of sophistication. Some people who have had a certain degree of training feel that they should be able to interpret their own dreams and if they are not able to do so they are failures or stupid or not worthwhile. In these instances we make it clear that we are really only concerned with their associations to the various elements of the dream, and not in their ability to interpret or understand the dream.

Sometimes patients who have had professional training or who have a degree of sophistication about dreams tend to report their dreams in a summary fashion, omitting many of the details and complexities of the manifest dream story. Under these circumstances the therapist may simply ask the patient to tell the dream in detail, and then inquire about the specific elements.

If the patient is uninformed about dreams, or only moderately informed, we may tell him that the dream that he remembers (i.e., the manifest dream) is like a puzzle, a rebus, or a message in code. To solve or understand the dream, we must divide it into pieces like a jigsaw puzzle and then see what comes to his mind with regard to each of the various pieces or *elements,* as they are called. The rationale of this technical suggestion is to undo the process of secondary revision (or secondary elaboration) that is so characteristic of the dream-work. It provides the patient an opportunity to bring up associations and reactions which would not be possible if the dream were viewed as a unity. There are exceptions to this rule, however, and these will be taken up later.

Freud provides the therapist a number of concrete tech-

nical suggestions for dealing with the manifest content of a
dream, both early in therapy and later on:

> [1] One can . . . proceed chronologically and get the dreamer
> to bring up his associations to the elements of the dream in
> the order in which those elements occurred in his account of
> the dream. This is the original, classical method, which I still
> regard as the best if one is analysing one's own dreams. [1923a,
> p. 109]

This method is particularly helpful if the patient does not
seem to be able to say anything spontaneously, or requests
some guidance as to where to begin. The therapist may then
suggest to the patient, "Why don't we begin at the beginning." This suggestion is actually ego-syntonic, as people are
used to beginning tasks and learning new skills at the beginning. They do it with books and academic courses and, as
they are beginning their analysis, it is an entirely "natural"
place to start.

The question may be raised whether suggesting to the
patient where to begin shapes the transference, and is too
dictatorial or too directive, thereby establishing a submissive
or dependent attitude toward the therapist at the beginning
of the therapy. While such a criticism may be valid, the
ultimate effect of the suggestion depends in part on the manner in which it is posed, whether it is said at the very outset
or only after the patient has had an opportunity to reflect and
to choose for himself where to begin. Presented as an open
suggestion, as one possible point of departure, especially if
the patient at the beginning of therapy wants or needs some
guidance, it provides the patient the option of beginning with
the first element or following one of the other possibilities
we will subsequently discuss.

The therapist's suggestion to begin at the beginning
may also help the patient establish some modicum of order
in an area that soon becomes pervaded by many associations
and often by a good deal of confusion. Whatever is done along
these lines, however, should certainly not be done in a way

that could give the patient the impression that the therapist is commanding him to proceed in a certain fashion; rather, it should be made evident that he is simply offering him one of several possible alternatives.

Frequently patients will introduce a dream by describing its locale or setting. Turning one's attention to this scene immediately provides the therapist important information about his patient's background or life situation. Thus, "In the dream, I was in the house where I lived when I was five years old. It was before we moved to the house on 'X' street." Or, "The dream relates to a time when I lived in a different city." Or, from the present reality, "In the dream, I was at my office" or "my house." "In my dream, I was in my bedroom." Or, "In my dream, I was in somebody else's bedroom."

Sometimes the patient may say, "I was in this building" or "in this room," etc. The emphasis here may be on the word "this" which identifies the locale as referring to the place where he is at the present time, i.e., the analyst's office building or consultation room. At times this identification is confirmed by the description of furniture or objects the patient has seen in the analyst's office.

Very early in his analysis, a patient reported a moderately lengthy dream in which he was standing near an old, rough, weatherbeaten, wooden fence. When asked why he was standing by such a fence, his first response was, "I don't know." But then, after a brief period of reflection, he said with some feeling, "That fence reminds me of a fence at my grandfather's farm where I used to go when I was a child. It was near where they kept pigs and I remember—I must have been five or six years old at the time—they were castrating the pigs and the pigs were squealing in pain. My grandfather had a knife that he used to sharpen on one of those large round grinding stones that spun around, that he worked with his feet. They kept it in a corner by that fence." It will readily be seen that the very first element of this dream referred to an extremely significant event in his childhood, one which was to influence his subsequent psychological development. Moreover, his associations revealed his anticipation that he would be treated by his analyst just as the pigs were by his grandfather. From a technical standpoint, it is important to point out that this material was obtained by simply inquiring about the first element of his early dream. It is possible, of course, that one of the other elements may have led to the same genetic material, or to the same anxieties in the transference.

> [2] . . . one can . . . start the work of interpretation from some one particular element of the dream which one picks out from the middle of it. For instance, one can choose the most striking piece of it, or the piece which shows the greatest clarity or sensory intensity. [1923a, p. 109]

In another connection Freud adds: "for we know that he will find it particularly easy to get associations to these" (1933, p. 11).

Freud's suggestion about picking out an element from the middle of a dream leaves the therapist a good deal of latitude in the event the patient does not turn to a particular element on his own. Here the therapist's experience, knowledge, and empathy will serve him in good stead. His intuitive feeling that certain elements may be especially important in the beginning stages of the analysis will prompt him to inquire about them. Those elements dealing obviously with the treatment, especially early manifestations of resistance or transference that could become a problem, may certainly be selected without impeding the emergence of other important material.

Freud's example of picking an element that is particularly striking, clear, or vivid provides another useful point of departure for associations, as such elements are usually greatly overdetermined. The clarity or vividness of a particular element is in itself often sufficient to stimulate the patient's desire to understand it. Questions directed to the patient about such elements often correspond to what has

7

impressed him and are therefore both ego-syntonic and relevant to an area he wants help with. Exploring the associations to such an element is an opportunity to facilitate a good working alliance. When, as is often the case, the intense clarity of a particular element (e.g., a color) is due to a great deal of condensation, many associations will immediately come into the patient's mind. We will return to this later.

We must caution the therapist, however, that in some instances very intense feelings are connected with especially clear or vivid elements in the dream. These feelings may be too disturbing for the patient to deal with at the time and, if this is so, the dreamer will shy away from pursuing his associations to this particular element. Any attempt to urge him to deal with these feelings will then prove counterproductive. The patient may feel that he is being pushed to deal with something that he is not able to, and that the therapist does not understand him. He may feel that his dream has revealed too much, and that the therapy poses a serious threat to his equilibrium. Fearing that the treatment may be worse than the disease, the patient's anxiety may bring about an increase in his resistance, and may bring about a cessation of the therapy before it has even begun. In these instances, one must deal with the patient's defenses and resistances before he can handle the anxiety-producing material. This may be the case when dealing with nightmares before the working alliance is sufficiently well established.

Among other dream elements the therapist may select for inquiry are, by contrast, those that are particularly vague or indistinct (1901a, p. 654). While these elements too may be nodal points around which many trains of thought converge, they are often made vague because of resistances that interfere with their openness or clarity. As a result, even though the therapist may choose to ask about them, the resistances responsible for their vagueness may extend to any attempt to understand them.

Freud suggests that

> [3] one can start off from some spoken words in the dream, in the expectation that they will lead to the recollection of some spoken words in waking life. [1923a, p. 109]

In another context, he emphasizes this point as follows:

> When anything in a dream has the character of direct speech, that is to say, when it is said or heard and not merely thought (and it is easy as a rule to make the distinction with certainty), then it is derived from something actually spoken in waking life—though, to be sure, this something is merely treated as raw material and may be cut up and slightly altered and, more especially, divorced from its context. [1900, pp. 183–184]

Inasmuch as speeches in a dream often refer, with modifications, to something that was said, heard, or read in the dream day, i.e., the day prior to the dream, they provide an excellent starting point for analytic investigation. The therapist should distinguish whether the speech itself or parts of it are important, or whether the particular incident or circumstances at the point in the dream at which the patient heard the remark are significant.

Another of Freud's suggestions for work on early dreams is the following:

> [4] . . . one can begin by entirely disregarding the manifest content and instead ask the dreamer what events of the previous day are associated in his mind with the dream he has just described. [1923a, p. 109]

The rationale for this is that "in every dream it is possible to find a point of contact with the experiences of the previous day" (1900, p. 165). Freud stresses that "a dream is invariably related to the events of the day before the dream" (1907, p. 57) but later modifies this: "experience," he writes, "has taught us that *almost* every dream [italics added] includes the remains of a memory or an allusion to some event (or often to several events) of the day before the dream, and, if we follow these connections, we often arrive with one blow at the transition from the apparently far remote dream-world to the real life of the patient" (1933, p. 11). He notes also, however, that often the connection of the manifest dream with some impression of the dream day "is so trivial, insignificant and unmemorable, that it is only with difficulty" that it can be recalled (1901a, p. 656).

Actually, even the most trivial reference, inasmuch as it has been brought into the dream at all, is significant in that it provides a point of departure for a chain of associations containing specific information. The patient may be informed of this fact in order to help him to get started working on the dream. The therapist can ask the patient directly, as Freud suggests, what in the manifest dream seems connected with an event of the previous day. Among the allusions to the dream day are specific references to material dealing directly or indirectly with the patient's reality conflicts, problems with business or professional activities, his marital situation, and relationships to love objects (children, parents, relatives, friends) or associates.

This technical device is very advantageous, as Freud indicates, because it immediately brings material from the world of reality into the treatment situation and gives the therapist a clear picture of what is going on in the patient's life. It helps eliminate the tendency for intellectualization, an especially common defense.

There is some danger, however, in using this technical suggestion to inquire about possible day residues. Although something in the dream day is associated with one or more dream elements, the patient may not be concerned with such connections, as these may not necessarily represent the main thrust of either the dream or the treatment at that time.

If over a lengthy period of time the patient consistently omits any reference to day residues or to stimuli in the dream day when discussing his dreams, the therapist should consider the possibility that the patient is suppressing something important in reality and should attempt to understand why the patient is holding back (Sharpe, 1937).

Freud writes:

> The fact that the manifest content of dreams is influenced by the analytic treatment stands in no need of proof. It follows from our knowledge that dreams take their start from waking life and work over material derived from it. Occurrences during analytic treatment are of course among the impressions of waking life and soon become some of the most powerful of these. So it is not to be wondered at that patients should dream of things which the analyst has discussed with them and of which he has aroused expectations in them. . . .
>
> . . . .the dreamer might quite well have reacted to the physician's remarks . . . whether . . . in harmony with those remarks or in opposition to them. [1923a, p. 114]

Being able to see some element in the manifest dream that refers to the previous treatment session is a great help in the therapy. Such elements in the manifest dream and the patient's associations to them usually will reveal direct as well as subtle references to the patient's transference resistances or defenses, thus providing an important means of communication between patient and therapist. This knowledge also helps them connect each session with the preceding one, revealing in great detail the continuity that exists between sessions. It thus provides both therapist and patient the opportunity to understand fully the dialogue and the interaction between them, often expressing reactions to the analyst's interpretation of which the patient may not have been fully aware. The therapist must be continually alert to such expressions. Failure to pick up material, especially if it alludes to negative feelings toward the therapist or disagreement with his comments, may be experienced by the patient as a criticism or a rejection, analagous in many instances to one participant in a dialogue ignoring or not responding to the remarks of the other.

Of special importance in the day residue material in the

initial stages of therapy are early manifestations of concern, hesitation, and anxiety about beginning treatment, and transference material dealing with the patient's feelings about the therapist.

As the therapy progresses, the patient's dreams reveal the themes he is dealing with at the time, and other day residues become subservient to these basic themes. Further discussion of day residues will be found in chapter 4.

Another technical device suggested by Freud which may be used, even early in treatment, is the following:

[5] If the first account given me by a patient of a dream is too hard to follow I ask him to repeat it. In doing so he rarely uses the same words. But the parts of the dream which he describes in different terms are by that fact revealed to me as the weak spot in the dream's disguise: they serve my purpose just as Hagen's was served by the embroidered mark on Siegfried's cloak. That is the point at which the interpretation of the dream can be started. My request to the patient to repeat his account of the dream has warned him that I was proposing to take special pains in solving it; under pressure of the resistance, therefore, he hastily covers the weak spots in the dream's disguise by replacing any expressions that threaten to betray its meaning by other less revealing ones. In this way he draws my attention to the expression which he has dropped out. The trouble taken by the dreamer in preventing the solution of the dream gives me a basis for estimating the care with which its cloak has been woven. [1900, p. 515]

The points at which his reproduction is defective owing to changes, and often owing to omissions as well, are the points which we fasten upon, because the inaccuracy guarantees a connection with the complex and promises the best approach to the secret meaning of the dreams. [1906, p. 111]

While one may pursue this technical suggestion to elicit certain details of the dream, its use is particularly impressive when the dream is composed of several sections. When one asks the dreamer to repeat such a dream, he rather conspicuously omits one of the sections. Under those circumstances it is easy to draw the dreamer's attention to his omission and then try to discover why he omitted that particular part.

Despite its value, we would not advise using this technical recommendation in the early stages of the analysis. If it is used at all, it is better to reserve it for patients who are already familiar with dream interpretation, or for therapeutic situations where many problems of transference and defense have already been dealt with, and where a good solid working alliance has been established. There are several reasons for this note of caution. Asking a patient to repeat a dream and then calling his attention to the parts that he omitted may make him feel that the therapist is being critical of him, or, what is even worse, may make him feel that he has been tricked or manipulated into revealing something that he wanted to conceal. Furthermore, it shifts the emphasis of exploration away from the patient's feelings, his resistances, and the problems in the transference, all of which can certainly be ascertained from the patient's initial comments and from the part of the dream that he did recall. If too much attention is focused on the dream and on the part omitted when the patient repeated it, his other methods of communication may be overlooked. As a result, this technical suggestion may serve to do exactly the opposite of what is intended.

There is another point. Sometimes rather than being an indication of resistance, it is actually helpful in understanding the main theme of the dream if the patient simplifies the dream when repeating it by omitting inessential details. Under such circumstances, the therapist would be advised to deal with what the patient has related, instead of turning to what the patient has omitted (1911, pp. 92–93).

Another technical suggestion given by Freud for beginning work with dreams is the following:

[6] It very frequently comes about that, to begin with, a portion of a dream is omitted and added afterwards as an adden-

dum. This is to be regarded as an attempt to forget that portion. Experience shows that it is that particular piece which is the most important; there was a greater resistance, we suppose, in the path of communicating it than the other parts of the dream. [1933, p. 14]

It not infrequently happens that in the middle of the work of interpretation an omitted portion of the dream comes to light and is described as having been forgotten till that moment. Now a part of a dream that has been rescued from oblivion in this way is invariably the most important part; it always lies on the shortest road to the dream's solution and has for that reason been exposed to resistance more than any other part. [1900, pp. 518–519; see also 1905a, p. 100n2.] And that, in all probability, must have been the only reason for its having been forgotten, that is, for its having been once more suppressed. [1901a, p. 677]

When a fragment of a dream is recalled in this manner, the other parts of the dream may be temporarily disregarded and attention focused upon this recollected portion. What has happened is that some resistance has been overcome during the course of the session, making it possible for the missing piece of the dream to emerge. Its appearance is then entirely ego-syntonic, and by remembering it the patient is actually inviting its exploration. It is appropriate, therefore, to disregard the other parts of the dream temporarily, to attend to the recalled portion and connect the associations surrounding this previously "forgotten" manifest dream with what is going on in the treatment, or with the other part of the dream.

A man with strong obsessive homosexual fantasies, though not a manifest homosexual, was talking about these feelings in connection with a dream that dealt with his wanting to fondle the buttocks and penis of a boy he had seen the previous day. His associations then led to his fear of men, authority figures, and his analyst as a transference object, who, he felt, would reprimand him for certain sloppiness in his work. When his fear that his therapist would be critical of him was discussed, he suddenly recalled another fragment of a dream he had had the previous night. In this dream fragment, he is fondling the breasts of a very attractive woman and is sexually very aroused. This part of the dream had been completely repressed and was only able to emerge into consciousness when he felt that his therapist would not be punitive with him for his heterosexual impulses which he experienced as forbidden. He had utilized homosexuality in the remembered first part of the dream as a defense against the more frightening and forbidden heterosexual oedipal impulses.

Sometimes a patient remembers the repressed fragment at the very end of the session when there is no opportunity to discuss it, or after he has left his appointment. In the first instance, when the patient has already reported the dream fragment, the analyst would not deal with it at the beginning of the next appointment unless the patient brought it up. In the second case, when the patient brings up a dream fragment that he recalled after he left the previous session, it would be preferable to deal with the current material before returning to the repressed fragment. Chances are that the new material would encompass the content of the emerged fragment. There are, of course, those patients who characteristically save important material to the very end of their session when there is no opportunity to deal with it. In those instances one must deal with the repetitive pattern of behavior before one can explore the recollected fragments with any feeling of conviction, as the same resistances that were responsible for the behavior will prevent any meaningful integration of the interpretation.

Freud's final suggestion for dealing with dreams is applicable at the very beginning of treatment as well as later on:

[7] If the dreamer is already familiar with the technique of interpretation, avoid giving him any instructions and leave it to him to decide with which associations to the dream he shall begin. [1923a, p. 109]

In actual practice, this is probably the most frequently used technique, as it allows the patient the greatest amount of flexibility and spontaneity. Beginning with the very first dream in analysis, as well as with any dream thereafter, it is a good policy to wait a bit to see what the patient brings up, in direct relationship to a dream element or otherwise, before making any comments or suggestions. The patient may appear to leave the dream altogether and go on to a discussion of matters that are seemingly unrelated. He may be totally unaware that he is really providing associations to the dream. It is then possible for the therapist to point out to the patient the connections between his spontaneous associations and the various specific dream elements.

It is important to bear in mind that a continuum exists between the reported dream and all of the patient's associations in the course of a given session. The patient may relate a dream along with a variety of other material, all of which is connected in some way. Frequently the patient's associations may precede his telling of a dream and may be in the form of direct statements or as a question. Sometimes the associations take the form of actions. Thus, a patient coming late for his appointment gave various plausible reasons for his tardiness. He then related a dream that he had had the night before in which he is late for some business engagement. It was evident that the dream was connected with his being late for his appointment. In his dream, the patient had already "planned" to be late for his session the next day. It was pointed out to the patient that he had anticipated being late for his appointment, a business engagement in his dream. After some reflection, he confirmed that his reluctance to come to his appointment was connected with his realization that he would have to reveal some very embarrassing material to the analyst.

As one looks at Freud's different suggestions as to where to begin working with a dream, one quickly realizes that they can all be used at different times and in combination. "It makes no difference," Freud wrote, "by which of these methods we approach the associations we are in search of" (1933, p. 11).

The reason it does not much matter which of these methods one uses is that "as a rule a single dream-thought is represented by more than one dream-element" (1901a, p. 653). The therapist is therefore guided to a great extent by what seems to be most appropriate for the patient at the particular time. This depends on his state of sophistication, what he brings up spontaneously, what is going on in his current life situation and what problems he is working on in connection with transference, resistance, defenses, etc.

The therapist should bear in mind, however, that

> a number of dreams which occur during analyses are untranslatable even though they do not actually make much show of the resistance that is there. They represent free renderings of the latent dream-thoughts behind them and are comparable to successful creative writings which have been artistically worked over and in which the basic themes are still recognizable though they have been subjected to any amount of rearrangement and transformation. Dreams of this kind serve in the treatment as an introduction to thoughts and memories of the dreamer without their own actual content coming into account. [1923a, pp. 110–111]

The writing down of dreams. Soon after the subject of dreams is brought up in an analysis, patients will often ask whether they should write down their dreams to help them remember them. Freud writes:

> we often find that a dreamer endeavors to prevent himself from forgetting his dreams by fixing them in writing immediately after waking up. We can tell him that that is no use. For the resistance from which he has extorted the preservation of the text of the dream will then be displaced on to its associations and will make the manifest dream inaccessible to interpretation. In view of these facts we need not feel surprised if a further increase in the resistance suppresses the

associations altogether and thus brings the interpretation of the dream to nothing. [1933, p. 14]

Some psycho-analysts, even, in giving the patient instructions to write down every dream immediately upon waking, seem not to rely consistently enough upon their knowledge of the conditions of dream-formation. In therapeutic work this rule is superfluous; and patients are glad to make use of it to disturb their sleep and to display great zeal where it can serve no useful purpose. For even if the text of a dream is in this way laboriously rescued from oblivion, it is easy enough to convince oneself that nothing has been achieved for the patient. Associations will not come to the text, and the result is the same as if the dream had not been preserved. No doubt the doctor has acquired some knowledge which he would not have done otherwise. But it is not the same thing whether the analyst knows something or the patient knows it . . . . [1911, pp. 95–96]

Abraham (1913) relates a case of a woman who was unable to remember a frightening recurrent dream; even though she was advised against it, she decided to write it down. Having overslept, she came late for her appointment the next day bringing the piece of paper with her, which she had not looked at since writing down the dream, and found that she had written, "Write down the dream against agreement."

Despite Freud's admonition to the contrary, some analysts have recommended that borderline patients write down their dreams so that they may be used as a starting point for discussion. Lorand (1956), for example, suggested that "the material thus obtained may yield clues which in themselves will help analyze this particular form of resistance" (p. 122). But even in these instances, I would question the basic wisdom of such a technical intervention, as there are many matters that can be taken up with these patients without the imposition of additional suggestions. Such advice may carry the connotation of an authoritative directive and preempt the study of transference, resistances, and defenses. Basically, we must remember that it is the patient and not the dream that we are trying to analyze.

Initially, it is better if no instructions at all are given regarding the writing down of dreams. The analyst should wait and see what the patient does on his own. Some patients never ask and never write down their dreams. Thus, to have given them any instructions would have been superfluous and could have colored the emerging transference situation. Other patients, as we said earlier, may ask outright if dreams are important and if they should write them down in order to remember them and bring them to their next session for discussion. Such a direct question provides the therapist the opportunity to advise him against doing it and to briefly explain the reasons. If the patient brings in dreams he has written down (or tape recorded) despite the therapist's advice, then the reasons for the patient's behavior must be understood. It is important to learn what purpose the dream served the patient, and what writing it down meant apart from communicating the specific manifest dream content. Is the patient, by his wish to preserve the dream, trying to placate the analyst or trying to undo the wish to conceal something, or is his writing down the dream, despite the therapist's recommendation, a way of expressing his defiance or rebellion? At times, the writing down or recording of dreams serves to control the patient's anxiety over what might spontaneously emerge during the session if he did not have something to bring in as an agenda.

Lipschutz (1954) describes a patient who, despite his advice to the contrary, wrote down his dreams on small 4 × 6 inch pieces of paper. He was able to demonstrate that the dreams were a fecal product and that the slips of paper upon which they were written were equated with toilet paper. The patient's dream production thus had the significance of a fecal gift to the analyst.

One married man jotted down a dream to help him

remember what it was. He wrote: "hi fi." Presumably, it was a note for him to call the serviceman about their high fidelity stereo equipment. Actually, he unconsciously hoped his wife would find the note to reassure her of his fidelity, even though he was having an affair. Another patient had a dream in which he was having an affair with X. Upon awakening, he took a slip of paper and wrote: "I am having an affair with X," and then wrote down the details of his dream. He put the slip of paper in his pocket and "forgot" about it. His wife went through his pockets prior to sending his suit to the cleaners and found the confession. The writing down of the dream served as a confession of his relationship with X, evoking a confrontation with his wife and a condemnation of his activity. The transference aspects of his action were apparent, as he was ready to blame the analyst for his slip. If he had not been in analysis, he rationalized, he would not have written down his dream.

One patient insisted on bringing in and playing a tape recording that he had made the night before of a dream that he had had. In this instance it was not so much the content of the dream that was important as his narcissistic pride in having the analyst listen to his production.

Chapter Two

General Considerations

When working with dreams, the therapist must continually keep in mind all that goes on during the session in which the dream is reported, what he knows about the patient from previous sessions, and—especially—what material was dealt with in the session immediately preceding. "As so often happens with dream-interpretation during analysis," Freud writes, "the translation of the dream does not depend solely on the products of association but we have also to take into account the circumstances of its narration, the behavior of the dreamer before and after the analysis of the dream, as well as every remark or disclosure made by the dreamer at about the same time—during the same analytic session" (1913a, p. 272).

The therapist keeps his attention open to allow for such observations to "register." In this respect it is in no way different from what the therapist does at any other time. He observes whether the patient is on time, early, or late. He pays attention to the patient's casual remarks as he enters the office. He notes his affect and general demeanor. Does he comment on the weather (e.g., "It's cold outside") and then later in the session mention a dream in which someone is cold to him, and complain about the analytic climate or temperature in the course of his subsequent associations?

Does he smile and act friendly or scowl? One physician in analysis greeted his analyst on entering the office with a professional "How are you today?" He acted as though he were making rounds. As he comes in, does the patient look at the analyst or at the floor? What does he do with his hands, his feet? A woman, who had dreamed about her marriage, played with her wedding band—taking it off and putting it back on throughout her session. One patient, a surgeon, reached into his pocket during his appointment and noticed that he had brought a hemostat with him. Does the patient wear his rubbers into the office or leave them outside? If he doesn't wear rubbers or boots, does he wipe his feet, and, if so, does he do it outside or inside? How does the patient get on the couch and what position does he assume? Are the patient's legs crossed or spread wide apart? One man who loved to ride motorcycles kept his legs stiff and wide apart as though he were on one. Does the patient look tense in the position he assumes, or is he relaxed? Does he thrash about from side to side or curl up in a fetal position? Does he unbutton his collar and pull down his tie? Does he begin talking? If so, does his voice have its usual quality and tempo or is he hesitant and talking more slowly (or more rapidly)? Is he silent, and, if so, for how long? At what point does the patient tell the dream and what is the character of the language that he uses? And so on.

It should be noted that although a portion of the dream will be related to current treatment matters, the rest of the dream may not be and may forge ahead of where the patient is at the time, or what he may be ready or able to discuss. In the course of his associations, especially early in therapy, the patient may leave the dream altogether, or "take off" on some element that refers to a current reality situation. The patient may find it important to explain to the analyst what is going on in his life with regard to business and professional situations, and to give background material about his family, friends, or associates so that the therapist may better understand him. At the same time, the patient himself profits from the explanation, as it serves to clarify his own thoughts. Under these circumstances discussion of this material may temporarily take precedence over the exploration and understanding of a dream.

Only the material from the dream connected with what the patient is saying or which gives particular insight or impetus to the progress of the treatment need be discussed by the therapist. Otherwise, there is a danger of turning the psychotherapeutic relationship into one which will seem to the patient to be geared only to his dream-life and to the uncovering of archaic conflicts that have little or no relevance to the world of reality as he perceives it. Although the analyst may learn a great deal about the patient's unconscious conflicts, it may not be possible for him to interpret them to the patient in any way that would be meaningful in connection with his present-day life situation. In this connection Freud cautions that

> one must in general guard against displaying very special interest in the interpretation of dreams, or arousing an idea in the patient that the work would come to a standstill if he were to bring up no dreams; otherwise there is a danger of the resistance being directed to the production of dreams, with a consequent cessation of them. The patient must be brought to believe, on the contrary, that the analysis invariably finds material for its continuation, regardless of whether or no he brings up dreams or what amount of attention is devoted to them. [1911, pp. 92–93]

Altman (1969) has neatly summarized the dangers inherent in an exaggerated preoccupation with dreams, stating that such an attitude "converts the unreal to real and reduces the real to the unreal" (p. 70).

Freud's admonition against displaying a special interest in the interpretation of dreams in an analysis is of crucial importance. Yet it poses a problem for the beginner as well as for experienced clinicians who feel more comfortable about what is going on in the treatment if the patient brings in at least some dreams. Dreams are, of course, important and when they are reported by the patient and are understood, they provide a "royal road to the unconscious."

Yet too vigorous a pursuit of the patient's associations to various dream elements may inhibit the patient's free associations and create the atmosphere of a teacher-student quiz. One patient, when asked about a particular dream element, said, "I don't know if this is right, but it makes me think of. . . ." The patient had evidently concluded that there was a right or wrong answer to the analyst's question rather than regarding it as one posed to allow him to elaborate on his thoughts and feelings. In some instances, injudicious questions may enhance a patient's compulsivity and scrupulosity.

The analyst must realize at the very outset that *no* dream can be completely analyzed in the course of any given session. Any attempt to do so would disturb the analytic process and create totally unnecessary difficulties for patient and therapist. Moreover, Freud writes, "when the interpretation of a dream has been discovered, it is not always easy to decide whether it is a 'complete' one—that is, whether further preconscious thoughts may not also have found expression in the same dream. . . . It remains possible, though unproven; one must become accustomed to a dream being thus capable of having many meanings" (1925b, pp. 129–130). He indicates that "it is only rarely that a dream represents, or, as we might say, 'stages', a single thought: there are usually a number of them, a tissue of thoughts" (1907, p. 59).

Freud writes:

The amount of interpretation which can be achieved in one session should be taken as sufficient and it is not to be regarded as a loss if the content of the dream is not fully discovered. On the following day, the interpretation of the dream is not to be taken up again as a matter of course, until it has become evident that nothing else has meanwhile forced its way into the foreground of the patient's thoughts. Thus no exception in favour of an interrupted dream-interpretation is to be made to the rule that the first thing that comes into the patient's head is the first thing to be dealt with. If fresh dreams occur before the earlier ones have been disposed of, the more recent productions are to be attended to, and no uneasiness need be felt about neglecting the older ones. [1911, p. 92]

Despite this recommendation, it does happen that both patient and psychotherapist may be frustrated because all of the material suggested by the dream has not been adequately explored. This is especially true with patients or therapists whose expectations for quick cure or understanding are inordinately great or unrealistically ambitious. Freud indicates that if one does not take up all the material or understand it, it will reappear in other dreams the following day or soon after, either in the patient's associations or in another dream which essentially deals with the same subject. He writes: "It often happens, therefore, that the best way to complete the interpretation of a dream is to leave it and to devote one's attention to a new dream, which may contain the same material in a possibly more accessible form" (1911, p. 94).

In the actual work of dream interpretation in the course of analysis, one is seldom able to pursue a dream to the point of uncovering the underlying wish. Usually it is only over a period of time and when the patient has progressed to a point where his ego can deal with the underlying wishes that a dream can be fully interpreted. Sometimes, later in an analysis, there may be an occasion to return to an old dream, one that was not understood at the time the patient first reported it, and find that it is now clear in the light of subsequent material (1901b, p. 269; 1925b, p. 129).

Even when the analyst does not understand all the determinants of a specific dream, he must make sure that he takes up pressing or embarrassing material, such as early expressions of negative or erotic transference. Otherwise the patient may feel that the therapist, for reasons of a countertransference nature, is avoiding the subject and is unwilling to hear his communication. In that case, the material may reappear only briefly or will become either suppressed or repressed. The patient will not talk about it nor even allow himself to dream about it.

I have seen instances in which a candidate analyst has missed the expression of intense affectionate transference in a patient's dreams. After a number of sessions, the patient brings in dreams in which he is angry with someone who obviously represents the analyst. The candidate can recognize the negative transference but may not be able to see its connection with his having missed the patient's positive feelings.

There are patients who insist on perseverating from one session to the next, sometimes even for several sessions, on a given dream. They may do this despite a recommendation that it is unnecessary, that surface, current, or more recent material (including more recent dreams) should be attended to first. They may even justify their efforts on the basis that this is what occurs to them, that they feel that the dream is important, that they want to "work on it" and "get more out of it," etc. In these instances, it is often an indication that certain resistances are operating and the perseveration represents a means to avoid dealing with current problems, especially those of a reality or transference nature. Generally, such perseveration has an intellectual quality and the associations do not carry any emotional conviction.

This is not always the case, however. At times the perseveration serves the function of gradually approaching material that is painful or embarrassing. After a period of several sessions, a patient may reveal something that he has known but kept secret. If one returns to the dreams he has had during this period, or even the dream that he has wanted to "work on" with such perseverance, one may sometimes find that one or more elements in such a dream were connected with this particular revelation. The therapist, however, should not make a point of bringing the patient back to that dream, but should allow the connections to it to be made spontaneously by the patient. Otherwise, there is again the danger of too much emphasis being placed on the importance of dreams in the treatment.

Perhaps the single most important guideline to be followed by the therapist is to know what is going on in the treatment situation. Often the reported dream helps him to do this, as it highlights the material with which the patient is really concerned. Thus, it may come as a revelation that while the patient has been talking about some current reality difficulty, his dream deals with what is going on in the transference. The reverse, of course, may also occur.

In general, the approach in exploring dreams follows the basic principles of therapy. The therapist proceeds sequentially through the various layers of material from the surface down. He proceeds from less repressed material to more repressed or less ego-syntonic material. To do this the therapist must be keenly sensitive to what will be acceptable to the patient's ego at the time. He must deal appropriately with the patient's resistances and defenses using language that is nontechnical and not readily reduced to jargon or familiar but meaningless catch phrases. He follows recognizable themes, helping the patient understand that his current problems, expressed in a variety of ways (e.g., in his relationship to different people or situations), are part of a continuum, as there were similar or parallel situations in the past, and that the same dynamics are operative in the transference. Ultimately the therapist is able to help the patient trace the origins of these conflicts to their genetic antecedents.

Freud continues: "If the dreams become altogether too diffuse and voluminous, all hope of completely unravelling them should tacitly be given up from the start" (1911, p. 92). While it is true that one cannot "deal with" all the elements that such dreams refer to, the character rather than the content of the dreams themselves, as also the way the patient works with his dreams, may reveal a great deal about the patient and his problems. Some patients may flit from one dream element to another or from one subject to another in a chaotic manner without dealing in depth with anything. Often this is characterological; these people deal with many things in their lives in the same fashion. Generally they have a great deal of anxiety and their ego structures are infantile in character.

Some patients over lengthy periods of time have a pattern of bringing in voluminous dreams. There are a number of reasons for this. The recitation of lengthy dreams occupying the greater portion of the therapeutic session may be an expression of a major resistance against the therapy, or against the emergence of feelings toward the therapist which are threatening to the patient. Sometimes this behavior is an indication of negative transference, as it effectively prevents the analyst from saying anything. Sometimes such dreams and the recitation of their content may indicate the patient's unconscious wish to continue his sleep in the analytic session (see Lewin, 1953a).

Voluminous dreams may also have the unconscious meaning of urination, seen at times in patients who have been enuretics (see Michaels, 1941, 1955). They may signify an aggressive urinary spray, an anal barrage, or an explosive diarrhea. The manner in which such dreams are told often discloses that the patient is replaying something in his analysis. This, rather than the content of the dream, is important.

One patient, for example, had such lengthy dreams that his analyst could not follow them, would become bored and at times even doze off. Analysis subsequently revealed that the patient's mother, a severe borderline character, would sit him down after he came home from school and insist that he listen to her while she rambled on and on. He would become so bored that he frequently dozed off. In his sessions he evoked the same feelings in his analyst that he had himself experienced as a boy.

Another patient, early in his treatment, flooded his sessions with dreams. He would begin a session by relating a dream and at the end of the session would still be telling the same dream. When it was time to stop he would become very frustrated because, he said, "I have not finished telling you the dream yet." In the next session he would not know where to begin because in the meantime he had had another series of lengthy dreams. After a number of such sessions, he telephoned his analyst following his appointment and complained that he did not feel that he was getting anywhere. When he returned for his next appointment, it was necessary to tell him to refrain from reporting any more dreams until some of his problems were better understood. As the sessions progressed, it became apparent that the plethora of dreams had been a means of concealing the many serious difficulties in his current daily life. He acted with his dreams like a delinquent who, when questioned about his role in a particular offense, gives a long involved circumstantial account that never quite gets to the point at issue. Because this patient had an extremely weak and fragile ego and was extremely anxious about the outcome of the explorations of his inner world, he used this type of dream production as a resistance.

It has been shown by workers engaged in sleep and dream research (Dement and Fisher, 1960a,b) that all people dream regularly throughout their sleep. Yet the actual number of dreams that people remember and report in therapy sessions is comparatively small. In certain instances, the quantity and character of the dreams seems to follow an almost characteristic pattern specific for the individual. Their style is difficult to explain on the basis of such matters as resistance, interest, or compliance with the therapist. Some people, no matter what their level of resistance, dream a good deal and report at least one dream in each session.

There may be some relationship between so-called good dreamers and people who are inclined to be more imaginative and creative. This would certainly seem to apply to Freud.

In a study of college girls, Adelson (1960) found that the more creative students, as rated by their teachers, had a greater number of dreams or dreams that were more creative.

Unlike these "good dreamers," however, some people seem to have a paucity of dreams. Some have gone through a lengthy analysis, lasting a number of years, during which they had very few dreams. Yet in these cases there was no dearth of material for analysis of the dreams they did bring in. Moreover, they were able to bring in fantasies and to understand their behavior in and out of the analysis in periods when no dreams were reported. With these patients, the question came up whether their production of dreams was curtailed for some inner reason, i.e., as a resistance or as the expression of an unconscious negative or defiant attitude in their analysis. These matters were discussed candidly and the resistances, defenses, and transference manifestations were understood and worked through without any appreciable difficulty. Yet the overall fact remained that these patients remembered only a small number of their dreams.

Some analysts, recognizing that dream analysis is related to the general problem of analyzability, doubt whether a patient who *never* dreams can be analyzed (Blum, 1976) and regard the absence of dreams as an indication of some "faulty working in the psychic apparatus" (Sharpe, 1937, p. 197). These patients are different from those just mentioned, who report few dreams but are able to deal with them. These patients rarely bring in fantasies and, for the most part, their associations are scanty and superficial. While some of this behavior may be due to resistance or to anxiety, we are often forced to recognize that their inability to deal with their inner psychic life may be an indication of deeply rooted characterological problems, perhaps stemming from some preverbal trauma. These people may therefore be unsuitable for depth-oriented therapy.

In general, Freud indicates that "all dreams that are dreamt in a single night belong in a single context" (1933,

p. 26) and that "the content of all dreams that occur during the same night forms part of the same whole" (1900, p. 333), or are "derived from the same circle of thoughts" (1901a, p. 661), or "need be nothing more than attempts, expressed in various forms, to represent one meaning" (1911, p. 94).

We may extend Freud's observations to dreams that occur between sessions in an analysis, such as those dreamt over a weekend, a vacation period, or some other interruption. These dreams, like the ones occurring during a single night, also deal with the same content and rework it in various ways. Quite often the manifest dreams which the patient remembers and reports after such an interval are more direct and summarize in an abbreviated manner his conflicts during this period.

Freud writes "that separate and successive dreams of this kind may have the same meaning, and may be giving expression to the same impulses in different material. If so, the first of these homologous dreams to occur is often the more distorted and timid, while the succeeding one will be more confident and distinct" (1900, p. 334; see also 1911, p. 94). We may observe, for example, instances in which the early manifest content in a series of dreams expresses a vaguely erotic scene, the subsequent dreams elaborate increasingly more outspoken erotic scenes, and the final dream culminates in an ejaculation. Rank (1912) presented clinical material with regard to a series of dreams about urination. The individual finally awakened, urinated, and returned to sleep. He then continued to have dreams of a similar nature which subsequently expressed frank sexual content.

The fact that dreams in a series often express the underlying conflict with increasing candor provides the therapist a useful technical adjunct to exploring dreams in therapy. In such instances the therapist would be advised to begin the analytic work with the *last* dream of the series. Inasmuch as the patient has already worked through some of his resistances to the material in the series of dreams, he is much more likely to deal with the material in his analysis.

Freud distinguishes, but "not too sharply" (1923a, p. 111), between dreams *from above* and dreams *from below*. With regard to the former, he writes that "we cannot understand the dream, but the dreamer—or the patient—can translate it immediately and without difficulty, given that the content of the dream is very close to his conscious thoughts" (1929, p. 203). In another connection, he writes: "Dreams from above correspond to thoughts or intentions of the day before which have contrived during the night to obtain reinforcement from repressed material that is debarred from the ego. When this is so, analysis as a rule disregards this unconscious ally and succeeds in inserting the latent dream-thoughts into the texture of waking thought" (1923a, p. 111).

Usually, what the patient "can translate" is the part of the manifest content of the dream that clearly represents his day residues, among which are his current conflicts and, often, his reactions (positive and confirmatory or negative and contradictory) to the therapist's comments, observations, and interpretations in the previous analytic session. Dreams of running away, missing an appointment, or going to another office or another therapist following the emergence of unpleasant material may clearly indicate the patient's anxiety and resistance in dealing with the material.

Freud remarks elsewhere that there "remain certain parts of [such dreams] about which the dreamer does not know what to say: and these are precisely the parts which belong to the unconscious and which are in many respects the most interesting" (1929, p. 203). And to this may be added: "Dreams from below are those which are provoked by the strength of an unconscious (repressed) wish which has found a means of being represented in some of the day's residues. They may be regarded as inroads of the repressed into waking life" (1923a, p. 111).

In working with dreams as an integral part of psychotherapy, the therapist must pay attention to what Freud terms the *pressure of resistance* and determine whether it is *"high* or *low*—a point on which the analyst never remains long in doubt" (1923a, p. 110). When the "pressure of resistance" is high, the dreamers' associations broaden instead of deepen. They relate a good deal of material about their life situations in a manner that appears to be quite superficial. "In place of the desired associations to the dream that has already been narrated, there appear a constant succession of new fragments of dream, which in their turn remain without associations" (1923a, p. 110). In another connection Freud indicates "that the longer and more roundabout the chain of associations the stronger the resistance" (1933, pp. 13–14). In these instances

one may perhaps succeed in discovering what the things are with which the dream is concerned, but one cannot make out what it says about these things. It is as though one were trying to listen to a conversation taking place at a distance or in a very low voice. . . . The majority of dreams in a difficult analysis are of this kind . . . [and one cannot] learn . . . from them . . . where the dream's wish-fulfilment may lie hidden. [1923a, p. 110]

Freud notes that in those instances where the *pressure of resistance* is high "one can feel confident that there is not much prospect of collaborating with the dreamer, one decides not to bother too much about it and not to give him much help, and one is content to put before him a few translations of symbols that seem probable" (1923a, p. 110). And further:

It is only when the resistance is kept within moderate limits that the familiar picture of the work of interpretation comes into view: the dreamer's associations begin by *diverging* widely from the manifest elements, so that a great number of subjects and ranges of ideas are touched on, after which, a second series of associations quickly *converge* from these on to the dream-thoughts that are being looked for. When this is so, collaboration between the analyst and the dreamer becomes possible; whereas under a high pressure of resistance it would not even be of any advantage. [1923a, p. 110]

Freud's remarks provide the therapist important guidelines for working with the patient's dreams. Assessment of
the patient's pressure of resistance will determine whether
and to what extent the therapist deals with the content of the
dream. Quite frequently, as we have noted, some elements
in the manifest dream will indicate the existence of a resistance and perhaps something of its nature. These resistances
may deal with timely reality considerations or may be due
to one or a combination of the five kinds of resistance Freud
distinguishes: "The ego is the source of three of these, each
different in its dynamic nature. . . . These [include] *repression* resistance . . . *transference* resistance, and the *gain
from illness.* . . . The fourth . . . arising from the *id,* is the
resistance which . . . necessitates 'working through'. The
fifth, coming from the *super-ego* . . . seems to originate from
the sense of guilt or the need for punishment . . ." (1926,
p. 160).

Helping the patient deal with his resistances gives him
a feeling of collaboration with the therapist, even in periods
when the "pressure of resistance" is high. It is especially true
in instances where the patient has brought in a dream and
the therapist can offer little or no help to him. While the
therapist may put forth "a few translations of symbols that
seem probable" it would probably be preferable to do so in
a general or thematic sense, thereby leaving an opening for
the patient to pick up whatever details in the dream come
to his mind. It is especially important that the therapist avoid
any approach that would lead the patient to intellectualization.

An analysis of the resistance usually brings about an
improvement in the working alliance and is frequently accompanied by a change in the "pressure of resistance." When
this occurs, the patient's manner of speech and tempo alter.
At times this change is preceded by some comment such as
"Oh, I remember now" or "This makes me think of something." Then one association follows another with increasing

rapidity, suddenly illuminating a sector of the dream. Other portions of the manifest dream may still not be understood or they may fall into line as peripheral, subsidiary, or supporting associations to the central topic. The therapist may then focus his attention upon the theme which is being expressed by this second "series of associations," which converge upon a central topic.

Analyzing the resistance is a problem when the pressure of resistance remains at a high level and the patient's dreams remain difficult to understand over a lengthy period of time because associations to them remain on a superficial level. The same problem occurs with patients who are sophisticated about the importance of dreams and are frustrated with themselves and with their analyst for not being more helpful in unraveling the meaning of their dreams. In these instances, the therapist must consider several possibilities. Is the patient purposely or for unconscious reasons attempting to conceal some material from the world of reality—something that he is ashamed of, guilty about, or is afraid will elicit criticism from the analyst? Does it have to do with transference material which is being suppressed? For example, is the unconscious intent on the part of the patient to bring about precisely that state of affairs in the interaction between himself and the analyst in which the frustration, the annoyance, and a feeling of "You won't or you can't help me" repeats a dynamic relationship that occurred at some time in the patient's past? Thus, by using his understanding of the situation, the therapist is able to convert an interference in the therapy to a most valuable therapeutic adjunct. This, it will be readily recognized, is precisely how other manifestations of resistance in therapy are handled.

Chapter Three

Initial and Early Dreams

Freud described initial dreams in an analysis as being "unsophisticated," betraying "a great deal to the listener" (1911, p. 95) that is useful in interpretation (1933, p. 10). They may also provide clues to the patient's diagnosis and prognosis (see 1922b, pp. 229–230). Unsophisticated dreams, which may also occur later in an analysis, may be "elaborate" and may be

> based on the entire pathogenic material of the case, as yet unknown to both doctor and patient (so called 'programme-dreams' and biographical dreams), and is sometimes equivalent to a translation into dream-language of the whole content of the neurosis. . . . The full interpretation of such a dream will coincide with the completion of the whole analysis; if a note is made of it at the beginning, it may be possible to understand it at the end, many months later. [1911, p. 93]

The wealth of material presented in these dreams stems from different layers of the patient's personality, from different events in the patient's life, and often expresses different conflicts with which he may be concerned. Freud cautions that "in the attempt to interpret such a dream all the latent, as yet untouched, resistances will be roused to activity and soon set a limit to its understanding" (1911, p. 93) and adds that "the more the patient has learnt of the practice of dream-interpretation, the more obscure do his later dreams as a rule become. All the knowledge acquired about dreams serves also to put the dream-constructing process on its guard" (1911, p. 95).

Frequently the patient himself quickly recognizes how much about himself such a dream reveals. As a result he may feel apprehensive and suppress any meaningful discussion of the dream. He may regret having told it, or what is even worse, regret having dreamed it. If he feels that his dreams have betrayed him, his subsequent dreams may become more obscure. The humiliation generated by an initial dream that is too revealing to the patient himself, or that he believes will be too revealing to the therapist, should not be underestimated. If such situations are not carefully handled, the patient may flee from therapy before it has had a chance to begin.

Some analysts feel that therapists should desist from any interpretation of dreams altogether until the therapeutic alliance is well established, largely because initial dreams are naive, betray too much, or are too complex (Reik, 1949). Certainly one should be cautious so that the patient is not overwhelmed by what he may feel the therapist has learned about him in this way. Quite often people attribute an aura of mystery to dreams and are awed if the therapist can understand them; they feel that he can thereby "read their minds." Some therapists are concerned lest such awe result in the patient's supplying the therapist with dreams in a "dependent submissive way" (Weigert, 1956, p. 123). Actually, there is little advantage to be gained by telling the patient everything the therapist may be able to see in a patient's dream. Even if the therapist sees a great deal, the patient cannot possibly understand it all or be able to make use of it at this point in his therapy.

In spite of the problems connected with interpreting early dreams, however, I share the opinion of those analysts who firmly believe that something should be done with the initial dream. It should not be passed over, as it is a communication from the patient which the therapist must accept. He shows his acceptance by making some comment in response to what the patient is trying to tell him by reporting the dream. He does so whether the patient spontaneously associates to the dream or not. Whatever comments or interpretations the therapist makes should be based upon the patient's genuine level of understanding. They should be ego-oriented, couched in simple and direct language, and should deal with surface material first.

Generally it is helpful to the patient if the therapist uses the patient's own words in his remarks, letting him know that he is quoting from the patient's description of his dream or his associations. A note of caution should be sounded, however, with respect to the use of vulgar and profane language even if the patient has used it. Some therapists justify their use of vulgarities by stating that it is the patient's language. Actually, this is demeaning both to the patient and to the therapist. It is neither necessary nor therapeutically advisable, as it lowers the level of communication from professional discussion to street talk or locker-room conversation. Such an approach may adversely influence the transference.

The therapist may choose to defer the discussion of some of the material in the dream until the therapy has progressed. But certain things, when alluded to by the dream, must be brought up and discussed at the time the dream is reported. Most pressing in this regard are the patient's current conflicts, his concern about the beginning of therapy, his anxieties about the therapist, and his worries about such reality considerations as time and financial arrangements. If one does not deal with these issues, the patient may feel that the therapist is unempathic and may decide to break off the treatment (see Arlow and Brenner, 1964; Spanjaard, 1969; Stolorow, 1978).

In his second session, a male patient reported a dream in which he was taking his car to a junky garage in a back alley to be serviced. The garage mechanic looked greasy, dirty, and disreputable and was going to charge him an exorbitant price to repair his car. In the dream, the patient doubted if this mechanic was competent and wondered if he was "just going to rip [him] off." It was important for the therapist to point out that the dream alluded to the patient's anxiety that the analyst might be like the dirty, greasy garage mechanic, might charge him an exorbitant price and take advantage of him.

A woman patient's first dream was that she was about to go to a hairdresser who had a very good reputation. When asked about this particular hairdresser, she related that she had actually gone to him a couple of years before on the advice of a friend. The hairdresser had put a solution on her hair which was "too strong" and it had burned her scalp. When the analyst questioned her about the hairdresser, the patient revealed in her associations her fear that even though she was going to an analyst who had been recommended to her as having a good reputation, in "working on her head" he would do a bad job, just as her well-recommended hairdresser had done. She was afraid that he would give her a "solution" (to her problems) that would hurt her. As she had not returned to the hairdresser after her experience, the implication was that if she were hurt by the analyst, she would not return to him either.

In this instance, it should be noted, the patient did not spontaneously see any connection between her dream and her anxiety about beginning analysis. The manifest content expressed the situation in positive terms, i.e., she was going to a hairdresser with a very good reputation. It was only *after* she was asked by the analyst about the hairdresser that the story of her "bad treatment" was revealed.

In her first week of treatment, another female patient dreamed she was at a counter buying some sexy lingerie; her parents were in the background, disapproving. This patient, who entered analysis because of some sexual problems, felt that her parents would disapprove of her going into therapy for such a reason. There was also a transference implication here, as the analyst was "in the background" too (i.e., he sat behind her as she lay on the couch). She was concerned that even though she was seeing him to help her with her sexual problems, he would disapprove of her sexuality, just as her parents did.

The manifest content and associations of the three preceding dreams aptly illustrate patients' anxieties about going into treatment and what could happen to them as a consequence. The first patient was afraid the dirty, incompetent garage mechanic–analyst would take advantage of him by overcharging him. The first woman patient was afraid the highly recommended hairdresser-analyst would do her harm, while the other woman feared that her parents would disapprove of what she was planning to do with her (sexual) life by going into treatment. In each instance, a brief or succinct discussion of the patient's fears was essential. In the first two examples, the required interpretation dealt directly with the anxiety about the relationship with the analyst. In the third, the required interpretation was specifically connected with the woman's concern about her parents' disapproval.

It should be emphasized that the comments made by the analyst under these circumstances should acknowledge the existence of the patient's anxiety and point out that the parallel or analogous situation in the dream or associations was a metaphor by which the patient expressed this anxiety. Verbalization of the problem by the analyst provides an opening for a free discussion with the patient. To ignore the message contained in the communication presented as a dream by the patient would be incorrect. It would imply to the patient that the therapist, for whatever reason, is unwilling to discuss these concerns with him. Rather than facilitating the development of a good working alliance in the therapy, it could hamper its development, perhaps for some time to come. This is especially true with timid patients or those who do not fully realize, out of transference reasons, that in their therapy they have every opportunity to discuss all their thoughts, hesitations, anxieties, doubts, and negative feelings. The initial interchange, played out by the patient's bringing in a dream and the analyst's response to it, immediately sets the tone of what is to come.

At some point in the early stages of treatment, if the patient is relatively unsophisticated and has not brought in any dreams, the therapist may ask about his sleep habits—whether he has dreams and, if so, whether he remembers any of them. This must be done with great caution, however, as the question may preempt the material or pull the patient away from the direction of his own associations; it may give him the feeling that the therapist is interested not in what he is or has been saying, but only in his dreams. If not used with great care, this technical maneuver may result in the patient's producing a never-ending succession of dreams which are difficult to deal with or in his having no dreams whatsoever.

Initial dreams are important in ascertaining the nature of the early transference situation; they provide a clue toward understanding the patient's inner emotional life, about which the therapist knows nothing. Because of her complicated work schedule and family pressures, a rather sophisticated woman had to see her male therapist in the evening. She very quickly developed an intense erotic transference toward him. Florid sexual fantasies emerged within a few sessions, puzzling both patient and therapist. The patient was not borderline, nor did she expect any type of overt gratification of these fantasies. After a few sessions she brought in a dream in which she was sitting on her therapist's lap, stroking the hair on his cheek. The hair was soft, downy, and silvery gray. She talked about relationships between secretaries and their employers and spoke of stories of secretaries sitting on their bosses' laps. She herself had worked as a secretary at one time but had not had an affair with her employer. Thus far her associations seemed to continue the theme of the erotic transference discussed in her previous sessions. No special comment was necessary, as the patient herself recognized this.

Finally, the therapist asked her why, if the dream actually referred to himself, she dreamed of his having such hair on his face; she must have observed that his hair was neither gray nor downy but dark, and that by evening he had a stubble of beard. After a moment's hesitation, the patient realized that the face and the fine hair she was stroking in the dream belonged to her grandmother, who had lived with the family and whom she loved dearly. The woman had died suddenly when the patient was quite young. She remembered sitting on her grandmother's lap, patting her cheek, cuddled warmly in her loving arms and feeling protected from her harsh and critical mother. Evidently, the patient's longing for her grandmother was transferred to her male therapist. Pointing this out to the patient was essential, as it helped her understand that her feelings toward her analyst were not based on reality but were an expression of her early feelings toward her grandmother. The explanation, based on her association to a detail in the dream, prevented her feelings from escalating to such a degree that out of anxiety she would have had to leave therapy.

In recent years a number of publications have noted the significance—for analyzability, diagnosis, or prognosis—of the undisguised appearance of the analyst in the manifest content of initial or early dreams. Concern has been expressed that "the patient in his unconscious is unable to differentiate between the analyst and a significant person in the past, or that the analyst in his appearance and behaviour really resembles such a person too closely" (Rappaport, 1959, p. 240). Other investigators (Harris, 1962; Yazmajian, 1964; Rosenbaum, 1965; Savitt, 1969; Fleming, 1972; Bradlow and Coen, 1975) believe that the significance of this type of dream may be "partially related to the patient's intense mistrust of the analyst because of his fear that the analyst would be like the parental transference figures" and that there is "an attempted denial of [the patient's] intense fear and mistrust in the service of a more powerful wish for gratification from the analyst" (Bradlow and Coen, 1975, pp. 423, 422). Some writers have suggested that patients reporting such dreams may have responded to countertransference reactions on the part of the analyst. Therapists should certainly be alert to this possibility.

Rappaport's statement that the "patient in his unconscious is unable to differentiate between the analyst and a significant person in the past . . ." is questionable. The "unconscious," after all, is not capable of any differentiation, and imputing such functions to it confuses both patient and therapist about the function of the dream altogether. To be sure, if a patient has difficulty in distinguishing transference from reality in the therapeutic situation, then the whole question of suitability for analysis must be dealt with. Generally in these instances, many other indications of severe ego disturbance would be present to corroborate the clinical impression. One would not need an initial dream in which the therapist appears as himself to reach a conclusion regarding suitability for analysis.

Judging from the available evidence, dreams of this type are not unique. They occur periodically, not only early but throughout the course of many analyses. The general significance of these dreams has not been completely settled, although their specific meaning in individual instances has been studied. When patients report dreams in which the analyst appears undisguised, he would do well to analyze these dreams as he would any other (see Martin, 1982). The patient's dream of sitting on her analyst's lap and stroking his face is a good example of this; it turned out to be a transference dream referring to her grandmother. The patient did well in her analysis.

Much more serious than initial dreams in which the analyst appears undisguised are dreams of another kind. Wild, vividly colorful initial dreams in which the individual himself or objects about him are dissolving, disintegrating, falling apart, or becoming fragmented, strongly suggest actual or threatening ego fragmentation. Kohut (1977) has indicated that the precarious condition of an enfeebled or fragmented self may be concretely depicted in the manifest dream imagery of narcissistically disturbed patients.

In other instances, where the manifest content deals with frankly cannibalistic or orally aggressive material, the possible presence of a schizophrenic psychosis, active or incipient, must be borne in mind. In these instances the therapist is urged to deal with the patient's particular condition rather than with the specific content of the dream. Utmost caution should be exercised in considering such patients for analysis (see Noble, 1951; Richardson and Moore, 1963).

With regard to prognostication from dreams, the therapist would be well advised to be cautious. Freud indicates that "there seems to be no reason why . . . any pathological idea should not be transformed into a dream. A dream may therefore quite simply represent a phantasy, an obsessional idea, or a delusion—that is, may reveal one or other of these upon interpretation" (1922b, p. 230). The presence of such material, however, while important in revealing the patient's problems, need not indicate in a specific way what the ultimate effects of the therapy will be upon these conditions.

Saul (1956) cited the example of "a woman who at the beginning of analysis dreamed of a trip for which she received a free ticket" (p. 125). This patient subsequently left therapy and never paid her bill. The report, however, does not indicate if the therapist understood the dream or discussed it with the patient at the time. The ability to predict whether a patient will continue in therapy or not, whether the patient will pay his bill or not, etc., can ultimately only be derived from what is done with the dream, how it is taken up, and what latent meaning it has for the patient. Neither the patient nor the therapist should confuse a wish that the patient may express in his dream with a reality. A patient may want some kind of gratification, have a dream about it, and yet deal appropriately with the realities in the treatment situation. Ultimately, the prognosis of therapy is determined by a great many factors of which dreams are only a part (see Bonime and Bonime, 1980).

Chapter Four

Specific Considerations of Dream Elements

Some of the most intriguing and challenging problems that confront the therapist dealing with dreams derive from the fact that any element in the manifest dream must be considered from a number of different standpoints. The therapist must decide

> (a) whether it is to be taken in a positive or negative sense (as an antithetic relation),
> (b) whether it is to be interpreted historically (as a recollection),
> (c) whether it is to be interpreted symbolically, or
> (d) whether its interpretation is to depend on its wording.
> [1900, p. 341]

We will discuss each of these points in detail, (a), (b), and (d), in this chapter, (c), in chapters 5–7. The therapist must bear in mind that any given element should be considered from all these standpoints; since the dream will often use them in combination, several meanings of a given element may be valid.

The Antithetic Relation

A dream element can "stand for its opposite just as easily as for itself" (1900, p. 471). Freud writes that "dreams feel themselves at liberty . . . to represent any element by its wishful contrary; so that there is no way of deciding at first glance whether any element that admits of a contrary is present in the dream thoughts as a positive or as a negative" (1900, p. 318) and recommends that "if a dream obstinately declines to reveal its meaning, it is always worth while to see the effect of reversing some particular elements in its manifest content, after which the whole situation often becomes immediately clear" (1900, p. 327).

This suggestion applies to all dream elements—nouns, verbs, adjectives, adverbs, etc.—and is pertinent to any part of the dream. In the main, nouns are seldom reversed, although there are examples of it. Freud notes that "the opposite of 'wet' and 'water' can easily be 'fire' and 'burning' " (1905a, p. 89). Locations may be given as nouns: "out west," "up north," etc. The manifest dream may refer to an event taking place on the West Coast while the associations clearly refer to some place in the East.

The designations for morning and afternoon, A.M. and P.M., may also be reversed. One patient, whose appointment was for 11 A.M., dreamed of coming for his appointment at 11 P.M. In this instance, the reasons for the reversal were connected with a libidinal wish implied in the 11 P.M. appointment. Another patient dreamed that he had been given a traffic ticket for a misdemeanor violation. His associations led to his anxiety that it would be discovered that he had cheated on his income tax declaration, i.e., a serious Federal offense.

Freud wrote that " 'a lot of strangers' frequently appear in dreams . . . and they always stand as a wishful contrary of 'secrecy' " (1900, pp. 245–246). "For obvious reasons the presence of 'the whole family' in a dream has the same significance" (1900, p. 246n1). In accordance with reversal, a " 'large party' [means] a secret" (1900, p. 288), i.e., a close or intimate relationship. The "secret" or "party" often refers in a metaphoric sense to a sexual party.

A large company, party, or group of people in a dream

can also stand for any gathering: business, social, professional, or political. It may refer to a joyous occasion like a wedding, anniversary celebration, confirmation, bar mitzvah, christening, or ritual circumcision, or to an occasion of sadness like a memorial service or funeral. The patient's specific allusions will reveal the nature of the material behind the dream element and with it the "secret" which has had to be repressed.

One patient dreamed of being present at a large party where many people were standing around. Her associations led to a wedding party she had recently attended. The secret implied in her associations was a deep erotic transference to her analyst and her desire to announce, to a large group, her wished-for relationship with him: "I would like to tell it to the whole world, shout it from the housetops and ultimately to be married to him."

The use of reversal constitutes a convenient defense against the recognition of impulses about which the dreamer feels guilty or impulses that are frightening or ego-alien to the dreamer. A woman dreamt that her husband left her for another woman. The dream referred to her own conflict about her wish to leave her husband for another man. As she had no reason to suspect that her husband was involved with another woman, she felt particularly guilty about her own wishes. Also, she feared that her husband would leave her if she got involved with another man.

In certain instances sexual material may screen aggressive impulses; the reverse may also be true. In such situations, the use of the particular defense often has specific significance for the dreamer. It may demonstrate, for instance, that he conceives of the sexual act as something violent and aggressive.

Inasmuch as all instincts have active and passive components, the dream may express any striving directly or by its opposite. It is up to the therapist to determine the dominant material from the patient's associations and what interpretation the patient may be able to accept at the particular time.

Since the position of passivity creates a great deal of anxiety, the individual may dream of a situation where he is the aggressor. He may be exhibiting his sexual prowess as a lover, may be expressing the wish to be active sexually and to penetrate his partner, either heterosexual or homosexual. Yet, the underlying or unconscious wish may really be the wish to be loved, to be passive in a sexual situation, and to be penetrated. If such wishes are intolerable to the ego, they are repressed and the reverse picture is permitted to enter the manifest content.

The presence of polarities in the unconscious makes it possible for many partial instincts to be expressed by reversal. An element dealing with scopophilia, for example, may actually refer to the unconscious wish to be looked at, i.e., to exhibit oneself. Particularly difficult to deal with, especially early in an analysis, are passive or masochistic strivings such as the unconscious wish to be sexually penetrated, to be hurt, to be crushed, to be beaten, to be devoured, to be killed. Great caution should be exercised in exposing such unconscious wishes by interpretation. These impulses are far more ego-alien than a reversal of such ego impulses as love and hate. In the latter case, the associations to the repressed material are often easy to follow and to demonstrate to the patient. But even here the therapist must judge the patient's readiness to accept an interpretation of this kind. When it is made, the interpretation is best given from the side of the ego, using such expressions as "You are afraid you may harbor feelings of hatred toward . . ." or "It may be that a part of you has thoughts or wishes about. . . ." Yet even when it is presented with the greatest tact and under the most obvious of circumstances, a patient may have difficulty in understanding or accepting an interpretation he regards as untenable at the time.

The utilization of reversal, of elements used in both a positive and a negative sense, is particularly impressive when dealing with bisexual conflicts. "It is remarkable to observe. . . ," Freud writes, "how frequently reversal is employed precisely in dreams arising from repressed homosexual impulses" (1900, p. 327). When a dream contains elements that have been reversed, therefore, the therapist should keep in mind the possibility that some reference to homosexual impulses will be present in the latent material that has been repressed or censored by the patient. This may be seen especially in openly heterosexual dreams that contain reversed elements, thereby providing the therapist the clue to look for homosexual material.

A patient dreamed of driving with the wife of a colleague the wrong way on a one-way street. He found himself very much aroused as she reached for his penis, at which point he had an emission and awoke. The dream had been prompted by his flirting with his colleague's wife at a cocktail party that afternoon. He admired her breasts and wanted to fondle them. In the dream, this wish is reversed, as the woman is about to fondle his penis. The element of driving the wrong way on a one-way street referred not only to his guilt feelings about wanting to have an affair with his colleague's wife (breaking a rule), but also to some unconscious passive homosexual wishes toward the colleague.

Dreams of homosexual patients who have great anxiety about revealing their heterosexual interests and strivings may also make use of reversal. Affects which are regarded by the dreamer as unpleasant, frightening, or forbidden are also subject to being expressed by their opposite. It is not uncommon for a peaceful, idyllic scene depicted in the manifest content to refer to death or to some episode of violent emotional turmoil. Freud indicates that dreams "show a particular preference for combining contraries into a unity or for representing them as one and the same thing" (1900, p. 318). Sometimes the idea of contradiction is represented by an "opposition in position," for example, "I sat opposite to her" (Sharpe, 1937, p. 27).

Freud's discussion (1910a) of Abel's *The Antithetical*

Meaning of Primal Words (1884) provides the therapist many useful hints to consider when dealing with the negative and positive sense of dream elements. In a footnote added to *The Interpretation of Dreams* in 1911, Freud cites the existence in ancient languages of single words denoting at once such antithetical pairs as "strong-weak," "old-young," "far-near," "bind-sever"; the contraries are differentiated only secondarily, by slight modifications in the common word (1900, pp. 318–319n3). Because the language of the dream is essentially primitive, it often utilizes similar elements, the precise meaning of which can be understood only in the context of the associations.

A dream may represent the dreamer as being in a *high* [altus] place, but his associations indicate that he is afraid he is getting in "too deep" or into *deep* [altus] water. In this example, the dreamer's being in a high place in the manifest dream was not attended by any anxiety, whereas his associations were. A woman dreamt that she was physically *cold*. She supposed that the stimulus for the dream was that her electric blanket had gotten unplugged. She went on to relate, however, that she had been considered sexually frigid. To some extent she agreed with this assessment, but then went on to relate that in a suitable situation, with the right kind of lover, she would be passionate, i.e., *hot*. In fact, she was afraid that if she really let herself go her lovemaking would be so vigorous that she would hurt her sexual partner. The antithetical words here, *hot* and *cold*, find a suggestion of their primal equation, both in the unconscious and in the original mother-tongue, in the Italian word, *caldo*, which means *hot*, and the English word, *cold*.

A reference to size in the manifest dream frequently provides the therapist the opportunity to consider the element from both a positive and a negative sense. A patient dreamed that he was in a cafeteria line and the woman cashier gave him a small slip of paper, like an adding machine tape, upon which was printed the total for his purchases. He noted that the amount was small, less than he had expected. The dream contained many references to his analysis. He viewed his coming for therapy as being in a kind of cafeteria line where he was one of a long line of patients, and regarded the therapist as providing his patients with a kind of fast food feeding (as opposed to leisurely dining at some fancy restaurant). He had turned the therapist, a male, into a businesslike female, somewhat indifferent toward the customers, who was interested only in giving him a bill. The day before, he had received a statement, typed on a professional letterhead, for the previous month of analytic sessions. The amount had "added up" and was greater than he had expected. The dream thus contained elements that were to be read directly, e.g., the reality of his having been given a bill; his assumption that the analyst had many patients; and his feeling that the analyst was like the businesslike, rather uncaring cashier. There were also elements that were to be read in a negative sense: the cashier was a female; there was a small bill on a small adding machine tape instead of the bill, larger than he had expected, on a professional letterhead.

But here we come to an interesting point. His feeling in the dream that the bill was small, *less* than he had expected, was a reversal of his reaction to his analytic bill which seemed large to him, *more* than he had expected. The smallness of the bill in the dream, in size as well as in amount, emphasized his wish that the analytic bill would be less than it was. Moreover, the reversal directly pictured hidden thoughts and impulses the dreamer had been unable to express. He felt that the real value of his therapy was far less than the amount he had to pay. This was graphically expressed in the dream, as well as his feeling that he was not getting the care and the love he wanted from his analyst, the businesslike female in the dream. The transference picture led directly to a consideration of the historical figures in this patient's past.

Once the therapist has ascertained that some dream elements are reversed, as illustrated by the previous examples, he must carry his investigation a step further and consider whether there is a specific meaning or purpose behind the mechanism of reversal. For example, in the case above, was the choice of smallness of the bill intended to reduce a threatening object or situation to one that is manageable and not so anxiety-provoking? Does the reversal succeed in expressing aggression, as in the example of the cafeteria bill? Does it refer to something in childhood? etc.

Reversal of affects in dreams is associated with the change of subject to object and the use of projection. Obviously, since both the affect and its negative counterpart may coexist, this greatly complicates the problem of understanding dreams. An anti-Semitic patient, whose analyst was Jewish, frequently and candidly discussed his prejudice in his analysis. One night he had a dream in which he was talking with a shadowy figure that clearly referred to his analyst. In the dream he says: "I hate Jews just like my father did." The manifest dream was a confession of what had been frequently discussed in his analysis, that his anti-Semitic attitude was an identification with his father's attitude. As he talked further, his associations led to his fear that his Jewish analyst would be "anti-Gentile." In the dream he was saying, "I, a Gentile, hate you, a Jew." What had been repressed was the opposite, his fear that his Jewish analyst would hate him, a Gentile. His continual baiting of his analyst by his anti-Semitic attitude proved to be an attempt to master and defend himself against his fear of being rejected and being regarded with contempt. He was sure that all Jews viewed Gentiles as "stupid goyim." Not well versed in Yiddish expressions, but wanting to display his knowledge, he had used this expression, but mispronounced "goyim" as "gayim." This parapraxis clearly voiced his concern that people would think him a homosexual; although not a manifest homosexual, he was often plagued by homosexual fantasies.

A further discussion of the use of reversal will be found in chapter 9.

Freud's Rules of Dream Interpretation

The Historical Standpoint

"Dreams," Freud writes, "can select their material from any part of the dreamer's life, provided only that there is a train of thought linking the experience of the dream-day (the 'recent' impressions) with the earlier ones" (1900, p. 168); "every dream [is] linked in its manifest content with recent experiences and in its latent content with the most ancient experiences" (1900, p. 218).

The continuity exhibited in dreams leads naturally to the approach which is, as we said previously, one generally followed in analytic therapy: from surface material to underlying material; from current material and conflicts to conflicts originating from the past; from transference expressions to their parallels and genetic determinants.

Inasmuch as the manifest content of every dream contains at least one allusion to the dream day (day residues), we may approach the dream by taking up this surface material. Careful attention must be paid to this material so that the analysis does not degenerate into an intellectual exercise unrelated to the real life situation of the patient. To maintain close contact with the patient's reality, it is essential that the therapist ask the patient for *specific* information and details about his associations to the dream. In principle, this is no different from asking questions about any material that is brought up in the course of the analysis. It is not enough for the patient to say, "Well, the dream had to do with a movie we went to see last night." The therapist must know *how* the dream "has to do with" the movie, to *whom* the "we" referred, *what* movie they went to see, *why* they happened to see that particular movie and not another, what the essence of the movie was, etc.

One patient dreamed he was "dining in some fancy restaurant." His associations led to his having met a girl a few days before. Then he added: "I invited her out for a bite to eat after work." The fancy restaurant in the dream turned out to be a McDonald's in real life; he had taken the girl there

54

for a quick hamburger and a cup of coffee. When he was asked why he had chosen to go there, his attitude was very revealing: "Why should I take her to a nice place? I didn't even know if she would go to bed with me." His dream of a fancy restaurant referred to other occasions when he had taken women to such places and found that they disappointed him. This, in turn, led to a consideration of underlying problems in his relations with women.

The technical suggestion to inquire about specific information is particularly valuable in the early phases of an analysis, when patients are in a sense being educated to develop an analytic attitude: an objectivity and appreciation for their own material so that the work may be maintained on a sound foundation. To be sure, if the material is proceeding rapidly in a particular direction, as in a discussion of recent events or of a crisis, the therapist would normally avoid interrupting the patient's flow of associations with questions about details. Such material is picked up later in the session or on another occasion. The whole matter of whether to interrupt a patient's associations, and when to interrupt them, requires a good deal of judgment and sensitivity. Sometimes patients may be only too eager to press forward with an account of an incident, thereby glossing over important details. At other times a patient's somewhat unclear account may be due to anxiety or to a narrative manner characteristic of children.

Early in an analysis the dream material may reveal problems which the patient has not yet mentioned and which he is not ready to deal with at that time. Sometimes in the manifest dream the patient finds himself in a conflict situation which expresses his current conflict. He may, for example, describe a struggle with wild animals that are pulling him in different directions. One patient dreamed of a cow standing between two haystacks not knowing from which haystack to eat. After some difficulty, he said: "The truth is, I feel like that cow. I can never make up my mind about any decision because each alternative seems as worthwhile as the other." The current conflict expressed in this patient's early dream referred not only to all the decisions which were so difficult for him to make because of his ambivalence, but also to his ambivalence about being in analysis altogether. Much later in his therapy, after he had become aware of his extreme passive feminine strivings, he realized the significance of having identified himself with a cow.

Sometimes the manifest content of a dream seems to be an incredibly banal rendition of the previous day's events. Freud writes that "it by no means rarely happens that innocent and unimportant actions of the previous day are repeated in a dream: such, for instance, as packing a trunk, preparing food in the kitchen, and so on. What the dreamer is himself stressing in dreams of this kind is not, however, the content of the memory but the fact of its being 'real': 'I really *did* do all that yesterday' " (1900, p. 21n2).

The real activities reproduced in the dream may contain an allusion to something about which the patient is apprehensive. One woman dreamed in great detail about her preparations for a dinner party. In the dream she was preparing the food, setting the table, etc., just as she had done in reality. What came out in her associations, however, was how much anxiety she had about the forthcoming party: whether her guests would be pleased with the meal she would serve them, whether they would appreciate her crystal, china, silverware, and flowers, etc. She was particularly concerned whether her husband, of whom she was afraid, would be critical of her for something, as he had been in the past: "He's always finding fault with everything I do. I don't seem to do anything right. He's just like my father—everything has to be perfect and then some. He'd even find fault with Jesus Christ." Behind this seemingly innocent dream was her conviction that her analyst would be critical of her, too.

Sometimes a banal dream that seems merely to rehearse the events of the previous day refers to something else that happened that day which the patient did not mention. It may pertain to some activity in which the patient was actually involved or was planning but for various reasons chose to exclude from his analysis. The omitted material may refer to transference feelings which were embarrassing to the patient. One man, a manifest homosexual, frequently had such dreams, which he tended to regard as unimportant because they were "merely reruns" of what he had done the day before. While the dreams indeed dealt with banal occurrences, they did not directly allude to his homosexual escapades, which he was ashamed to discuss, not only because of their content but also because he was acting out his homosexual feelings toward his analyst. The "rerun" elements in the manifest dream referred to the reality of his homosexual activity as well as to what he felt were real but embarrassing feelings toward his analyst.

Sharpe (1937) observed that "uncamouflaged dream[s] of hostility" of "actual death wishes, [are] forthcoming only if in reality there has been the direct stimulus of hearing actual appreciation of the person who afterwards figures in the dream as the object of hostile wishes" (p. 93). The expression of aggression may be associated with any stage of libidinal development.

Apart from reality conflicts in which the individual may find himself and which are often referred to in the manifest content of dreams, dreams may express all aspects of the individual's inner psychic life. These may appear directly in the manifest content or be referred to in the course of the patient's associations, which in turn lead to the latent dream thoughts.

The day residues, whether they appear overtly as elements in the manifest content of a dream or are uncovered via the patient's associations, are only "such stuff as dreams are made on." It is not enough for the therapist merely to point out how specific elements in the manifest content of the patient's dream are connected with certain of his associations. He must go further. As Freud indicates, "an association often comes to a stop precisely before the genuine dream-thought: it has only come near to it and has only had contact with it through allusions. At that point we intervene on our own; we fill in the hints, draw undeniable conclusions, and give explicit utterance to what the patient has only touched on in his associations" (1933, p. 12).

The therapist attempts to verbalize for the patient the underlying meaning of his communication: whether it deals with current reality problems or refers to the transference or the therapy situation. At times the therapist does this by indicating to the patient that he is speaking in a metaphor, as the patient who dreamed of taking his car to a back alley mechanic who would take advantage of him, or the woman whose associations led to the hairdresser who would burn her scalp. In these instances the therapist intervened, "fill[ed] in the hints, dr[e]w undeniable conclusions, and g[a]ve explicit utterance to what the patient ha[d] only touched on"—that the latent dream thoughts behind his associations alluded to his concerns about the therapist and the therapy. In other instances, when the material is close to the surface, or when the patient is sensitive to his own dynamics, no intervention on the part of the therapist is necessary, as the patient can provide the connections himself and understand what he is saying. The therapist's task then will often go a step further, as he may help the patient see from what he has said how the metaphors relate also to similar experiences in the past.

The therapist must pay particular attention to the *manner* in which the patient talks about the conflicts he has alluded to and discussed in his associations to the dream. He must be aware of and sensitive to the patient's eagerness or reticence to talk about these matters. The nature of the patient's resistance will often reflect a characterological attitude which typifies his general approach to internal conflicts.

A patient who had problems with potency when he

attempted to have sexual relations with women avoided putting himself in a humiliating position by being an entertaining conversationalist. In his analysis he would avoid dealing with sexual matters even when the material in his dreams clearly alluded to his problems. Instead of pursuing these issues directly, he would often launch into lengthy theoretical discussions on philosophy, politics, movies, restaurants, etc.

It will be seen that when an attempt is made to understand any element, the patient's associations to it, together with his style or manner in dealing with the material provide the therapist a wealth of information about him. The therapist must sift through and understand the totality of the patient's communications in order to get to the latent dream thoughts and, if possible in the particular session, to the underlying dream wish behind them. In the above example, it was imperative to demonstrate to the patient how he used intellectuality as a defense against dealing with the sexual material in his dreams, just as he used it in real life situations with women.

By virtue of their connection with the latent dream thoughts, many of the patient's associations lead to the disclosure of the nature of his early relationships to friends, teachers, relatives, lovers, and, of course, close members of his family. Among the wealth of associations that patients bring up, there may be references to stories, novels, movies, plays, etc. Freud notes that "elements and situations derived from fairy tales are also frequently to be found in dreams" (1913c, p. 281). "Snow White and the Seven Dwarfs," partly because of the movie, "Cinderella," and "Sleeping Beauty" are stories frequently mentioned. The thoughts and feelings behind these memories lead to the revelation of such nuclear complexes as the patient's bisexuality, infantile sexuality, oedipal conflicts, castration anxiety, and primal scene material.

Apart from references to specific people and situations and to early conflicts and memories, dreams also provide valuable information, either directly in the transference or by some reference to a situation outside the therapy, about the individual's dynamics, including his defenses.

A man had a three-part dream. In the first part he is chopping violently at a snake. In the second part he is in a store buying a suit, and his father is severely criticizing him for buying such an expensive one. He feels humiliated in the presence of the salesperson. In the third part of the dream he finds himself submitting passively to a man who is about to perform anal intercourse on him. The dream contains the dynamic elements of his problems. As a child he had repeatedly been humiliated and criticized by his overly harsh, abusive father, who restricted him at every opportunity. On many occasions he had been so angry with his father that he had wanted to kill him. He was especially furious at his father for having boasted to him of his sexual conquests of women; the patient had had fantasies of hacking off his father's penis. He was extremely afraid of his father but had never been able to express any of his anger toward him and had become a woefully passive person. While not a manifest homosexual, he was nonetheless continually preoccupied with homosexual fantasies. His fear of and anger at his father, together with the flagrant passive homosexual defense, emerged in this dream and were seen repeatedly in the transference situation.

Sometimes the patient's dynamics are expressed by the specific use of the dream in therapy, rather than by its content. In these instances, the patient brings in dreams either to placate the analyst or as a gift to him. In the example of the patient who wrote down his dreams on slips of paper similar in size to pieces of toilet paper, the specific content of the dreams was not as important as the fact that he was giving his analyst a fecal gift, thereby repeating behavior that went back to a very early period in his childhood.

Dreams and acting out. The example just given is one of many situations in which the patient provides the analyst associations to his dream, not only on a verbal level but also by acting out. To a greater or lesser degree, all patients "act out" in or out of their analysis, and this behavior is, of course, subject to analytic scrutiny.

Our concern here is the pertinence of the patient's behavior to the dream, bearing in mind that a continuity exists between all of the patient's associations and the dream. The behavior may occur before a dream, i.e., in the dream day, and the dream may allude to it or explain it in some way. It may occur after the dream, in which case the behavior may be a continuation of the material dealt with in the dream, may provide an association to it, or be a reaction to or defense against some material in the dream. In any event, the therapist must regard the acting out as part of the overall continuum of material which the patient expresses.

Some acting out, while important as a communication, is, in and of itself, of no *major* consequence. A patient may, for example, tell his spouse a dream, which appropriately, he knows, should be related solely to his analyst. It is almost axiomatic "that one feels impelled to relate one's dreams to the very person to whom the content relates" (Ferenczi, 1912b, p. 349). That the patient tells his analyst that he told his spouse a dream is itself an association to the dream; it says, in essence, that the dream in some way deals with the spouse.

The patient's behavior on the couch, what he does with his hands, etc., are all motoric expressions underlying his verbal productions and should be carefully observed. A woman reported a dream that led to a chain of associations dealing with her unhappy marriage. While talking, she began playing with her wedding band, eventually removed it, tossed it back and forth from one hand to the other, and finally accidentally dropped it. The ring fell to the floor and rolled under the couch. Her actions clearly continued the thoughts in her dream and her associations about wanting to terminate her marriage.

Analytic patients often respond to the statement for professional services, appointment changes, cancellations, and other interruptions in the regular flow of the analysis by bringing in dreams that relate to these realities. Frequently, too, some concomitant acting out is to be found. The patient may hold back payment of his bill, may be a few minutes late for his appointment, may cancel or "forget" an appointment, miss the street or the office building, etc. This acting out derives from the patient's dynamics and expresses in a dramatic way conflicts that are reported in a dream.

Before lying down on the couch for her analytic appointment, a woman reached into her purse, took out some hand lotion, and rubbed it into her hands. Asked about this behavior, which was most unusual for her, she shrugged her shoulders and said that her hands were chapped. After several minutes she recalled a dream of the previous night in which she was about to have intercourse with her husband; instead he had an ejaculation as she was fondling his penis. Her dream was a repetition of what had actually happened the night before. She spoke of her reactions to this occurrence and complained about her husband's sexual performance. What had happened was not unusual, but this time it frustrated and disturbed her greatly. She wished that she had a better lover. Her dream, playing out her husband's sexual inadequacies, and the symbolic incident with the hand lotion in her analytic session had obvious transference implications: the wish for sexual gratification as well as the expectation that the same thing would happen there as happened with her husband, with the same frustrations and anger on her part. All men were a disappointment.

Sometimes the acting out is an attempt to defend against strong impulses. In a most uncharacteristic act a patient brought several bottles of Scotch whiskey to his analyst as a Christmas gift. He then reported a dream in which he was engaged in a saber duel with a masked opponent. His gift served to ward off and appease the analyst (the masked adversary), whom, in his dream, he had wanted to slash with a saber (see also R. Sterba, 1946b).

Other acting-out behavior can be extremely destructive or self-destructive, involving "accidents," promiscuous or inappropriate sexual activity, occupational or professional entanglements, and the like. Unfortunately, there are times when children become the innocent victims of such behavior. It is a major achievement indeed, if the patient brings in a dream that foreshadows his intentions and the therapist is able to discuss openly this material with him and prevent some tragedy from occurring.

A bitterly depressed alcoholic woman, profoundly resistant to hospitalization or drug therapy, dreamed that she was going on a long journey with her infant son in her car. On the basis of the manifest content of this dream the analyst was able to discuss her suicidal plans with her. In the course of this discussion, she revealed that she had planned to take her child, wrapped in a blanket and with his cuddle toy, get into her car in the garage, and turn on the motor so that they might die together of carbon monoxide poisoning. The discussion helped. While she continued to be depressed, she did not carry out her plan.

It has been suggested (Greenacre, 1950; Lebe, 1980) that patients who have a tendency to chronically act out probably have some early, preverbal fixation. It may then be presumed that the behavior itself, or the material which is expressed in this way, is of a preverbal nature. Careful study of the material is necessary in each instance to verify the pertinence of such an hypothesis.

Associated with the problem of acting out in connection with dreams, which people are inclined to view as being to a certain extent under the individual's conscious or voluntary control, is the subject of dreams and illness. Dreams may contain some reference to underlying physical disease or conditions about which the patient may be only dimly aware, if at all. "In dreams," Freud writes, "incipient physical disease is often detected earlier and more clearly than in waking life, and all the current bodily sensations assume gigantic proportions" (1917b, p. 223).

In these instances the individual has probably been aware that all was not well with him, but managed to ignore it and put off seeing a physician. The sensations and thoughts which such patients have may be the day residues that are then taken up in a dream. One man, who prided himself on being an athlete and in excellent physical shape, dreamed that he was attending some primitive ritual in which a medicine man dressed in an elaborate costume was leading a group of people in a wild dance to the sound of huge drums. His associations led to his revealing that for the past several months he had been having headaches (in the dream magnified to pounding drums) and that he had had some fleeting thoughts about seeing a physician (a "medicine man" as opposed to a psychoanalyst). He did in fact do this some time later and was found to have hypertension.

In other situations the patient may not be dealing with an incipient illness, but may incorporate some physical sensation such as an ache or a pain into his dream. The dream attempts to deal with this stimulus that might awaken the dreamer, just as it would some external stimulus as, for example, the ringing of the telephone. Freud noted that the actual experience of pain does not occur in a dream "unless a real sensation of pain is present" (Breuer and Freud, 1893–1895, p. 189). This occurs with toothaches, gall bladder attacks, kidney stones, ulcers, labor pains, etc.

Sometimes the response to an affect in a dream may coincide with or initiate a physical response, i.e., a psychosomatic disturbance. Ernest Jones (1911) writes, "It is incorrect to regard the dream as the cause of the symptom that subsequently arises. They both have a common cause in some buried thoughts. The same thoughts can come to expression in both a dream and a neurotic symptom, thus illustrating the near relationship of the two" (p. 255).

A patient who often expressed his anger by developing a migraine headache responded in this way in a dream which, as his associations revealed, referred to fury directed toward a colleague. He awoke from the dream and found that he was in the midst of a full-blown attack of migraine. He then recalled that in the dream he had begun to experience an aura.

The development of psychosomatic symptomatology poses many unanswered questions, however, insofar as the interrelationship between the psychic and the physical is concerned (see Dunbar, 1947, 1954; Seguin, 1981).

A man who had been working on the problem of his aggression toward his mother, whose somewhat eccentric characteristics strongly suggested a borderline character, dreamed one night that he was kicking her violently in her buttocks with his foot. As his big toe hit the mother's buttocks, he suddenly experienced a sharp, excruciating pain in his big toe. The pain, more severe than he had ever had, was so intense that he awoke. The pain continued without abatement, so his wife drove him to a nearby hospital emergency room. The diagnosis of gout was confirmed by laboratory studies that revealed hyperuricemia. He had no previous history of gout and did not even know he was susceptible to it. Why the attack of gout occurred just at the time he dreamed of kicking his mother could not be determined. It remains an open question whether the attack of gout was triggered primarily by psychic factors or primarily had an organic basis and was "translated" by his dream in accordance with the aggressive wish he had toward her at the time.

Another patient, a woman, who had been dealing in her analysis with her problems with her mother and her discovery that her husband was having an affair with her best friend, brought in the following dream. She is in a kind of cable car suspended between two mountains. The cable suddenly breaks and the cable car with her in it plunges to the depths below. She is frightened and awakens. In her associations to the dream, she talked about the possibility of leaving her husband and divorcing him. She was determined to break off her relationship with her friend, who she felt had betrayed her, as had her husband. She discussed her infantile relationship with her mother and realized that it, too, must cease. She thought the two mountains referred to her mother's breasts, to which she still clung as if a child, and said she felt she would die if she gave up that relationship. Later that day she began to develop an abdominal pain which became so severe that she had to be hospitalized. A diagnosis of an acute abdomen was made and surgery was performed the next day. A thick band of adhesions from previous abdominal surgery was discovered to be the cause of her acute symptoms. This was successfully removed and the patient's surgical wound was closed. Within less than an hour the patient suddenly went into irreversible shock and died. One can only speculate about the relationship of this patient's dream and her death so shortly after.

Wording

Paying attention to the wording of a dream, while listening to its account, provides both therapist and patient a sense of deeper understanding, as well as aesthetic pleasure and delight in the inner workings of the mind.

While all people make use of these mechanisms in their dreams, the dreams of some people literally abound in the use of puns, witticisms, switch words, and neologisms, some of which may strike one as "corny" or even childlike. Why this is so is unclear. Some of these people are particularly clever and witty in their daily lives, but not all are. Other people seem to have a run of such dreams for several nights, but do not continue to use this device in their dream-work with any notable regularity. The talent and sensitivity of therapists, enabling them to understand patients' use of wording in dreams, varies. Unfortunately, some therapists seem to have an especially difficult time in this area and are often frustrated when this type of material appears. Feeling they don't understand, they may as a result discourage their patients, either actively or unconsciously, from using dreams as vehicles for communication.

The therapist is usually able to understand the patient's dream by following his patient's associations closely. In many instances the patient himself will spontaneously recognize that some element in the dream has been used as a pun or switch word.

Words in the manifest dream frequently relate to names of people and places. As some names are more suited than others to be represented in this manner, the manifest dream will be more inclined to use these names. References to the transference are often made in this fashion, using the analyst's name or that of some other analyst.

My own name is often represented by references to "green" and to "stone." One woman dreamed that she was looking at her menstrual pad, on which there was an emerald clasp. The noun "clasp" was a pictorial representation of the verb "to clasp." The dream pictured an unconscious erotic wish to clasp the green stone. The libidinal transference was further continued in her reactions to her menstruation and her thoughts and fantasies about pregnancy.

Another patient dreamed of looking at a sheet with a grass stain on a bed. Her associations led her to recall making the bed the previous day and noticing a stain on the sheet from her husband's dried ejaculate. The transference implications of the dream, utilizing a pun on my name (a green stain), were immediately obvious to her.

The first part of my last name has also been expressed pictorially by a smiling or grinning face, and the last part as a beer mug or stein. The first two syllables of my first name have frequently appeared in dreams represented by the initials "L. X."

Members of the analyst's family may also be referred to in the dream by the use of words or pictures. A patient who had seen my wife in the audience at a scientific meeting dreamed of a blue delphinium. His associations led to his having noticed that she was wearing a delphinium-blue dress. The dream element was also a pun on her name, Adele.

Another patient dreamed that he was attending a large dinner party. Two men he had recently met, whose names were Davidson and Richardson, were also present. While he had actually met these people recently, the dream referred to my two sons, David and Richard, and his wish to be present at a dinner party at my house as a member of the family.

Important determinants of the individual's symptomatology or personal history are at times expressed by the use of the mechanism of *plastic word representation*. One patient saw a large wicker basket in his dream. He went on to say that he was "a basket case," that he was in such a depressed state he might as well be dead. The basis for his depression was that he felt like a castrate. He had tried to have intercourse with a new girl friend and had been completely impotent. He felt that his penis was dead. Another patient dreamed of walking on a grassy lawn and noticing a number of depressions in the earth, each deeper than the next. These "depressions" were a pictorial representation of his basic symptom, i.e., episodes of depression, and his concern that each would become deeper than the previous one. The grassy lawn referred to a cemetery and his fear that his depression would ultimately result in his death. A woman dreamed of a Valentine card on which there was a large heart in pieces. It referred to her being "heartbroken" about the breakup of a love affair.

An extremely narcissistic man with homosexual tendencies dreamed of putting a baby cream on his face. In his associations he revealed that he did in effect want to keep his face from wrinkling and to maintain a youthful appearance so that he could attract young homosexuals. But it also referred to his feeling ashamed for many of his practices and his wanting to "save face"—not be humiliated. Historically, the baby cream referred to medications applied to his skin for eczema when he was an infant.

A medical technician who had been trained in parasitology dreamed of a parasitic infiltration called "schistosercosis." The word puzzled him at first. He knew of the disease *schistosomiasis*, which is caused by the worm *Schistosoma japonicum*. The word "schistosercosis," however, was not the name of a real parasitic disease, and he could find no reason for dreaming about it. Then he suddenly realized that the dream element was a pun on his *sister's psychosis*. His older sister had been severely emotionally disturbed for many years and her condition contributed greatly to his difficulties during childhood.

Another man dreamed of a little boy with sawed-off legs to which wooden sticks were attached. The dream referred to his brother's club feet. During his childhood, the patient was continually hurt and angry because of the concern and attention given to his younger brother by his parents because of his condition. He felt that they ignored him.

Still another patient dreamed of being in a church in which "weepy organ music" was being played. The "weepy organ" referred to his symptom of urinary urgency, which at times bordered on incontinence. He would be so overcome by his need to urinate that he would have to stop whatever he was doing and find a place where he could urinate, at times in situations that could well have led to rather compromising circumstances. The patient's mother had died when he was a small boy, and he vividly recalled the organ being played, both during her funeral and on the anniversaries of her death, when a church service was dedicated to her memory. The "weepy organ music" in the dream referred to his wanting to weep during those occasions, but never allowing himself to do so. His urinary symptom was a displacement of these feelings.

Consideration of the wording of a dream element will often reveal the nature of the patient's resistance or defenses. One man dreamed he was safely "holed up" in a gigantic castle with thick stone walls, a huge moat, and a drawbridge, while the enemy was vainly trying to attack him. The scene was taken from a television movie he had watched the night before, but the enemy that was unsuccessfully trying to penetrate his defenses was the analyst and the analysis. The choice of the word "holed up" referred to deeply rooted passive wishes and a fantasy that he had a hole at the base of his scrotum which could be penetrated by a man.

Another man, who had been raised on a farm, dreamed of a broken fence. He immediately recognized that what he was saying in his dream was that his *defense* was broken (the fence = de = fence defense). Some time later, when he dreamed that he was in a peach orchard similar to the one on the farm where he lived as a boy, the reason for his anxieties became clear. In the dream he is looking at the peaches in the trees and says to someone near him, "The fruit is ripe to pick." The dream announced the emergence of intense passive strivings in the transference.

Frequently, sexual and aggressive material may be expressed in the wording of a particular dream element. A patient dreamed that he was bald. The dream referred to his having "balled" a woman the night before. Another man, a male homosexual, reported a two-part dream. In the first part of the dream, he said that he was "blowing a young man." In the second part, he was so furious with another man that he felt he would "blow up." Finally he "slugged him so hard" he thought "the blow" would have knocked him out. The dream makes use of the word *blow* as a switch word referring to fellatio as well as to violent aggression, expressed outwardly as well as being internalized. In his case, the homosexual behavior was in part a defense against his intense aggression against men. Similarly, the word *stroke* may be used in dreams both as an expression of aggression and to denote an affectionate gesture.

In a previous communication (1954) I was able to demonstrate from a number of cases that the element *convertible* in the manifest content of dreams in men often referred to, or was used as a switch word for, sexual *convertibility*. Some time after its publication, a patient who was in the mental health field read my paper and raised some questions about it during one of his sessions. That night he dreamed about having the turntable of his phonograph repaired. His discussion of my paper on *convertible* during his session became the day residue behind the element *turntable* in the manifest content of his dream. His associations to the turntable being repaired led to his anxiety that he would be turned into a homosexual as a result of his analysis.

A Jewish patient, in treatment with a woman analyst, dreamed that he was looking at a beautiful Spanish stamp on which a nude painted by Francisco Goya was reproduced. As a boy the patient had seen this stamp in his father's collection. The dream referred to the patient's therapist, whom he regarded as forbidden, a "goya," i.e., a Gentile woman. The dream expressed his oedipal wish in the transference to see his therapist in the nude, and to have a sexual relationship with her. Originally, he had seen his mother in the nude and had entertained sexual wishes toward her.

Often the therapeutic situation, in any of its aspects, appears in a dream. A man dreamed of his analyst's office. In the corner was "a large plant, on the leaves of which were some bugs." The dream referred to his thought that the analyst had a "plant" and was "bugging" his communications. Another patient dreamed that he was at an airport ready to board a plane which was Flight Number 45. His dream referred to his wish to take flight from his analysis because of his fear of acting upon his aggressive fantasies of shooting his analyst with a .45 caliber pistol he had inherited from his father.

A young woman consulted a woman therapist about going into treatment with her. As the therapist had no available time, she referred the young woman to a male analyst for analysis. Prior to going to see him, the woman had a dream in which the woman therapist she had consulted was serving her some mints on a silver tray. The dream expressed her wish that the woman therapist would give her her "treat-mints" on a silver tray or platter. After a few sessions, she brought in another dream, in which she was buying an Impala car. The dream referred to her fear of being impaled by her male analyst and was connected in her associations to her memory of repeated myringotomies as a child. Her treatment by a doctor and her position on the couch reminded her of those experiences.

From the illustrations cited it is possible to see the vast scope of the use of wording in dreams. There does not seem to be any relationship, however, between the use of this particular mechanism of dream-work and the content of the material or the degree of repression present.

Chapter Five

Symbolism

Thus far we have discussed three of the ways any element in a manifest dream must be considered: in its positive or negative sense, from an historical standpoint, or from its wording. We come now to the fourth method: consideration of the dream from a symbolic standpoint.

The term *symbolism* has come to have many meanings in language and popular literature. It refers, in its broadest sense, to the metaphoric or allegorical significance of a term, a thought, or an object (E. Jones, 1916). It may be an allusion to something: e.g., the flag standing for the country, a church standing for a religion, a government building standing for the government itself or a government agency such as the FBI. Such a metaphorical significance must always be considered when examining any dream element. The use of symbols in a metaphorical sense is often very idiosyncratic; the "same" symbol may have *different* meanings not only in different cultures, but also to different people, and even to the same person at different times. Any *ad hoc* interpretation of the symbol by the therapist would preempt the patient's thoughts about it.

In analytic work, the term symbolism refers to a rather narrow, albeit extremely important, list of subjects that deal primarily with the most intimate aspects of life. The symbols are quite "standard" and generally mean the *same* thing in different cultures, to different people, and to the same person at different times. Symbols deal primarily with the individual's relationship with the various important members of his immediate family (parents and their substitutes, siblings, and offspring); various parts of the person's body, particularly the sexual organs; love and sex in all their manifestations; and birth and death. Only in this respect does psychoanalysis come close to offering a small dictionary for the translation of symbols in dreams.

  Frequently the strictly symbolic meaning of an element may actually overlap or be combined with its metaphorical significance. A snake, for example, may refer to a penis, but it may also refer to attributes of deceptiveness, sneakiness, or trickery, or to the dangerous qualities in a person (the proverbial snake in the grass).

  Freud warns strictly against overestimating the importance of symbols in dream interpretation and of "restricting the work of translating dreams merely to translating symbols" and "abandoning the technique of making use of the dreamer's associations" (1900, p. 360).

He emphasizes that the patient's associations to a dream element must be given precedent in *every* instance, whereas the translation of elements into their possible symbolic meaning is only to be used as an "auxiliary method." The result is a "combined technique, which on the one hand rests on the dreamer's associations and on the other hand fills the gaps from the interpreter's knowledge of symbols"; he urges caution "in order to disarm any charge of arbitrariness in dream-interpretation" and advises that one bear in mind, because symbols frequently have multiple meanings, that "the correct interpretation can only be arrived at on each occasion from the context" (1900, p. 353). He stresses that

> often enough a symbol has to be interpreted in its proper meaning and not symbolically; while on other occasions a dreamer may derive from his private memories the power to

employ as sexual symbols all kinds of things which are not ordinarily employed as such. If a dreamer has a choice open to him between a number of symbols, he will decide in favour of the one which is connected in its subject-matter with the rest of the material of his thoughts—which, that is to say, has individual grounds for its acceptance in addition to the typical ones. [1900, pp. 352–353]

And again:

Quite apart from individual symbols and oscillations in the use of universal ones, one can never tell whether any particular element in the content of a dream is to be interpreted symbolically or in its proper sense, and one can be certain that the *whole* content of a dream is not to be interpreted symbolically. A knowledge of dream-symbolism will never do more than enable us to translate certain constituents of the dream-content, and will not relieve us of the necessity for applying the technical rules which I gave earlier. [1901a, p. 684]

Freud indicates also that symbols "are generally known and laid down by firmly established linguistic usage. If one has the right idea at one's disposal at the right moment, one can solve dreams of this kind wholly or in part even independently of information from the dreamer" (1900, p. 342).

Despite Freud's warning and his careful exposition of the general rules governing the utilization of symbols in dream interpretation, for a time psychotherapists insisted on interpreting or translating dreams solely on the basis of their symbolic content or equivalents without exploring the patient's associations regarding his selection of the symbol and its context both in the dream and in the total communication. Often *ad hoc* interpretations were offered in which the therapist was really giving *his* associations to the patient instead of vice versa. The results proved disastrous for patient and therapist alike, as in the long run neither could profit from such interpretations. The pendulum then swung the other way. Students and even experienced therapists became so wary of the use of symbolic interpretations that even when such interpretations were valid and necessary, they hardly ever used them.

Although the analyst may think that a particular element or group of elements may be understood symbolically, he must assess the patient's readiness to accept such an interpretation before suggesting it to him. Generally, the most useful technique is to follow the patient's associations to the various dream elements first and then, if possible, to convey one's interpretation to the patient on the basis of these associations. Should the patient's associations not seem to lead to material that the therapist can interpret in a useful way, the therapist may *suggest* that the patient consider the element or elements from a symbolic standpoint. By doing so, the therapist opens the door to any considerations that may come from the patient in the form of additional associations, or he permits the patient to examine and then discard the symbolic significance in favor of other specific associations.

These days one must be especially perceptive when working with people who have an intellectual or superficial knowledge of dream interpretation. These people are particularly prone to use symbolic interpretations themselves as a defense against pursuing their associations to the dream in directions that might prove threatening. A man who worked as a mental health professional in a large hospital described a dream in which a dentist was working on the inlays of his teeth. After telling the dream, he promptly remarked, "Oh, that is obviously a castration dream. You are the dentist. The teeth represent my penis and you are grinding or doing something to my penis like removing it." He then went on to discuss various matters and finally, after a period of silence, said, "I haven't told you this, but I got a big raise in my job last week." After he talked about his raise, and what he wanted to do with the extra money, the significance of his dream became clear. He was very fearful that, as he had received a substantial salary increase, the analyst, like the dentist in the dream, would take the gold out of his mouth, i.e., he would raise his fees. While it is true that on a deeper level the patient's own interpretation, that he feared the analyst would castrate him, was probably correct, what he feared most at this time was that his analyst would take away his recently acquired funds. This had more meaning to him than the symbolic interpretation he had given as a defense. In this instance it was much more useful to deal with the metaphorical communication in his manifest dream than with a strictly symbolic one.

A similar point may be made about various objects commonly employed as anatomical symbols. Patients who dream of guns, for example, will often talk about them as being "obvious phallic symbols," yet will frequently omit or ignore the aggressive significance of the guns as offensive or defensive weapons. One patient dreamed of a cigar and spoke quite intellectually about its being a penis symbol. He bypassed, for a time, the specific associations that led to a business meeting in which a particularly officious and unscrupulous business adversary was smoking a large, black, and, to the patient, particularly foul-smelling cigar. Eventually he said, "I was so mad at the son of a bitch, I was boiling inside. I felt I wanted to take his goddamn cigar and ram it down his throat till his eyeballs popped!" Again, interpreting the phallic and fellatio significance of this communication would have ignored the more pressing issue of the patient's fury and his internalizing his rage ("I was boiling inside").

On one occasion, a Jewish woman dreamed of wearing a gold cross on a chain around her neck. She dismissed the dream by indicating that it was obviously an expression of her penis envy. She then went on to talk about her relationship with a non-Jewish man and, fearing that her parents would be angry with her, her feelings of guilt about it. By referring to the anatomical significance of the cross, she sought to give her analyst the kind of theoretical explanation that she thought would please him rather than risking the possibility that he might be displeased with her (as her parents were) for having a relationship with a non-Jewish man.

In general, although a strictly symbolic interpretation may have validity, a great deal of care should be exercised in assessing the patient's associations to determine the level at which an interpretation should be made. Quite frequently, considering the element in a metaphorical sense will be a good deal closer to what is ego-syntonic for the patient. Should the patient's associations indicate that one can go deeper and deal with the content more along id lines, then one may offer a symbolic interpretation. Sometimes the use of a sexual symbol in a dream foreshadows the emergence of frankly sexual material in later sessions.

We may categorically state that it is in every instance important for the therapist to know *why* a particular symbol is used in the dream. Freud's comment that the dreamer's choice of a symbol will be "in favour of the one which is connected in its subject matter with the rest of the material in his thoughts" is especially pertinent in this regard. It is up to the therapist to ascertain the connections between the symbol and the underlying dream thoughts.

Keeping in mind the general considerations about viewing an element in the manifest content of a dream, let us now discuss the various symbols. The reader should realize that the list is far from complete. Patients can select any object from their particular realm of experience to serve as a symbol in a dream. Due to the progress of civilization and technological development, new symbols are constantly created which become quite popular, while old symbols seem to be used less frequently, especially by the younger patient population. The reader will notice, moreover, that some symbols can represent more than one thing. Their specific significance therefore can be ascertained only from the patient's associations.

Marriage

Freud writes that marriage is symbolized in a dream by the lottery, "a short-lived state of happiness" (Freud and

Oppenheim, 1911, p. 186); a married couple by "two horses" (1922a, p. 214).

Often marriage is symbolized by a *house*. The destruction of a house in the dream refers to the destruction of a marriage by divorce, separation, remarriage, or the death of a spouse. If the dreamer finds himself in someone else's house, he may be expressing the wish to be married to someone else.

Family

Parents are symbolized by people of high authority: emperor and empress or king and queen (Freud, 1900, pp. 353–354); czar and czarina; president and first lady; governor and his wife; mayor and his wife; great or famous people, etc. The reference may be to the rank or position itself, e.g., the presidency, or to specific people, e.g., Mr. and Mrs. Franklin D. Roosevelt or Mr. and Mrs. Dwight D. Eisenhower.

The associations that emerge in connection with the "royal couple" often lead directly to an insight into the actual, fantasied, or wished-for attributes of the patient's family. It is not sufficient to understand that the dream was about a "king and queen" and that these royal personages represent the dreamer's parents. As we have discussed earlier, in connection with other dream elements, the therapist must inquire or elicit specific information from his patient about *which* king and *which* queen were in the dream. What are their characteristics? Were they young or old, kind or cruel, peace-loving or warmongering, etc.? Were they real figures or fictional? Frequently, inquiry into the associations behind the royal couple in dreams results in associations that lead specifically to one or the other, i.e., to the male or to the female figure.

At times the characterization of royalty serves not only to extol the parents but to convey their remoteness and unattainability. At other times the designation serves to express an early family romance fantasy. In the vernacular of some patients, "throne" in the expression "to sit on a throne" refers to the toilet. With these people, the characterization of the royal couple on their respective thrones may be an expression of their great derision and contempt for their parents, one that is obscured by placing them in an elevated position. This derives from the individual's earlier ambivalent view of his parents.

The selection of degraded figures to represent the parents expresses the individual's negative feelings toward them.

> Robbers, burglars and ghosts, of whom some people feel frightened before going to bed, and who sometimes pursue their victims after they are asleep, all originate from one and the same class of infantile reminiscence. They are the nocturnal visitors who rouse children and take them up to prevent their wetting their beds, or who lift the bed-clothes to make sure where they have put their hands in their sleep. Analyses of some of these anxiety-dreams have made it possible for me to identify these nocturnal visitors more precisely. In every case the robbers stood for the sleeper's father, whereas the ghosts corresponded to female figures in white night-gowns. [Freud, 1900, pp. 403–404]

Here once more it is important to obtain specific details about these dream criminals. A distinction should be made as to whether the crime is one of stealth and secrecy or one in which the criminal is assaultive, as in a robbery; whether the criminal is armed or unarmed; and what he is after. If armed, the type of weapon and the specific threat made to the dreamer are important. Careful attention should be paid to current events when such elements are present. When we get material about nocturnal visitors who helped to control enuresis and tried to prevent masturbation, it is important to elicit further information about the manner in which this was done and also about the patient's fantasies at the time.

Ghosts figuring as dream elements may stand for female figures in white nightgowns, but specific information must be obtained, as the reference may be to some book, drama, movie, or television production, or possibly to someone who has actually died. A great deal of information can be obtained with regard to the dreamer's notions about death from the type of ghosts present in the dream. In addition, the characterization of a ghost may refer to death wishes directed toward a parent.

At times the presence of a black man and woman in the manifest content of the dream represents either passion in general or, more specifically, the dreamer's parents in their nighttime activity ("act of darkness"), i.e., sexual relations. The aggressive connotations here may then refer to the child's conception of parental coitus as a violent act. The "black" figure in dreams may also refer to the analyst, about whose personal life the patient is "in the dark."

The father may be represented by any figure of authority or any great man, e.g., Goethe (Freud, 1900, p. 354), a chief, a general, a commander; or commanding officer, the pope (*il papa*), a rabbi, a judge, a conductor, a policeman, a guru, a radio or television anchorman or commentator such as Walter Cronkite. The father may also be represented by the sun.

One patient dreamed of a king who reminded him in his associations of King Lear, whom he regarded as a stupid fool for giving away his kingdom. He would never give everything away like that to his daughters, who he felt were selfish. Then he went on to talk about his resentment of his senile father, who was being cared for in a nursing home at his expense. Another man dreamed of the Emperor Claudius after seeing a movie about him. The reference was to the emperor's cruelty, which led to the patient's own experiences at the hands of a sadistic surgeon. The patient feared that his analyst would treat him similarly. Behind this was a childhood memory. While camping in the woods with his father, the patient had gotten a large splinter in his thumb. His father removed it by cutting into the thumb with his pocketknife after sterilizing the blade by holding it over a flame. His father had not used any anesthetic other than putting some cold water on the thumb "to freeze it." While the patient understood that there were no doctors around, he still felt that the manner in which his father cut into his thumb had been sadistic. Still another man, who dreamed of a Turkish nobleman, referred in his associations to the original Count Dracula, who had impaled Christians. The patient feared his analyst would treat him in the same fashion. His associations led to his father's having held him down as a child to give him enemas while his mother watched.

One man dreamed a lengthy dream about the conquests of Alexander the Great. The day residues led to his having seen a book about the great general. By the ready reference to my first name, the patient's associations led from the conqueror to myself. Subsequent associations indicated, however, that he had been impressed to learn that Alexander the Great had had a violent temper, was reputed to have had such rages that he killed men, that he had had incestuous relations with his mother, that he was homosexually inclined, and that he was an epileptic. The patient's description of the Macedonian's personality was an allusion to how he regarded me in the transference situation. He was afraid that I had similar tendencies, that I would become violent and kill him or that I might attack him sexually. Ultimately his fear of me referred to his dread of his father, who did have a violent temper.

Freud indicates that "a dreaded father is represented by a beast of prey or a dog or wild horse" (1900, p. 410). An enraged bull may symbolize masculine strength (Ferenczi, 1916). These symbols must be considered carefully, as they may also contain the dreamer's dread of his own wild impulses projected upon the image of the father. At times the wild impulses characteristic of some animals may represent a wished-for freedom to express impulses that are not really wild but which the individual believes would be considered wild by society or by his superego.

The mother may be represented by a highly esteemed female authority figure (a teacher, a mother superior, a school principal, an actress) or some important social or political figure (Queen Elizabeth, Catherine the Great, Maria Theresa). She may be represented by a nurse or waitress, or by Mother Earth, Mother Church, or the Alma Mater. She may appear as the good fairy godmother or a multibreasted Magna Mater. Sometimes the mother is symbolized by the moon, the sea (*la mère* and *la mer*), or by a dais or desk (Klein, 1923). "Heavy objects" refer to the pregnant mother (Freud, 1917a, p. 155). The mother may also be symbolized by some female figure with frightening, malevolent, bisexual, or sadistic attributes: a witch or some mythological goddess such as Kali or Rati. She may also be represented by a church (the Cathedral of Notre Dame) or house, or by some other architectural construction. The choice may be based on aspects of the structure that lend themselves to anatomical symbolism: arches, domes, balconies, etc. Very often the mother may be represented by an institution such as the army or some organization that cares for the needs of the people, e.g., a hospital, clinic, school, library, museum, university, store, bank, restaurant, company, firm, loan company, shopping center, or corporation.

Again, it is important that the therapist know why the specific imagery or symbol in the dream has been chosen; whether it fits in with the general concatenation of the patient's associations or is glaringly discordant; and whether the allusion is to be viewed in a complimentary or derogatory manner.

The dreamer himself may be symbolized as a prince or princess (Freud, 1900, pp. 353–354) or may appear as a child. One of the dreamer's children, especially a child of the same sex, will often stand for the dreamer and refer to the time in his life when he was a child. A "little bird may also be a symbol for a child" (Freud, 1922a, p. 215). At times the dreamer appears as himself but the surroundings in which he finds himself are large, thus indicating that the dream scene alludes to something from his childhood, i.e., when he was small.

The dreamer's siblings as well as other children are often represented as small animals, birds, or bugs. Vermin in dreams represent babies (Freud, 1918, p. 82n2; 1921, p. 136). If the dreamer regards children as undesirable, an unwelcome intrusion into his life, this fact may be expressed in this type of symbolism. A sister is represented as a nun or by a river (Niederland, 1957), a brother by a monk or fraternity brother.

The Human Figure as a Whole

"The one typical—that is regular—representation of the human figure as a whole is a *house* . . ." (Freud, 1916–1917, p. 153). When dealing with the human figure as a whole, one must bear in mind that the ego is essentially a body ego. The individual's view of himself, his self-percept, may be expressed in adjectives describing the house itself, a part of it, or the area in which it is located.

One patient, a highly narcissistic male homosexual, dreamed of a beautiful classic Greek building, something like the Parthenon. Part of the building was covered by a plastic tarpaulin such as is used on construction sites. Under this was a lot of rubbish, dirt, garbage, and rot. The building represented himself as he wanted to appear, a kind of Adonis. He selected physically beautiful young men for his homosexual lovers, their physical appearance representing how he himself wished to be perceived. Underneath was his belief, stemming from early childhood, that he was ugly and deformed and that his skin was rotten as a result of his past episodes of atopic dermatitis.

Used in describing a house appearing in a dream, such expressions as "I felt the house was old and crumbling" may refer to what the person presently thinks of himself or what he may have thought of himself at an earlier time. It can also be that when the patient dreams of a house as being old, built in some bygone era, or located in an old decrepit neighborhood, the reference is to an earlier period in the person's life. Sometimes the patient may note a specific detail in the dream, e.g., a particular wallpaper design, that may effectively date the material to which he is referring.

The size of the house or building is another matter for consideration. Big buildings or houses may refer to what the individual thinks or has thought of himself, i.e., a grandiose view of his ego. It is significant, too, whether the individual finds himself *in* the house or outside looking at it. If he is in the house, this may refer to the "house" of the mother's body (fantasies of intrauterine life) or to the house in him, i.e., his idea or conception of the interior of his own body cavities: mouth, bowel, vagina, uterus. If the dreamer is on the outside of the house, he may be looking at someone else, e.g., the mother (see Kestenberg, 1975). Quite often a big house or building dates the events to which the dream refers to the individual's childhood, when he was small and the people around him seemed gigantic.

A woman dreamed that she was in a large building when a large powerful locomotive, such as she remembered seeing when she was a child, suddenly rammed through the front door and into the lobby. Next she was walking someplace and discovered she had lost one of her shoes. The dream referred to a fantasy she had had as a child: that she had been damaged *in utero* by her father's penis (i.e., she had lost her own penis) when her parents were having intercourse.

Attention must also be paid to references to various openings and parts of the house such as windows and doors. The former often refer to eyes, ears, or nose; the latter to vagina or anus (back door). The therapist must note the specific location *in* the house, if this is mentioned, as well as the general description about it. Thus, the attic or upper story will often refer to the head. Attention may then be directed to comments made about the attic, e.g., the presence of dirt, cobwebs, etc. Sometimes such comments refer to the patient's notions about having mental problems.

A patient dreamed that he was in the attic of an old house and a fire broke out. He was afraid he might be trapped, the whole building would collapse, and he would be destroyed with it. His associations led to his fear that his whole personality would collapse and he would be completely destroyed if he dealt with certain highly traumatic material from his childhood.

Houses with extensions may refer to the arms or legs, to the breasts or genitals. The basement or cellar usually refers to the genital organs as well as the "base" impulses or drives of the person. Quite frequently people who have had some difficulty, abnormality, or deformity will dream of a house partially deformed or misshapen. A patient who had one leg smaller and weaker than the other as a result of polio in childhood had frequent dreams in which a part of the house or building was damaged in some way. When the house refers to somebody else, any reference to a deformity must also be noted.

In his discussions of these themes, Freud notes the following:

> It may happen in a dream that one finds oneself climbing down the façade of a house, enjoying it at one moment, frightened at another. The houses with smooth walls are men, the ones with projections and balconies that one can hold on to are women. [1916–1917, p. 153; see also 1900, p. 355]

> Smooth walls over which the dreamer climbs, the façades of houses, down which he lowers himself—often in great anxiety—correspond to erect human bodies, and are probably repeating in the dream recollections of a baby's climbing up his parents or nurse. [1900, p. 355]

> Tables, tables laid for a meal, and boards also stand for women—no doubt by antithesis, since the contours of their bodies are eliminated in the symbols. [1900, p. 355]

> Materials, too, are symbols for women: *wood, paper* and objects made of them, like *tables* and *books*. [1916–1917, p. 156]

We may add that "tables laid for a meal" often refer to the mother's breasts. This is especially true if the symbol is overdetermined by descriptions of the china, plates, cups, goblets, and wine glasses as well as of specific foods or beverages (grapefruit, rolls, sundaes, etc.). Often, Freud adds, "a table . . . has to be interpreted as a bed" (1916–1917, p. 262). Chairs are also well suited to represent the human body: they have legs, a back, a seat, and arms. The seat of the chair may also refer to a lap, especially the mother's lap.

An automobile or other conveyance (such as a bus) in which the individual finds himself may also stand for the individual's body ego. The headlights appear there as eyes, and the motor, whether in front or back, refers not only to sexual organs but also to such vital organs as the heart. Fenders frequently refer to extremities, especially the arms (the fenders = de-fenders). The trunk of the car often represents the back, the lower bowel, the rectum, or the anus. The steering wheel or gearshift lever and the tires often refer to the genitals, male and female respectively.

As the patient describes the car, the therapist should note the make, type, and size of the vehicle. Some individuals, especially men who are very "car conscious," may describe the car according to the year and model, e.g., "It was a '42 Dodge sedan," etc. Often such dating of the vehicle serves to express the approximate year that some event occurred. The size of the car, especially if it is represented as large, may also reveal the individual's age when the event occurred. Cars are often associated with specific experiences, accidents, trips, or scenes of the individual's family when they were in close quarters and a good deal of the family dynamics were expressed and compressed in a short space of time.

In addition, Freud mentions some miscellanous symbols that pertain to the body:

Clothes and *uniforms*, as we have already seen, are a substitute for nakedness or bodily shapes. [1916–1917, p. 158]

'Down below' in dreams often relates to the genitals, 'up above', on the contrary, to the face, mouth or breast. [1900, p. 410]

At times this representation is to be considered from a metaphoric standpoint: the "down below" refers to "base instincts" (such as lust) and the "up above" to their opposites (love in a platonic, spiritual, or intellectual sense). The reference to the latter strivings, however, may be used as a displacement to obscure or deny the existence of other, less noble impulses. With some patients it is the other way around. This is especially true with some patients with homosexual impulses; often they confuse their wish to be loved and the sexualization of this wish. One patient's desperate need to be loved by someone was freely expressed by frantic homosexual acting out, but the thought of loving or being loved by a man was anathema to him. Frequently during his analysis he had frankly homosexual dreams involving his male analyst, but he could not bring himself to recognize either his love for him or his wish to be loved by him in turn.

Chapter Six

Sexual Symbols

Freud remarks that "the very great majority of symbols in dreams are sexual symbols" (1916–1917, p. 153). It is far more common for the genitals to be symbolized than for them to appear as themselves in dreams.

The Male Genital Organ

Ernest Jones (1916) notes that "there are probably more symbols of the male organ itself than all other symbols put together" (p. 103). Freud begins his list by observing that "for the male genitals as a whole the sacred number 3 is of symbolic significance" (1916–1917, p. 154).

Objects resembling the male genital in shape. Freud notes that the male organ "finds symbolic substitutes in the first instance in things that resemble it in shape—things, accordingly, that are long and up-standing" (1916–1917, p. 154). These include "all elongated objects, such as sticks, tree-trunks and umbrellas (the opening of these last being comparable to an erection) . . . (1900, p. 354). To these may be added scepters (Freud and Oppenheim, 1911, p. 181), as well as "high or tall objects or buildings, church spires, monuments, minarets" (p. 199). Trees may at times take on the added significance of the "tree of life." In addition, the number 1 and objects with the shape of cylinders, cones, triangles, and tripods may also represent the male genital, the last three suggesting, of course, the "sacred number 3" as well as a certain quality of upstandingness.

Objects with a penetrating function. Overlapping the first category are "objects which share with the thing they represent the characteristic of penetrating into the body and injuring—thus, sharp *weapons* of every kind, *knives, daggers, spears, sabres,* but also fire-arms, *rifles, pistols* and *revolvers* (particularly suitable owing to their shape)" (1916–1917, p. 154; see also Freud and Oppenheim, 1911, pp. 183–185). Needles, scalpels, currettes, lances, trocars, and other invasive instruments capable of penetration for medical or surgical procedures are important symbols of the male genital organ. The laser beam, with its capability of exact destruction, is becoming increasingly important as a male genital symbol. Various types of weaponry such as cannons, rockets, and launching devices, especially those with recoil mechanisms, may also be included.

The characteristic of penetration may be modified to some extent into the capability of opening things, e.g., keys (1905a, p. 97), combination locks, screwdrivers, awls, can openers, drills, and certain types of wrenches. Animals with a capability for burrowing, such as moles, mice, rats (the latter with its long tail), gophers, and woodchucks are also appropriate symbols in this regard, though here the possibility of reference to oral sadism should be kept in mind.

Objects emitting fluids. Also somewhat overlapping the first category are, in Freud's words, "objects from which water flows—*water taps, watering-cans,* or *fountains*" (1916–1917, pp. 154–155). Pipettes, syringes, enemas, and fire extinguishers are also properly included here, as are various propellant devices such as aerosol cans that spray substances, sometimes at long distances. As they are activated by hand after the container is shaken, they may have an added masturbatory significance. Semen itself is represented by jelly, jam (especially jam with seeds), glue, worms, small fish, etc. In addition, "thread . . . like all things analogous to it (cord, rope, [wheat], twine, etc.), is a symbol of semen" (Freud and Oppenheim, 1911, p. 194).

Objects capable of being lengthened. Included by Freud in this category are hanging-lamps and extensible pencils (1916–1917, p. 155; see also Freud and Oppenheim, 1911, p. 193). Telescopes and automobile antennas are still other examples of such objects, whose significance is rather obvious.

Elongated objects that are grasped in the hand. Here Freud mentions "*pencils, pen-holders, . . . hammers,* and other *instruments*" (1916–1917, p. 155). All writing instruments such as chalk, fountain pens, and ball points of various kinds are included here. Those that appear hooded in some way may represent the uncircumcised penis or the clitoris. Also included are nail files, "possibly on account of the rubbing up and down" (Freud, 1900, p. 354).

Machinery. Freud remarks that "the imposing mechanism of the male sexual apparatus explains why all kinds of complicated machinery which is hard to describe serve as symbols for it" (1916–1917, p. 156). The list here includes boilers, pipes, tubes, hoses, and the like. Revolving governors are also a frequent symbol, as they contain two balls, as are such vehicles as horsecarts (Freud and Oppenheim, 1911, p. 194), cars, locomotives, motorboats, tractors, and plows.

Sharpe (1937), however, suggests that "all kinds of machinery and movable apparatus can be transferred bodily sensations, especially those experienced at an early age" (p. 87). Kohut (1971) adds a metaphoric significance to machines in dreams, indicating that they can be "understood as the result of amalgamations and compromise formations between current and archaic aspects of the self representation" (p. 246).

Various musical instruments may also be included here, as well as such gadgets as hair dryers, electric massagers, etc. In addition, the hair dryer (or "hair blower," as it is sometimes called) and the "snow blower" are often used as switch words for fellatio. Sports equipment of various kinds—bats, racquets, golf clubs, and all such extensions of the extremities—may symbolize the male genital, especially if used in connection with balls.

Objects which rise up in defiance of gravity. This characteristic, "one of the phenomena of erection," according to Freud (1916–1917, p. 155), leads to its representation by bread and its ability to rise when baked, breadsticks, long French loaves, etc. In this connection Freud specifically mentions *"balloons, flying-machines* and most recently . . . *Zeppelin airships"* (p. 155). The list of such objects also includes rockets, kites, and birds—"little birds" (Freud, 1922a, p. 214). The stork is especially well suited to represent the male organ, with its long legs and neck and the myth that it brings babies (1910c, pp. 125–126; see also Margolis and Parker, 1972). The swallow, while it may represent the penis, may also be connected with food or with fellatio (Sharpe, 1937).

In a metaphoric sense, these objects may also represent ambition (Gutheil, 1951). The symbolic meaning of balloons is further complicated, as they often stand for breasts or, because they are filled with gas, for flatus. Finally, dreams "can treat the sexual organ as the essence of the dreamer's whole person and make him himself *fly*" (1916–1917, p. 155).

Reptiles and fish. These, according to Freud, are "less easily understandable male sexual symbols"; they include "above all the famous symbol of the *snake*" (1916–1917, p. 155).Freud "remarked that snakes are . . . also female *symbols*: having no legs, they are totally castrated" (Nunberg and Federn, 1962–1974, vol. 3, p. 220nl).

While a snake in dreams generally refers to the penis, in a number of instances I have seen it refer to large coiled feces, sometimes excreted by the patient but at other times by someone else (e.g., the parents). Reptiles, especially crocodiles or alligators, often refer to the aggressive and orally sadistic aspects of male sexuality, while fish often prove to have bisexual significance through reference to the "fishy smell" attributed by some people to the vaginal odor. One man, after a dream about being in the fish market area in New York City, commented about the "cunt market" in New York. Then, in the course of his associations, he recalled a vulgar ditty about a woman's genitals: "You can wash it and clean it and powder it well, but you can never get rid of the fishy smell."

Other animals. Freud writes that "many of the beasts which are used as genital symbols in mythology [e.g., the unicorn] and folklore play the same part in dreams: . . . snails, cats, mice (on account of the pubic hair) . . . (1900, p. 356). With respect to mice, Freud also regarded them as a symbol for the female genital (Nunberg and Federn, 1962–1974, vol. 4, p. 157). Other animals, such as the giraffe (Freud, 1909a, p. 40), rhinocerous, bull, boar, and elephant, may also symbolize the male genital.

Articles of clothing. Freud notes that "an overcoat [German '*Mantel*']" is often used to symbolize a penis, "though in this case it is not clear to what extent the use of the symbol is due to a verbal assonance" (1900, p. 356). And in another connection he writes, "an *overcoat* or a *cloak* means a man, perhaps not always with a genital reference" (1916–1917, p. 157). The use of the overcoat as a symbol is elaborated by Ernest Jones (1927).

Elsewhere Freud reports a patient's dream in which a "transparent grey garment," later described as "a long black coat and grey trousers," symbolized a condom (1913c, p. 282). Coats, especially plastic raincoats, even when they are not gray, frequently have this meaning. In some dreams of coats and jackets, reference is made to a fur collar or a fur piece, which is a reference to the pubic hair.

One patient dreamed that he was wearing a long coat which he felt was going to be shortened. While taking a shower the day before the dream, he noticed that he had accumulated a small amount of smegma under his foreskin and had wondered whether he should have been circumcised.

Coats or jackets with zippers are often a displacement upward from pants that have to be unzipped for sexual relations to proceed.

A woman's hat, Freud notes, "can very often be interpreted with certainty as a genital organ, and, moreover, as a *man's*" (1900, pp. 355–356). This is particularly well symbolized in dreams of hats from which a large feather protrudes or which have tassels or other ball-like ornaments attached to them. The hat, however, is also a bisexual symbol.

"In men's dreams a necktie often appears as a symbol for the penis. No doubt this is not only because neckties are long, dependent objects and peculiar to men, but also because they can be chosen according to taste—a liberty which, in the case of the object symbolized, is forbidden by Nature" (Freud, 1900, p. 356). Necktie dreams are also common in women. A chain or neck ornament worn by either sex may be a substitute for the necktie. Ropes and cords of all kinds may symbolize the male genital or the umbilical cord or stalk, or may refer to a tie in a metaphoric sense (e.g., *Silver Cord*, by Sidney Howard).

Others parts of the body. "The genitals," writes Freud, "can also be represented in dreams by other parts of the body: the male organ by a hand or a foot" (1900, p. 359). In addition to these, and in accordance with displacement from below upward, the penis is frequently represented by the head or nose, the penis and/or testicles by the eyes or eyeballs. A mustache may represent the pubic hair. "And finally," writes Freud, "we can ask ourselves whether the replacement of the male limb by another limb, the foot or the hand, should be described as symbolic. We are, I think, compelled to do so by the context and by counterparts in the case of women" (1916–1917, pp. 155–156).

Language makes use of such expressions as "middle leg," "third leg," "short arm," etc. to symbolize the penis. The popular expression that one can tell the length of a man's penis by the length of his nose or the size of his feet bears this out. The fingers or thumb and the toes, especially the big toe, can also be used in this way. Oppenheim writes: "pushing a ring down on a finger [depicts] erection. The lower the ring goes, the longer the penis becomes" (Freud and Oppenheim, 1911, p. 193n1). Pushing a ring onto a finger also refers to intercourse.

Persons. "The male organ," Freud notes, is "represented by persons" (1900, p. 366). These may include a specific figure (e.g., the father) or a nonspecific one, most often a man or a child (Freud, 1913c, p. 282). Sometimes dreams make use of figures that are mythological, folkloristic, or derived from fairy tales: dwarfs, gnomes, elves, little men, etc. Modern-day figures who perform tasks, such as service men, repairmen, etc., may also be used. Often men's names—John, Dick, Tom, George—are used to refer to the penis in dreams. The therapist should note, however, that not only can a person represent the male genital, the reverse is also true: when the genitals appear in a dream, they may represent the dreamer himself. This is in accordance with the principle that a part can stand for the whole. Sometimes the use of a penis symbolizing the person is a means of expressing a grossly derogatory view of the individual.

Plants. "The four-leaved clover," Freud writes, "has taken the place of the three-leaved one which is really suited to be a symbol. . . . The mushroom is an undoubted penis-symbol: there are mushrooms [fungi] which owe their systematic name (*Phallus impudicus*) to their unmistakable resemblance to the male organ" (1916–1917, p. 164). The stinkhorn mushroom is particularly well suited because of its shape. The allusion to mushrooms also includes the question of their being edible or poisonous. These are often important characteristics attributable to the penis, especially if there are fellatio fantasies.

While the therapist rarely has a problem recognizing any of the symbols we have outlined as representing the male genital, in clinical practice the question remains what to do about this recognition. The task becomes easier if, as we have said earlier, the therapist refines his understanding by questioning the dreamer to elicit specific information about the particular symbol involved. Adjectives added by the dreamer in his description of the dream element will enhance the therapist's understanding.

A patient brought in a dream about a gun. From a symbolic standpoint both therapist and patient readily recognized its phallic significance. The specific details about the gun were that "the barrel was crooked" and "it went off at a funny angle." The dreamer, a man who was concerned that his penis "was crooked," was worried that he might be suffering from Peyronie's disease. As a boy he used to bend his penis when he masturbated to prevent the ejaculate from staining the sheets of his bed. He was convinced that he had damaged himself irreparably.

Sometimes the description of the symbol in the dream will reveal the patient's comparison of his genitals with those of other men, his father, or his brothers. Concerns about circumcision may, in some instances, be a determinant of this comparison.

The following dream is an instance in which the specific nature of the phallic symbol revealed significant historical material. A male patient dreamed he was having difficulty climbing a flagpole which was covered with grease and had "rusty spots on it." His associations led to his having had himself circumcised as an adult in anticipation of getting married in the hope that this would make him more potent. The grease of the flagpole referred to the Vaseline gauze which had been wrapped around the shaft of his penis at the site of the circumcision, while the rusty spots referred to some bits of dried blood he had observed during the period of healing. The patient's difficulty in climbing the flagpole referred not only to his concern that he had been damaged as a result of his circumcision, but also to an earlier concern that he had damaged himself by masturbating. By having himself circumcised he attempted to undo what he feared were the harmful effects of his masturbation. The dream was also determined by underlying guilt feelings for his masturbatory fantasies.

The specific way in which the male genitals are symbolized in the manifest dream often clearly indicates the individual's concern about his sexual potency. One analytic patient dreamed that he was unable to start his very powerful car; another, that he could not "engage the clutch" of his sports car after he had started it; a third, that one of his tires was flat or deflated. Still another patient, who suffered from premature ejaculations, dreamed that his car was going out of control. His associations provided an understanding of one determinant of his symptom. He feared that if he "let himself go" sexually, he would become a rapist and rip women apart with his penis.

Transference material must also be carefully kept in mind, even though the dream appears "simply" symbolic on the surface. A Catholic woman had decided after a period of time that her analysis might run counter to her religious education and therefore determined to stop. The night prior to her planned last session, she had a dream in which she was wearing a bishop's miter (a pointed headpiece with a large cleft in it). On one side, there were two balls, one of which hung lower than the other. Someone came up behind her and gently tugged at these balls. On one level the dream expressed her anxiety that her analyst (someone behind her) would pull away her Catholicism (the bishop's miter). On a deeper level, however, it referred to her feeling that her analyst might in some way pull away her testes (the balls) and thus threaten her masculine position and leave her with a large cleft.

The Female Genitals

The symbolization of the female genitals may be divided into symbols that refer to the external genitalia, those parts directly or readily visible, and symbols that refer to the internal genitalia, those which are not. With regard to the former, a prominent feature is the pubic hair, even though it is evident in both sexes (the actual difference in male and female distribution of pubic hair is not often represented in dreams). The pubic hair of women is most often symbolized by fur, fur pieces, and muffs, and by woods, bushes (1916–1917, p. 156; 1905a, p. 99), forests, thickets, or clumps of trees. One patient dreamed of "pussy willows."

The image of Medusa's head, with its writhing snakes the sight of which turns men to stone (i.e., the opposite: makes men turn soft—impotent—instead of hard like a stone) is mentioned by Ferenczi (1923b) as a symbol of the penis-lacking external female genital. In actual clinical practice in this country, the appearance of Medusa's head as a symbol in the manifest content of dreams is rare.

Often a beard or the face of a bearded man may symbolize the external genitals. The character of the fur, thicket, etc. readily reveals whether the dreamer views the genital area as comforting or potentially menacing. One patient dreamed of wandering through a thick wood with many brambles, tangled vines, and scratchy raspberry bushes; there he was startled by a large, ferocious dog or wolf with big white, pointed, shining teeth. The dream referred to his belief that the pubic hair was hurtful and dangerous (brambles, tangles, and scratchy raspberry bushes) and that hidden in it was the vagina dentata (the dog or wolf with big teeth). The therapist should in each case try to understand whether the patient regards the pubic hair as representing a penis substitute, or whether he regards it as concealing a hidden penis or some dreaded object.

Natural and artificial features of a landscape. "*Doors* and *gates*," Freud writes, ". . . are symbols of the genital opening. . . . The complicated topography of the female genital parts makes one understand how it is that they are often represented as *landscapes*, with rocks, woods and water . . ."

(1916–1917, p. 156). He mentions also bridges and wooded hills (1900, p. 356); churches and chapels (1916–1917, p. 156); and cemeteries, vestibules, and railroad stations (1905a, p. 99). To this list may be added caves, glens, grottoes, hedgerows, valleys, craters, bogs and swamps, areas of quicksand, mine shafts, and gardens. While at times the dream imagery is specific (e.g., a vestibule, a station, a bus terminal), at other times it is vague and the surroundings are confusing. An ambiguous or hazy description corresponds to the dreamer's view of the female genital, i.e., to the fact that at some past time it was confusing to him.

Numbers and names. The letter or number "0" or "nothing" refers to the vagina. The number "8" refers to the openings of the vagina and rectum. Certain names in dreams may refer to the female genital: Kitten, Candy, Honeypot.

Animals. Freud holds that snails and mussels "are undeniably female symbols" (1916–1917, p. 156; see also 1918, p. 70). Shells and shellfish generally, bivalves such as clams and oysters, and crustaceans such as crabs and lobsters (especially the pincer claws of the latter) may be included here.

The cat is a common symbol for the female genital, which in vulgar parlance is often called "pussy." A female patient who had been frigid dreamed that her cat, which had been dead for several years, had come back to life. The dream signified a return of her sexual feelings. Only the patient's associations, however, can substantiate the meaning of a symbol used in a dream. Thus, while the cat is a common symbol of the female genital, it need not necessarily refer to it, at least not directly. In one instance, a man dreamed of a cat lying curled up on a couch. The patient's associations led to the fact that he had been planning to take the family male cat to the veterinarian to have it "neutered and declawed." The patient had identified himself with the tomcat and the analyst with the veterinarian, the castrator who would emasculate him and make him into a neuter.

Jewelry and Jewel cases. Sometimes, however, "jewels," may refer to its use in the vernacular as the "family jewels" in which case it has male genital significance. Finery of all kinds may symbolize the external female genital. (Freud, 1905a, p. 91; 1916–1917, p. 156).

Other parts of the body. Freud mentions the mouth "as a substitute for the genital orifice" (1916–1917, p. 156), and to this may be added the anus and the urethral opening. Elsewhere he refers to "an ear or even an eye" in this connection (1900, p. 359). The iris of the eye with its black pupil is especially appropriate.

Miscellaneous symbols. "The horseshoe," writes Freud, "copies the outline of the female genital orifice . . ." (1916–1917, p. 164). Elsewhere he asserts an equation between a crown and the vagina (Freud and Oppenheim, 1911, p. 182). A saddle is yet another common symbol of the external female genital and the region around it. It is important to distinguish in each case whether it is an English saddle or a Western type with a horn in front of it. Tables and wood are "puzzling but certainly female symbol" (Freud, 1916–1917, p. 158).

The internal female genitalia, i.e., the vagina or the uterus, are symbolized by:

Objects enclosing a hollow space. Freud mentions pits, cavities, and hollows; vessels and bottles; receptacles, boxes, trunks, cases, chests, pockets, and so on (1905a, p. 77; 1916–1917, p. 156). To this he adds "hollow objects, ships, and vessels of all kinds" (1900, p. 354).

To Freud's list we may add such objects as handbags, purses, wallets, refrigerators, freezers, toasters, ovens, microwave ovens, furnaces, incinerators, jukeboxes, and items of plumbing such as bathtubs, sinks, wash basins, toilet bowls, and bidets.

It is important in these instances for the therapist to know whether the reference is to the size and shape of the container, whether it is open or closed, whether it is hot or cold (i.e., whether it refers to passion or frigidity), whether the container retains its temperature or dissipates it, whether it is "turned on" or not (a reference to sexual arousal), whether it is functioning or not, whether in the case of such objects as radios and televisions the reception is good or not, etc.

Modern technology has added other objects to the list of female symbols besides those enclosing a hollow space. These include kitchen devices used in food preparation—mixers, blenders, food processors, grinders, slicers, etc.—as well as large appliances like automatic washers, driers, and garbage disposals and compactors. There are also many tools and instruments that may symbolize the vagina: pincers, nippers, pliers, nutcrackers, etc. Various machines also fit into this category: rollers, mills, vises, presses, etc. The significance for the patient's dynamics is readily understood, as most of these symbolize the patient's concept of the vagina as a powerful, grasping, and potentially destructive object.

"Some symbols," writes Freud, "have more connection with the uterus than with the [external] female genitals: thus, *cupboards, stoves* and, more especially, *rooms*. Here room-symbolism touches on house-symbolism" (1916–1917, p. 156). "We are acquainted already," he writes, "with *rooms* as a symbol. The representation can be carried further, for windows, and doors in and out of rooms, take over the meaning of orifices in the body" (1916–1917, p. 158; see also 1900, p. 354). "In this connection interest in whether the room is open or locked is easily intelligible" (1900, p. 354; see also 1916–1917, p. 158). Additionally, references to subterranean regions, "where [these] occur *without* any reference to analytic treatment, stand for the female body or the womb" (1900, p. 410).

It may be regarded as a rule that when the dreamer finds himself in a room, it is the room in the dreamer or in someone else which is under consideration. Quite significantly, the number of rooms often refers to three openings or cavities in the female pelvis: the bladder, the vagina, and the rectum. Two rooms in the manifest content may refer to any two of the above or may allude to the vagina and the uterus. Freud writes of the

> interesting link with the sexual researches of childhood when a dreamer dreams of two rooms which were originally one, or when he sees a familiar room divided into two in the dream, or *vice versa*. In childhood the female genitals and the anus are regarded as a single area—the 'bottom' (in accordance with the infantile 'cloaca theory'); and it is not until later that the discovery is made that this region of the body comprises two separate cavities and orifices. [1900, pp. 354–355; see also 1913b, p. 195; 1933, p. 101]

He indicates that

> a dream of going through a suite of rooms is a brothel or harem dream. But, as Sachs (1914) has shown by some neat examples, it can also be used (by antithesis) to represent marriage. [1900, p. 354]

Sometimes dreams in which an individual goes through many rooms refer to multiple sexual affairs. A male patient, who had frequent sexual affairs, sometimes several in the course of a day or an evening, had a dream in which he was jumping down a hall and from room to room on a pogo stick that he was holding with both hands. The dream expressed his jumping from one woman to another and his narcissistic pride in his sexual prowess. His holding the pogo stick with both hands referred also to his masturbatory practices.

As in other instances, the specific meaning of a symbol as well as its wording must be considered. A man dreamed he was standing in a closet and there were clothes hanging around him. He remembered that as a child he often played hide and seek. His favorite hiding place was inside his mother's clothes closet. He recalled the smell of his mother's clothes and the pleasant sensation of rubbing her silken dresses around his face and arms. Because he had been impotent when he attempted to have sexual relations with his wife, he thought that perhaps he was really a homosexual—a "closet homosexual." In this respect he identified himself with a woman who would be passive in relation to a man. His passivity, however, was a defense against an early oedipal wish in which he wanted to be in his mother's closet in a genital sense.

Much of what was said earlier regarding the understanding of the symbols of the male genitals has equal pertinence here. Considering the nature of the problems people have in their sexual lives, the therapist should be particularly attentive to the modifiers that are used to describe the symbols. In this instance the therapist should ascertain: Are the rooms large or small? Clean or dirty? Is the equipment (furnace, compactor) safe or dangerous? etc. Quite frequently there are indications that at one time the dreamer was confused about the nature of the opening, i.e., whether it was genital or anal. What the dreamer is doing with regard to the particular symbol is important, as is his affect in connection with this activity—e.g., does he experience his entrance into a tunnel with pleasure or with anxiety?

Menstruation

Dreams of both sexes often refer to menstruation, which may be symbolized in various ways. Elements dealing with blood directly or with the color red (e.g., a Bloody Mary), especially in connection with the female genital, often refer to menstruation. Red fluids of various kinds (e.g., red wine) and berries (e.g., strawberries, raspberries, currants) and pomegranates, the juices of which may stain clothing, are common symbols in this regard. Cherries, however, may signify defloration. The spring flower, bloodroot, condenses the idea of defloration with that of blood. Sometimes menstruation is signified in dreams by a visit, or by the pictorial representation of someone falling off a roof. The slang expression "the curse" is depicted pictorially, in some instances, by a pronouncement from a malevolent witch who usually represents the dreamer's mother.

Breasts and Buttocks

Freud writes:

The breasts must be reckoned with the genitals, and these, like the larger hemispheres of the female body, are represented by *apples, peaches,* and *fruit* in general. [1916–1917, p. 156]

In dreams sweet things or sweetmeats stand regularly for caresses or sexual gratifications. [1918, p. 107]

I have come across undoubted cases in which 'sisters' symbolized the breasts and 'brothers' the larger hemispheres. [1900, p. 358]

To this may be added the symbolism of hills and mountains, especially twin peaks. Popular, too, are cream puffs and cupcakes, sundaes or grapefruit halves decorated with maraschino cherries. Aerosol cans dispensing whipped cream or shaving cream, as well as milk or cream cartons or bottles, may often refer to breasts (or to baby bottles), as does the letter "B" because of its shape and its position as the first consonant in the word "breast." Certain types of wine goblets and buildings, especially capitol buildings with round domes, may also be used to symbolize breasts. Sometimes breasts, as unconsciously signifying nurturing comfort and bliss or providing security to the individual, are symbolized by a drug or an alcoholic drink. The term "cocktail" may have bisexual significance when it appears in the manifest content of a dream.

Because of their shared qualities of roundness and firmness, and their association with the production of fluid, the breasts and the testicles may be used to symbolize one another (Bell, 1961, 1965; Grinstein, 1962). Tausk thought that sisters sometimes represented testicles (Nunberg and Federn, 1962–1974, vol. 3, p. 251). Inflated balloons often refer to the breasts, as well as to the erect penis or to the "perfect object-self" (De Saussure, 1971, p. 91).

Inasmuch as breasts and buttocks both have the quality of being hemispherical and protuberant, it is possible for dreams to use one to symbolize the other. At times the scene of the dream may appear to be projected as on a "blank screen," which Lewin (1946) identified as the mother's breast (see also Isakower, 1938). Such dreams in analysis usually have transference significance.

Sometimes the buttocks may stand for the male genitals, which "stick out in front as the buttocks do behind." The moon—"slang use of the word *'lune'* in French [viz. 'bottom']" (Freud, 1900, p. 400)—may often stand for the buttocks. This is related to the vulgar expression "mooning" for showing the bare buttocks out of a car window.

Bisexual Symbols

Freud writes:

the tendency of dreams and of unconscious phantasies to employ sexual symbols bisexually betrays an archaic characteristic; for in childhood the distinction between the genitals of the two sexes is unknown and the same kind of genitals are attributed to both of them. But it is possible, too, to be misled into wrongly supposing that a sexual symbol is bisexual, if one forgets that in some dreams there is a general inversion of sex, so that what is male is represented as female and *vice versa*. Dreams of this kind may, for instance, express a woman's wish to be a man. [1900, p. 359]

The ubiquity of bisexuality necessitates the therapist's consideration of any sexual symbol as potentially bisexual in nature. The genitals of either sex may be represented by buildings, stairs, and shafts (1900, p. 364). An elevator shaft in a dream, for example, may represent the female genital as the space or opening in which the elevator moves. The elevator itself and the word "shaft" easily represent the male genital with its capacity for elevation.

Another example of a bisexual symbol is an astronomical observatory. The building has a large dome (breast). It has an opening like a slit (vagina) in which there is a telescope (penis). The instrument is used to observe the heavenly bodies at great distance at night (primal scene significance).

In addition, though hills and rocks are symbols of the male organ (1916–1917, p. 158), mountains are frequently used as symbols for the breasts. Another bisexual symbol is a volcano. The shape refers to the breasts, the explosion of lava to ejaculation, and the crater to the female genital. After the eruption of Mount St. Helens, a patient dreamed of the eruption. The dream expressed his anxiety that if he allowed himself to experience an orgasm (eruption), he would be left with a crater, i.e., be totally castrated.

Bisexual characteristics may be attributed to any figure in the dream. When a male figure signifying a parent appears in the dream, for example, the therapist must understand whether the reference is to the patient's father or to the phallic mother. By the same token, clear references to the phallic mother in a dream must raise the question as to whether the reference is actually to the father. One sees this frequently in transference dreams pertaining to the male therapist which must be understood as referring to the therapist as a woman or as the phallic mother. Similar bisexual considerations are applicable to women therapists as well.

A woman patient was able to trace her mother's ancestry back to the eleventh or twelfth century. The family had a crest with various heraldic symbols emblazoned on the family escutcheon. One night the patient dreamed of this crest with a lion rampant upon it. In place of the lion's penis, however, there was a long enema tube which the lion held in one of his paws. The patient's associations to the dream led first to her ancestors and the meaning of the various symbols in heraldry. The specific connotation of the enema, however, was connected with her mother's interest and enthusiasm in administering enemas to her as a child. These experiences played a significant role in the development of her neurosis. Her characterization of her mother as a phallic woman caricatured her phallus as an enema tube.

Obscure Sexual Symbols

Our comments about bisexual symbols permit us to understand more readily the various symbols Freud finds obscure.

Hats. "The *hat*," Freud writes, "is an obscure symbol of this kind—perhaps, too, head-coverings in general—with a male significance as a rule, but also capable of a female one" (1916–1917, p. 157; see also 1916, p. 338). Since a hat is capable of being removed or lost, it provides a ready symbol for the male genital, which the individual feels may also be detached. We have already mentioned the Catholic woman who dreamed that she was wearing a bishop's miter from which were suspended two ornamental balls. The cleft in the miter was definitely feminine in its significance, whereas its generally pointed shape and the two balls referred to the penis and testicles.

In other dreams, the symbolic meaning of the hat as masculine or feminine can be readily determined from the description of the hat in the manifest content, or from the dreamer's associations. A woman dreamed of wearing a tuxedo with tails and a stovepipe opera hat that clearly symbolized the male genital. A man, who was frequently preoccupied with the notion that his penis was too small, dreamed one night that he was wearing a very tall chef's hat and was preparing some exotic dish.

In the following dreams, however, the symbol of the hat is clearly feminine. A woman dreamed of wearing a helmet, like a knight, with a visor in front that had a number of slits in it. She noticed that the visor could snap shut and offer her protection. A man dreamed of wearing a conventional type of dress hat but the top of it was crushed or crumpled and one corner of it was frayed (reference to "a-fraid"); there also appeared to be a hole in it.

Underclothing and linen in general. These Freud considers female (1916–1917, p. 158). Lingerie, bathing suits, brassieres, leotards, camisoles, panty hose, and the like may be included here. The emphasis placed on the sexually stimulating or provocative quality of such attire by pictures or photographs of women wearing it in advertisements makes it a convenient symbol. Generally, the article of clothing in the dream refers directly to the body of the girl wearing it—"There's nothing between me and my Calvins," says a young starlet in a designer jeans commercial.

Careful attention should be paid to the condition of undergarments in the manifest dream. Any references to blood, dirt, or stains of any kind are particularly significant. The presence of undergarments in the manifest dream provides the therapist an opportunity to find out how the dreamer obtained his knowledge of sexual matters. In these instances, the dreamer may be asked whose undergarments they are, thus leading to a discussion of a genetic nature. "I used to look in my mother's dresser drawers and examine her underpants," responded one patient. Of great importance, too, is the clue these dreams often provide regarding a male dreamer's having tried on or worn his mother's or a sister's clothing. Does he want to "get into their drawers" from a heterosexual standpoint, or is he identified with the woman who wears them? Obviously, cross-dressing has a different significance for a girl.

A woman's dreams of underclothing may also indicate her self-image as a woman. One woman dreamed she was in the bargain basement of a large department store and was buying the cheapest underpants she could find. Her associations led to her comment that she "never spent much money on things like that anyway. Who would know?" She viewed herself, and especially her genital area, as dirty and disgusting.

Another woman dreamed of going to a supermarket and buying a bag of Gold Medal flour. In the dream she felt ashamed and embarrassed at the checkout counter. The dream referred to her mother, who had recently visited her. The patient took her mother to her own gynecologist because she had complained of vaginal bleeding. When they got to his office, the mother was asked to undress and the patient saw, much to her humiliation, that instead of a regular slip her mother was wearing one made out of a large flour sack with the Gold Medal logo imprinted on it. While the manifest content of the patient's dream did not deal with underclothes directly, it was evident that her associations did. At one time, her own view of herself as a woman was similar to the one expressed by her mother's attire.

Shoes and slippers. These, according to Freud, represent female genitals (1916–1917, p. 158). The specific sexual significance here may be readily ascertained by the details given about articles of footwear. While the notion of a shoe, slipper, or boot as a container into which a foot is put may allude to the female genital, the type of footwear will often have bisexual significance. A man dreamed of women's shoes with sharp, pointed heels three or four inches high. His associations led to thoughts about women having a sharp penis which can pierce or damage the man in sexual relations. He was having an affair with a call girl who he thought would dig her heels into him as she danced on his nude body. One woman dreamed of open-toed shoes through which she could see her big toe. Her associations led to her idea that a penis was concealed in her vagina. Another woman dreamed she was looking at her boots and noticed that the joint on her big toe was pushing through the leather. She recognized that like various members of her family who had to have painful and incapacitating bunion operations, she, too, might require such surgery. Her further associations, however, led to her fear that the analysis would be like a bunionectomy, a painful procedure that would result in a part of her anatomy being removed. A dream in which a woman loses her shoe after a large locomotive rams into a hotel lobby represents the shoe symbolically as the penis.

Another woman dreamed that her male analyst was wearing moccasins, which she thought very casual and sporty.

In her associations, she commented that the shoes referred to her view of him as being rather uninhibited sexually. She went on to relate that her father always wore shoes with laces and immediately recognized that she meant her father, unlike her analyst, was "straight-laced."

Gardens. These too are "common symbols of the female genitals" (Freud, 1916–1917, p. 158). The significance of this symbol, like so many others, can be determined only by its context. Often the specific references are to planting the garden (implantation or impregnation), to flowers, to defloration, to procreation and growth. The therapist should pay attention to the patient's description of the garden as well as to his comments as to what if anything should be done in it or to it, and by whom. A woman reported a dream in which she was looking at her garden and found that it was messy. "I knew that I had to get it cleaned up and would have to call my gardener to take care of it and plant some new things in it." There were obvious transference implications to this dream.

Blossoms and flowers. These, Freud notes, "indicate women's genitals, or, in particular, virginity. Do not forget that blossoms are actually the genitals of plants" (1916–1917, p. 158). Symbolism of this type used by adult patients may refer to a time in their psychological development when virginity and defloration were very important areas of concern and conflict. As blossoms and flowers contain both male and female elements, they readily lend themselves to use as bisexual symbols. The therapist must determine their precise meaning in each case.

Fruit. According to Freud, fruit "stands, not for children, but for the breasts" (1916–1917, p. 158). It is up to the therapist to find out from the patient what type of fruit is present in the manifest dream. Apples, pears, peaches and the like, because of their shape, readily represent breasts. Pineapple, however, while it very often symbolizes the breasts, often refers to the hurtful, harmful breast, nongiving and prickly. This is also true of the prickly pear and the quince. The type of juice or the taste of the fruit will also indicate the dreamer's ideas about breast milk and his thoughts and fantasies about the kind of loving or nursing he received from his mother.

Other fruits, such as bananas, for example, because of their appearance, must be considered phallic in nature. Whatever oral significance they have may refer to fellatio fantasies.

Apart from the strictly symbolic meaning mentioned by Freud, fruit can have a somewhat different connotation when viewed from the aspect of its wording. Language and literature (e.g., the Bible) commonly equate fruit with children, i.e., "the fruit of the womb." This approach may be applied, for example, to a male patient's dream that "the fruit was ripe to pick." In that instance the verbal significance of "fruit," i.e., its use as a slang expression for homosexual, accounts for its appearance in the manifest dream.

Diminutives. "Some symbols," Freud notes, "signify genitals in general, irrespective of whether they are male or female: for instance, a *small* child, a *small* son or a *small* daughter. Or again, a predominantly male symbol may be used for the female genitals or vice versa" (1916–1917, p. 157). Both baby and penis are referred to as "a little one." Freud writes: "It is a well-known fact that symbolic speech often ignores difference of sex. The 'little one', which originally meant the male genital organ, may thus have acquired a secondary application to the female genitals" (1917c, pp. 128–129). To this we may add that a child or midget may refer to the clitoris. In addition:

> The penis appears . . . as a *worm* ('fat earthworm'), which has crawled into the girl, and at the right time crawls out again as a *little worm* (baby). [Freud and Oppenheim, 1911, p. 182]

> Relatives in dreams usually play the part of genitals ([Stekel, 1909,] p. 473). I can only confirm this in the case of sons, daughters and younger sisters—that is only so far as they fall into the category of 'little ones'. [1900, p. 358]

One night, a man dreamed he was driving his car on a dirt road and saw his small son riding on a tricycle in the middle of the road. He could not stop in time and realized that he must have hit him. When he stopped his car and looked back, he saw his son lying in the road, crumpled up and bloody. He felt horribly guilty. In his associations he stated that the dream might refer to some deeply rooted hostile, aggressive wishes that he had toward his son, although he was not aware of any such impulses. As the session progressed, he revealed that he had had intercourse with his wife the night before and had discovered that she had begun to menstruate. He had gone to the bathroom and noticed blood on his penis, which he thought was particularly shrunken. He wondered momentarily whether it was his blood or his wife's on his penis. It will be seen that the bloody, crumpled child in the dream referred to his penis. The dirt road referred to his idea that the menstruating woman was dirty. His being unable to stop in time led him to thoughts that his orgasm might have been somewhat premature.

Plans, maps, charts, and diagrams. These in Freud's view "represent the human body, the genitals, etc. . . . In the case of unintelligible neologisms, too, it is worth considering whether they may not be put together from components with a sexual meaning" (1900, pp. 356–357). At times, maps, plans, charts, and diagrams may refer to anatomical drawings the dreamer looked at as a child or adolescent in an attempt to learn about the anatomy of the sexual organs. Incomprehensible neologisms may refer to medical terms the dreamer came across and did not understand while looking at such diagrams. The incomprehensibility of the charts and neologisms is significant, as it may refer to the dreamer's own lack of understanding concerning the genitals. Introducing this material into the dream is a means of indicating to the therapist that the patient does not understand things about sex and hopes the therapist will enlighten him. In addition, by the use of unintelligible neologisms the patient may attempt to evoke a reaction of incomprehension in the therapist, similar to what he himself felt as a child.

Quite often the patient may feel frustrated because he feels the analyst does not understand this type of dream or will not explain it to him. The patient thus repeats in the transference situation an earlier situation in which he felt frustrated because his parents did not provide adequate sexual enlightenment. One patient remarked after just such a dream, "I am sure you know what it's all about. Why don't you tell me?"

Luggage. This "often turns out to be an unmistakable symbol of the dreamer's own genitals. Luggage that one travels with is a load of sin, [Stekel (1909, p. 479)] says, that weighs one down" (1900, p. 358). In our experience, luggage or baggage often refers to the female genitals, especially the uterus in which a fetus is carried. The symbolism of heavy luggage usually refers to pregnancy. The term "baggage" or "old bag" is sometimes used as a derogatory term for a woman. When luggage or baggage is used metaphorically, attention must be paid to whether it is heavy or light, carried easily or with difficulty. Sometimes luggage refers to the patient's relatives or immediate family, who are experienced as burdensome. This is especially true when the patient is responsible for the care and support of aged, enfeebled, ill, or senile parents. In such cases, the wording of the dream element rather than its strict symbolism is significant.

In dreams men may express a feeling of genital engorgement in the scrotum and testes as the luggage or "load" they carry. Among homosexuals, the term "basket" specifically refers to the scrotum and testes.

Masturbation
Freud writes that "satisfaction obtained from a person's own genitals is indicated by all kinds of *playing,* including *piano-playing.* Symbolic representations *par excellence* of masturbation are *gliding* or *sliding* and *pulling off a branch*"

(1916–1917, p. 156). The "playing" may be any activity which is pleasurable or rhythmical and usually involves only one person. Popular language uses this symbol in the expression "playing with oneself." In dreams the patient may present such imagery as "I was playing solitaire," "I was practicing my tennis, hitting a ball against a backboard," "I was exercising, doing chin-ups, sit-ups," or "I was sewing or knitting."

Playing or practicing a musical instrument such as a piano or string instrument, when presented in the manifest content of a dream, often has reference to masturbation. The emphasis here is on an activity that involves the hands or fingers. One patient who dreamed of practicing the piano, which he said he had not touched for years, was reminded of a joke: "They laughed when I sat down to play. I didn't know the bathroom door was open." His remark about not having touched the piano for years referred to his not having sat on the toilet and masturbated, as he had done during his adolescence.

Obviously, dreams of practicing or playing woodwind instruments or brasses may have an oral or anal significance (e.g., fellatio or flatus). Gliding or sliding activities often include some reference to working with wood or metal: e.g., planing or sanding. One patient, for instance, dreamed of sanding a long dowel with some fine sandpaper or steel wool, and feeling its smooth texture by rubbing his fingers gently over the surface. "It felt good," he added.

In a rather unusual dream, a man reported that he was frying some eggs. This patient, after considerable embarrassment, spontaneously related how as an adolescent boy he had learned that the Jewish word for testicles was "batesim," from the Hebrew word meaning eggs. Having learned this he wondered if the product of his ejaculation was like the white of an egg and could therefore be fried; one day when his mother was not at home, he actually tried to fry his ejaculate in a frying pan.

The symbolism of pulling off a branch or "pulling one

out" (Freud, 1899, p. 319) refers directly to masturbation. There are many other expressions that appear or are pictured in dreams that deal with the same subject: "to jerk," "to jerk off," "to jack off," "to knock one off," "to tear off a piece," etc. A patient related a dream in which he was driving a car and had a flat tire. He stopped and jacked up the wheel to change the tire. Suddenly the jack gave way, the car settled down, and he saw that the tire was still flat. The patient's associations led to his having masturbated before going to bed the night before and his noticing how flaccid his penis had become.

While language and dream symbolism use imagery where something "comes off" to express the idea that a product (semen) separates from the body, the imagery also carries the implication of punishment by castration.

In each instance, the therapist must distinguish whether the symbol stands for masturbation or for sexual intercourse, as the identical symbols may be used to refer to either activity (e.g., "to knock off, or tear off, a piece"). Important clues as to whether the patient is dealing with masturbation may be given by such details as whether the activity is solitary or involves another individual of the same or opposite sex.

There is a problem here, however. The manifest dream content may not involve another person, while the patient's associations do. The therapist is then left to determine whether the sexual wishes or fantasies are or are not associated with masturbation. At times it is easier for patients to reveal their heterosexual fantasies than to confess that they have masturbated, either recently or at some earlier time, and to discuss the fantasies and/or techniques that have accompanied this behavor. The patient's difficulties in disclosing such material frequently depend upon the status of the transference. If the patient feels the analyst will punish him for sexual thoughts and fantasies associated with masturbation, he may suppress this material. The dream may then symbolically refer to masturbation, while the associations lead only to some actual heterosexual event. Similarly, a dream symbolizing masturbation may lead to associations about a heterosexual experience, while the patient omits any reference to homosexual fantasies connected with the material.

"The *falling out of a tooth* or the *pulling out of a tooth*," Freud observes, "is a particularly notable dream symbol. Its first meaning is undoubtedly castration as a punishment for masturbating" (1916–1917, pp. 156–157). This is one of those dream presentations where the therapist may deduce the "crime" from the nature of the "punishment"in accordance with the law of Talion: "Eye for eye, tooth for tooth. . ." (Exodus 21:23–25). Since the punishment must fit the crime, if the punishment is that a tooth (genital) is lost or pulled out, the crime must be a genital one. Even though a tooth is used to express a genital symbol, however, the therapist should keep in mind that it may have other meanings. A further discussion of the meaning of teeth in dreams will be found in chapter 13.

Another symbol associated with masturbation is the presence in the dream of someone who is being beaten, hurt, or humiliated in some way. Quite often such imagery leads to the unraveling of masochistic masturbatory fantasies in which the dreamer assumes a passive but highly exciting position. In this connection, masturbation may be directly symbolized by such expressions as "flogging the dummy," "beating the meat," etc. (see Freud, 1919a).

Sexual Intercourse

"We come across special representations of sexual intercourse less often than might be expected," Freud writes; ". . . .Rhythmical activities such as *dancing, riding* and *climbing* must be mentioned here, as well as violent experiences such as *being run over;* so, too, are certain *manual* crafts, and, of course, *threatening with weapons*" (1916–1917, p. 157). Dreams involving this symbolism may refer to actual experiences of intercourse, including oral or anal intercourse.

Other representations of sexual intercourse as "violent experiences" include such manifest dream elements as being hurt, beaten, tortured, shot, stabbed, crucified, or murdered. These are entirely passive experiences, but their active concomitants may also be represented. It will be noted that acts of cruelty or aggression depict sexual relations in accordance with regressive or infantile fantasies of sexual relations. The dreamer conceives of the sexual act as a sadomasochistic encounter in which someone attacks, punishes, debases, or humiliates a victim. These dreams often contain an allusion to an oral or anal assault of some kind.

One woman dreamed of getting an injection of penicillin in her buttocks, an obvious pun on the medical procedure. Another dreamed of getting a transfusion. "Transfusion" expressed the idea of sexual relations symbolically as well as verbally, as "trans" referred to the *trans*ference of her relationship to the analyst as a physician. The nature of the activity may symbolize the individual's problems in sexual relations, e.g., "The gun went off too soon"; "I was practicing archery but missed the bull's-eye"; "The motor of my refrigerator kept running, but it didn't cool" (reversal of frigidity).

With regard to one type of "rhythmical activity" Freud writes as follows:

> Steps, ladders or staircases, or, as the case may be, walking up or down them, are representations of the sexual act. [1900, p. 355; see also 1910b, p. 143.]

> It is not hard to discover the basis of the comparison: we come to the top in a series of rhythmical movements and with increasing breathlessness and then, with a few rapid leaps, we can get to the bottom again. Thus the rhythmical pattern of copulation is reproduced in going upstairs. [1900, p. 355n2]

This symbolism may be expressed by other activities involving a crescendo of excitement, e.g., musical compositions: "Rhythmically moving water vessel [is] a good symbol of the female genitals in the act of copulation" (Freud and Oppenheim, 1911, p. 199); "The narrow door and the steep stairs . . . [represent] intercourse" (1913c, p. 282). When symbols of this type are present in the manifest dream, we urge the therapist once again to inquire into the specific associations to them. For example, in one instance, the stairs about which a patient dreamed referred to a house in which he lived as a child. He and a neighbor girl used to play doctor under the stairs. Thus the dream about the stairs, while referring to sexual relations, also referred to a childhood scene involving sexual activity of another kind. Another man, who dreamed of a ladder, recalled that a friend of his had fallen from a ladder and broken his leg. Here, the symbolism of the ladder referred not only to sexual relations, but also to its dreaded consequence.

Freud notes that sexual intercourse may also be symbolized by those activities that are "immediately justified by linguistic usage (such, for instance, as those derived from agriculture, e.g., 'fertilization' or 'seed') and others whose relation to sexual ideas appears to reach back into the very earliest ages and to the most obscure depths of our conceptual functioning" (1901a, p. 684).

At times sexual intercourse is represented by other types of activity. It may be expressed as urination into some container, on a wall, or on a house. In these instances, the dream clearly expresses a child's conception of coitus, i.e., that the man urinates into or on a woman. Patients may dream of conversations, as on a telephone, of musical performances, such as a vocal or instrumental duet, or of a party of some kind which they are either giving or attending.

Weaving is another symbol for sexual intercourse. In this symbolism, the loom represents the bed; the shuttle the penis; the thread stands for semen and the material is the child (Sharpe, 1937). Referring to another sphere of domestic activity, Freud writes that "the ugliest as well as the most intimate details of sexual life may be thought and dreamt of in seemingly innocent allusions to activities in the kitchen . . ."

(1900, p. 346). The content of the dream will reveal whether the material is to be regarded as genital or oral. The use of various types of machines in culinary operations reveals many of the dreamer's ideas and fantasies about sexual intercourse. We have already discussed many of these devices in reference to the female genitals. In this connection, however, the devices are represented as functioning and are to be understood as verbs symbolizing copulation and the individual's ideas about it. Dreams dealing with such objects as mixers, food processors, or any other equipment that blends, creams, grinds, slices, or cuts will often express the dreamer's anxieties in regard to sexual relations and their real or fantasied consequences. For example, a man may fear that his penis will be ground up like coffee or meat, or a woman may express an unconscious wish to destroy the male organ.

After her alarm clock rang, a woman had gone back to sleep for a few minutes before getting up. During this interval, she dreamed that she was putting coffee beans into an old-fashioned grinder and turning the crank. Her associations led to her grandmother, whom she used to watch doing this, and to her grandfather, who had lost part of his hand in a farming accident. Somehow she vaguely held her grandmother responsible for her grandfather's mishap. Her associations then led to some pejorative comments about her husband, who was a "coffee freak" and who suffered from premature ejaculations, especially if she took an active part in sexual relations. The morning of the dream, she had wanted to have sex with her husband rather than getting up and fixing breakfast. She thought, however, that if she made her feelings known and was active, her husband would ejaculate prematurely. Her dream expressed this wish to have sexual intercourse. The symbol of putting the coffee beans into the old-fashioned coffee grinder identified her with her grandmother, who, she believed, was responsible for her grandfather's symbolic castration.

It is important to note that the symbolism for sexual

intercourse among manifest homosexuals is often identical to that used by heterosexuals. With homosexual patients the therapist must distinguish whether the reference is to a homosexual activity or to the patient's heterosexual wishes and fantasies.

By the mechanism of displacement, a table, especially one covered with a white tablecloth, often alludes to a bed and to sexual activity. "Since 'bed and board' constitute marriage, the latter often takes the place of the former in dreams and the sexual complex of ideas is, so far as may be, transposed on to the eating complex" (Freud, 1900, p. 355). One may note, however, that the oral symbolism may refer to oral sexual activity or directly to some oral impulse such as sucking or biting. One patient had a dream in which he was "eating at the Y." He referred to a familiar joke in which "Y" stands for YWCA but is a switch word for cunnilingus. Where there is a specific reference in the manifest dream to a table set with certain foods, it is important to inquire about their nature. There is a considerable difference in implication between foods that are hard and have to be bitten and chewed and those that are soft and creamy.

One final symbol for sexual intercourse that was mentioned prominently by Freud is that of "the chimney-sweep, who carries the ladder"; he "appears in this company on account of his activities, with which sexual intercourse is vulgarly compared. . . . We have made the acquaintance of his ladder in dreams as a sexual symbol" (1916–1917, p. 164). Although dreams dealing with chimney sweeps are not common these days, they do occur. Sometimes the men are represented in full attire, with black tails and tall stovepipe hats, carrying the long-handled brooms and brushes of their trade. Some patients have dreamed of the huge vacuum cleaner equipment used in cleaning chimneys. Various sexual practices may be symbolized in this way. One man dreamed of a large vacuum hose, several feet in diameter, coming out of the front door of a house. As he watched, "the machine instead of sucking up the contents, blew them all over the street." The man, a homosexual, had seen such a hose some days before while he was cruising for a "blow job."

The significance of these dreams lies in their reference to the soot and the dirt in the chimney that needs to be cleaned out. The imagery here points to the dreamer's conception of sexual relations as being a dirty business. In their associations, patients have sometimes metaphorically referred to analysis as a dirty job or a dirty profession. The transference aspects of the analyst as the chimney sweep (sewer cleaner, well digger, etc.) are clearly expressed in the choice of symbol. Some physicians, whose dreams of chimney sweeps were stimulated by movies or television productions, noted in their associations that cancer of the scrotum was a frequent occupational hazard of chimney sweeps. The castration allusions are obvious.

Chapter Seven

Miscellaneous Symbols

Psychic Equivalents in the Unconscious

The secretions of the human body, Freud writes—"mucus, tears, urine, semen, etc.—can replace one another in dreams. . . . what in fact happens is that significant secretions, such as semen, are replaced by indifferent ones" (1900, p. 359). In another connection, Freud quotes Rank as follows:

> The same symbols which occur in their infantile aspect in bladder dreams, appear with an eminently sexual meaning in their 'recent' aspects: Water = urine = semen = amniotic fluid; ship = 'pump ship' (micturate) = uterus (box); to get wet = enuresis = copulation = pregnancy; to swim = full bladder = abode of the unborn; rain = micturate = symbol of fertility; travel (starting, getting out) = getting out of bed = sexual intercourse (honeymoon); micturate = emission. [Rank, 1912, p. 95, in Freud, 1900, p. 403nl]

Urination may also be expressed as sheets—i.e., "it was raining sheets" (which may also refer to wet sheets)—or by a man running (Sharpe, 1937). Urination and its control may be represented by such objects as faucets, spigots, and petcocks. These objects often refer to the dreamer's anxiety about being able to control urination, e.g., enuresis, or to weeping.

The means of representation employed, however, is important, and it is not sufficient merely to realize that "significant secretions, such as semen, are replaced by indifferent ones" such as urine or tears. In each case, the therapist must understand why a substitution has been made. Thus, the use of urine in a dream symbolizing semen may refer to the childhood conception that the only product that emerges from the penis is urine, that the man urinates into the woman during intercourse, or that something sad or painful happens during sexual relations that leads to tears.

Oppenheim (Freud and Oppenheim, 1911) writes that "comparisons [can be made] between virility and wealth and between the thirst for gold and libido" (p. 186nl), while Freud himself writes as follows: "Dreams with an intestinal stimulus throw light in an analogous fashion on the symbolism involved in them, and at the same time confirm the connection between gold and faeces which is also supported by copious evidence from social anthropology" (1900, p. 403; see also Freud and Oppenheim, 1911, p. 190).

Freud summarizes his conception of psychic equivalents in the unconscious by the formula Penis = baby (little one) = gift = money = feces (1917c, pp. 127–133). Feces may also be symbolized by eggs (Ferenczi, 1915; see also Bourke, 1891). Money may at times be equated with love or with payment for sex to a prostitute. Frequent references to this connection are often found in the transference and in the patient's reaction to the payment of his analytic bill. Flatus is expressed in dreams by various references to wind or to gas. The latter may be expressed in turn by a reference to a hot air balloon, to getting gas for a car (the revere of passing it), or to something concerning natural gas. A compulsive man, whose mother had given him enemas for constipation during his childhood, dreamed that someone was putting a nozzle into the back end of his car to put gas into it. Then a balloon, covered with a brown sticky (stinky) material came out of the fuel (phew[l]) opening.

As a consequence of these psychic equivalents and the capacity of symbols to have multiple meanings and to replace each other, the therapist is faced with a wide range of possible meanings of his patient's dreams. As we have emphasized before, he is guided in his interpretations by the thrust of the patient's associations. Moreover, he should continually bear in mind that any one of these symbols may have an aggressive as well as a sexual meaning.

A patient described his father as wealthy and extremely penurious. When the patient was a boy, his father always gave him "a hard time" whenever he asked for even the smallest amount of spending money. Before going home for a Thanksgiving holiday during his analysis, he dreamed of a Thanksgiving dinner with the whole family gathered around the table. In the dream he was supposed to bring in the turkey on a platter and to set it before his father so he could carve it. Instead of the turkey, however, he carried in a platter on which a large pile of feces was heaped and placed it before his father. While both the manifest content of the dream and his associations clearly expressed his aggression and fury with his father for his meanness and stinginess, his underlying thoughts dealt with his longing for his father, his wish that his father would love him and that he in turn would love his father and present him with a baby.

Freud states that "defaecation-dreams can . . . be impotence-dreams" (Freud and Oppenheim, 1911, p. 200) and indicates also that "those defaecation-dreams which are concerned with treasure contain little or no fear of death, whereas the others, in which the relation to death is expressed directly (dreams of an assumption to Heaven), disregard treasure and motivate the defaecation in other ways" (p. 197).

The unconscious significance of vaginal dreams may refer to the anal or rectal antecedents of vaginal eroticism. Thus, a woman dreamed of a black penis or a black dildo penetrating her vagina. Her associations led to memories of enemas received or observed. The reverse is also true: dreams of the lower bowel or rectum may refer to the vagina. The juxtaposition of anal and vaginal symbolism will frequently provide the opportunity to explore cloacal theories of the female genital as well as ideas about childbirth and conception.

Spiders

Freud writes that "according to Abraham (1922) a spider in dreams is a symbol of the mother, but of the *phallic* mother, of whom we are afraid; so that the fear of spiders expresses dread of mother-incest and horror of the female genitals" (1933, p. 24). The black hairy nature of the spider's body often refers to pubic hair and to the anxieties referable to it. In their associations patients will often identify the spider specifically as the black widow spider, a species in which the female destroys the male after intercourse. The extreme dread evoked by this symbol is that the woman, or specifically her genitals, will castrate or kill the dreamer, suck the blood out of him, and destroy him just as the black widow spider kills her mate after he has fertilized the eggs and is of no further use to her. Men may have such dreams in connection with impregnation and/or childbirth, thereby expressing the fear that when their biological usefulness has been realized, they will be destroyed by the woman.

Spiders in dreams not only refer to the dreamer's anxieties about himself, however, but may also allude to a whole host of ideas about what the dreamer's mother may have done to his father, especially if the father was a passive man, was ill, or had died. In his elaboration of spider symbolism in dreams, Abraham (1922) observes that the spider's web represents the pubic hair, while a single thread symbolizes the male genital. In addition to a horror of the female genitals, the spider may refer, at times, to a similar horror of oral sadism (R. Sterba, 1950). Finally, the spider and the web it spins with a barely seen thread may allude to the bond of the dreamer with his mother, a bond that may ultimately lead to his destruction.

Bridges

Of the bridge as a dream symbol, Freud makes the following remarks, drawing on the work of Ferenczi (1921, 1922):

> First it means the male organ, which unites the two parents in sexual intercourse; but afterwards it develops further meanings which are derived from this first one. In so far as it is thanks to the male organ that we are able to come into the world at all, out of the amniotic fluid, a bridge becomes the crossing from the other world (the unborn state, the womb) to this world (life); and, since men also picture death as a return to the womb (to the water), a bridge also acquires the meaning of something that leads to death, and finally, at a further remove from its original sense, it stands for transitions or changes in condition generally. It tallies with this, accordingly, if a woman who has not overcome her wish to be a man has frequent dreams of bridges that are too short to reach the further shore. [1933, p. 24; see also 1913a, pp. 275–276]

While the sexual significance of this symbol is readily apparent, its multilayered determinants must always be kept in mind. The following illustration will demonstrate this. A woman patient, a native of Canada, dreamed she was back in Canada, just across the river from Detroit. The scenery was beautiful, very green and hilly. She was trying to cross into the United States by going over the Ambassador Bridge but somehow was not able to reach the other side. "I was almost there but I couldn't quite make it."

A number of years before, while she still lived in Canada, she had been in treatment with a Canadian psychotherapist, but had had to terminate her treatment when her husband's employment necessitated an abrupt and precipitous move to Detroit. She did not like Detroit, which she found provincial and stultifying, and longed to go back to the beautiful area in Canada from which she came. One element of her dream, that she "couldn't quite make it," referred to her general adjustment to the way of life in Detroit. But, to complicate the situation, she had had to go into analysis here and had great difficulty establishing a relationship with her analyst. Not having worked through the separation from her Canadian therapist, she felt she "couldn't quite make it" with her Detroit analyst. On another level, the move to Detroit meant giving up her rather infantile attachment to her mother, who remained in Canada, and adapting to a new environment. She resented her husband for having made her move. "I had to do it because he's the man and makes the money," she complained. On a deeper level, the dream expressed her wish that she had been the man, as she would have done things in such a way that she would not have had to move.

Fire

"Kindling fire," Freud writes, "and everything to do with it, is intimately interwoven with sexual symbolism. Flame is always a male genital, and the hearth is its female counterpart" (1916, p. 162). "The interpretation of dreams of fire," he remarks elsewhere, "justifies the nursery law which forbids a child to 'play with fire'—so that he shall not wet his bed at night" (1900, p. 395).

Freud (1932) later indicated that in men the impulse to urinate on a fire is homosexually tinged. Keeping this formulation in mind, we may suspect that many dreams of fire, especially in men, refer to the emergence of urethral erotism or are the symbolic expression of a homosexual conflict. In my own practice I have seen a number of dreams in which the element of fire in the manifest content was associated in the latent dream thoughts with oral and anal material (see Grinstein, 1951). I would therefore recommend that the therapist be attentive to references to all stages of libidinal development in such dreams.

Dreams of fire may refer in a general metaphorical sense to any passion, whether libidinal or aggressive, that may erupt out of control and destroy everything about it. Sometimes such dreams are a part of a "story line" that deals with war or bombing, or one in which the individual was directly or "inadvertently" responsible for a fire. In one dream, for instance, a patient dreamed he was camping with a group of people whose identities were not clear. They were gathered around a campfire, which was then extinguished. The fire was not properly put out, however, and he suddenly observed that it had spread and the adjacent woods were ablaze. His associations led to his anger with many people, including his wife and children, with whom he was planning to go on a camping trip. He complained that he hated the bother and the primitive conditions of such a trip. "I prefer camping at the Plaza in New York," he said. The dream expressed his intense anger with everyone in his family.

Dreams of fire need not necessarily be interpreted from a symbolic standpoint. They may be connected with historical events in the individual's life. Fires are very impressive, especially to children. If a fire has occurred in the dreamer's house and there has been destruction of the individual's property, references to the traumatic event occur at various times in the course of an analysis. One patient related that a fire had destroyed his home when he was a child and his family had had to move. He had few memories of living in the house that burned. One day, after a dream about a fire, he recalled the events of that fateful night, and remembered that when his father grabbed his baby sister and rushed out of the house, he had thought that his father was going to leave him behind in the burning house. A whole host of feelings toward his parents and his sister that had formerly been screened by the "memory" of the fire then emerged.

The destructive aspects of fire in dreams may also be connected with fears of ego dissolution or bodily disintegration in a violent manner. One patient remembered that during his adolescence he had had a dream of a fire that consumed everything around it. As he watched in the dream, he saw that the sky was red, as buildings and various structures toppled. It was clear from his associations that at that time he had been concerned about his sexual impulses and his intensely furious hatred of his parents, who he felt were trying to control his life by telling him where to go to school, what to study, etc. But then his associations led to his revealing that at that time he was also concerned that he was becoming psychotic; everything about himself seemed to be going to pieces and undergoing a kind of destruction. He felt he was "falling apart." The dream heralded the onset of a disturbed state which required him to be hospitalized for a period of time.

Swimming

"People who have frequent dreams of swimming," Freud writes, "and who feel great joy in cleaving their way through the waves, and so on, have as a rule been bed-wetters and are repeating in their dreams a pleasure which they have long learnt to forgo" (1900, p. 395).

With swimming dreams, specific information should be obtained from the dreamer about the setting in which the scene occurs, whether other people are present, and what their reaction is to the great enjoyment the dreamer is experiencing. Such information provides clues to the parents' reaction to the child's expression of instinctual impulses. Sometimes such dreams refer to fantasies of intrauterine existence which the patient has had about himself or a sibling.

Patients who have a history of enuresis will frequently have dreams of fire also.

Déjà Vu

Freud writes:

> In some dreams of landscapes or other localities emphasis is laid in the dream itself on a convinced feeling of having been there once before. (Occurrences of '*déjà vu*' in dreams have a special meaning.) These places are invariably the genitals of the dreamer's mother; there is indeed no other place about

which one can assert with such conviction that one has been there once before. [1900, p. 399]

In these dreams, the allusion may be to observations or fantasies regarding the mother's genitals. They may be accompanied by the dreamer's fantasies about his birth or his prenatal existence. Special attention should be paid to the details of the landscape in these dreams, as they will often provide specific information not only about the observation, but also about the dreamer's reaction to it.

Some *déjà vu* dreams contain a reference to a house or location where the dreamer lived when he was a small child. In such instances, the patient's feeling of conviction that he has been there before derives from the fact that the dreamer really has been in such a place and that "things were different then."

Sometimes the allusion is to a kind of Shangri-la or Garden of Paradise, and the idyllic happiness refers to a time before a younger sibling made his appearance or before the family had to move to another location. People who have had to emigrate from their homeland to a country where a different language is spoken, or people who have simply had to relocate, are apt to have such dreams. Often these may be associated with a feeling of homesickness, which may refer to a longing for the mother's breast (see E. Sterba, 1941).

Castration Symbols

"To represent castration symbolically," Freud writes, "the dream-work makes use of baldness, hair-cutting, falling out of teeth and decapitation" (1900, p. 357). We have referred to dreams dealing with falling out of teeth in chapter 6 above, and a further discussion will be found in chapter 12.

Dreams of haircutting, representing castration, are common in analytic work, especially since the position of the analyst behind the patient on the couch facilitates his representation as a barber or hairdresser who is going to do something to the patient's hair. In an earlier chapter we gave the example of the woman patient who used hairdresser metaphors to express her fear that her analyst would damage her head. Often the choice of symbol refers to the dreamer's childhood anxieties about haircuts. The Biblical story of Samson, who lost his strength (sexual potency) when his hair was cut off, is often alluded to as an association to dreams of this kind. Freud writes that a mannikin with short hair in a dream refers to castration (1913c, p. 283).

While baldness in dreams usually symbolizes castration, it is also used as a switch word. A man dreamed that he was bald. The dream represented his wish "to be balled" or to "ball" a woman he had recently met, and his fear that he would be made bald (i.e., castrated) for his sexual wishes. Losing hair in dreams is often linked to thoughts about cancer, chemotherapy, and the hair loss that ensues.

Decapitation and dreams involving the guillotine are particularly vivid symbolizations of castration and are often accompanied by a great deal of anxiety. Freud notes, in the case of castration dreams in youth, that a round ball is interpreted as "the head of the dreamer's father" (1916, p. 339). Dreams of decapitation sometimes refer specifically to the head of the penis and to concerns about some infection involving it. It should be noted also that the word "head" is used in slang to refer to fellatio, and may express the dreamer's wish for fellatio and his anxiety about castration as a fantasied consequence.

"If one of the ordinary symbols for a penis occurs in a dream doubled or multiplied," Freud writes, "it is to be regarded as a warding-off of castration. The appearance in dreams of lizards—animals whose tails grow again if they are pulled off—has the same significance" (1900, p. 357; see also 1919b, p. 235).

In addition to the symbolic representations mentioned by Freud, castration or its result may sometimes be directly represented. A male patient may dream that he does not have a penis at all, but only a smooth skin in its place, or that his penis has been injured or is bleeding. An uncircumcised male may dream that his penis has been circumcised. There may also be a displacement to some other part of the body—testicles, legs, feet, toes, arms, fingers, etc. Damage, wounding, disfigurement, or distortion of any appendage or extension may be used to represent castration. In addition, the eye (Freud, 1919b, p. 231), the ear (van Gogh), the nose, or the tongue may be similarly employed. More generally, the dreamer may dream of a loss of some kind, of a hat, purse, wallet, pen, etc. If the patient is a man he may dream of himself as a woman or dream of a prepubescent girl with no pubic hair. A man may dream of having breasts, thus equating himself with a woman and symbolically providing himself two projections in the upper part of his body but none below.

Displacement from below upward and the equation of the eyes with the genitals permits the ready symbolic equation of blindness with castration, as in *Oedipus Rex* or the Earl of Gloucester in *King Lear*. For example, a patient had a dream in which he saw a blind man with a cane. His associations led to an account of an episode of impotence the previous night and his fear that he was a castrate. The long, round cane in the dream symbolically undid his feeling of being castrated (blind) and provided him with a long phallus.

One man dreamed that his ring finger was bent and he could not straighten it because of some obstruction. A man sawed off the ring and it was then possible for him to straighten his finger. The dream referred to the patient's feeling that his marriage interfered with his relationships with other women. He thought that if his analysis made it possible for him to divorce his wife, he would be freed of that impediment and would be potent again. But the dream also expressed his fear that his analyst would castrate him if he left his wife and had sexual relations with another woman.

Another man dreamed that he was standing over a toilet bowl filled to the brim with dark reddish water, urine, feces, toilet paper, etc. He had a straight razor and then sliced off his penis so that it fell into the toilet bowl. In the dream he experienced no affect. The patient's mother was psychotic during much of his childhood and would not allow the toilets to be flushed. The picture of the toilet in the dream reminded him of the toilet in his childhood. Although the patient was married, sexual relations with his wife occurred only episodically. He viewed the vagina as a toilet or cesspool full of urine and feces. In the dream he expressed a feeling he had had many times, that for him to have intercourse would be like deliberately cutting off his penis and putting it into that dirty toilet bowl. As the straight razor in the dream referred to his father's razor, the patient was also expressing his fear that his father would castrate him for his underlying oedipal wishes. He succeeded in mastering his anxiety about the vagina and his fear of his father by actively severing his own penis in the dream.

Pregnancy Symbols

Being plagued with vermin (Freud, 1900, p. 357); being infested; being infected or having cancer or a growth of some kind are symbols of pregnancy. In addition, pregnancy may be symbolized by parasites such as worms (e.g., tapeworms, pinworms, echinocci, amoebae) or by some poison or toxin.

Various animals may also be used in the manifest dream to symbolize pregnancy. Freud indicates that "the pig is an ancient fertility symbol" (1916–1917, p. 164). The kangaroo or the opossum, with their marsupial pouches, are frequently used in dreams to symbolize pregnancy. The elephant, while a bisexual symbol, may serve also in this capacity, not only because of its size (which may allude to the child's conception of the pregnant mother as a monstrous figure) but also because of its "trunk"; used as a switch word (trunk as in steamer trunk), it may be viewed as capable of holding objects (e.g., babies). Other large animals may also be used to express pregnancy: the cow, the hippopotamus, the camel (the hump or humps representing breasts), or various large prehistoric animals.

Sometimes pregnancy is symbolized by figures that are heavy or obese, or by overeating or its reverse (vomiting). Inanimate objects may also serve in this capacity: heavy luggage or a carriage or grocery cart being pushed. References in the manifest dream to menstruation or to lactation are other symbols of pregnancy. Freud notes that a young married woman's dream that she was having her period meant in fact that she had missed her period (1900, p. 126), an interpretation based upon reversal. Sometimes such dreams occur during ovulation (Benedek and Rubenstein, 1939) and the dreamer responds to the hormonal stimulation within her body with a wish to be pregnant and a reaction to this wish.

In considering dreams dealing with impregnation the therapist should bear in mind the possibility that the patient may be expressing infantile sexual theories of impregnation. Such notions may derive from any level of the patient's psychosexual development.

A woman who was rather slim dreamed that she was dining at a very posh French restaurant and was served some ice cream for dessert that was shaped like an erect penis. "Then there was a space in the dream and then I was looking at a full-length mirror and saw I was very fat and my stomach was sticking out." The patient's dream referred to a fantasy she had had as a child when her mother was pregnant (fat) with her sister. She thought her mother had gotten pregnant by eating something. Later she connected this with a fellatio fantasy (the French restaurant and the penis-shaped ice cream).

Lactation

Freud recounts that a friend of his had written to him that "his wife had dreamt that she had noticed some milk stains on the front of her vest. This too was an announcement of pregnancy, but not of a first one. The young mother was wishing that she might have more nourishment to give her second child than she had had for her first" (1900, p. 126).

Dreams dealing with lactation often refer to the person's thoughts about breast feeding and the conflicts around it. In a woman these dreams may refer to her childhood, her relationship to a sibling, or to her thoughts about whether her mother had had enough milk for her. Sometimes lactation dreams express the fantasy that because her mother did not have sufficient or properly nutritious milk, or did not breast feed her at all or did so only briefly, she did not develop properly and therefore became a girl. In men, lactation dreams may also refer to sibling rivalry, especially if they have had the opportunity of seeing the mother breast feed a younger sibling. In some instances, when a man learns that his wife is pregnant, he may have lactation dreams which refer to his rivalry with the coming infant.

Symbols of Birth, Parturition, and Intrauterine Life

Passing through narrow spaces or coming out of a room of some kind or out of a body of water, often accompanied by anxiety, is a frequent symbol of birth (1900, pp. 399–400). The dreamer may find himself trapped underwater in a submarine, or in some confining space, but then with great anxiety he emerges out of the trap and at times even gasps for air.

One patient, for example, dreamed that the front door of his house opened and a flood of water poured in. Although the day residues referred to his having read about some recent flooding, his associations led to his having observed the birth of a younger brother. Another patient dreamed of seeing a submarine rising to the surface and the hatch opening. The dream was overdetermined, as the word "hatch" was used as a switch word: he had recently watched the hatching of baby chicks in a movie.

At times the idea of birth is symbolized by someone bringing a gift, by a bird (the stork), or by the arrival of a messenger or telegram. A patient, whose wife was pregnant, dreamed of the front doorbell ringing in his home and a Western Union messenger, dressed in uniform, handing him a telegram while singing the message: "Welcome to the new-born king."

Sometimes the reference to birth is symbolically expressed in dreams in accordance with an infantile sexual theory. In the dream "things" may emerge from objects or locales of various kinds. One patient, for example, dreamed of a hill that suddenly developed a large "sinkhole" into which a car and some trees fell. He could see the "limbs of the trees" protruding from the hole. The day residue for the dream was a newspaper account about a sinkhole into which some buildings and cars had fallen. His thoughts led, however, to his childhood and his seeing his mother's pregnant abdomen, her protrudent umbilicus, and the *linea nigra*. He recalled asking her what it was and her joking reply: "One of these days it will burst open and something will come out." Later, when his brother was born, the patient fantasied that his brother's arms and legs (the "limbs") somehow tore his mother's abdomen apart along the *linea nigra*.

Sometimes the idea of birth is symbolized by a baby coming out of another part of the body, e.g., the mouth. By means of a further process of substitution, the loss of a tooth may come to symbolize childbirth, as will be seen in greater detail in chapter 13. Children, Freud notes, often have the notion that "babies come out of the anus" and that "men can have babies just as well as women"; "according to the technical rules for interpreting dreams, the notion of coming *out of* the rectum can be represented by the opposite notion of creeping into the rectum . . . and *vice versa*" (1909b, p. 220). Similarly, in many dreams birth is represented by a reference involving water, either coming out of it or the reverse. Rather than coming out of some body of water, for example, the patient may dream of diving into a lake (Freud, 1900, p. 400) or swimming pool.

In dreams symbolizing birth it is important to distinguish *whose* birth the patient is referring to. Sometimes the reference is to an early fantasy about his own birth, but it may be to the wish to give birth to a child or the fear of giving birth or of having a child. It may also refer to an historical event such as the birth of a sibling.

In summary, Freud maintains that "to poison oneself = to become pregnant; to drown = to bear a child; to throw oneself from a height = to be delivered of a child" (1920b, p. 162nl). The dreamer may express the underlying symbolism of childbirth in the dream by acting it out as, for example, by falling out of bed (1922a, p. 213).

Rescue dreams, according to Freud, are a specific variant form of birth dream:

> Rescue dreams are connected with birth dreams. In women's dreams, to rescue, and especially to rescue from the water, has the same significance as giving birth. [1900, p. 403]

> If one rescues someone from the water in a dream, one is making himself into his mother, or simply into *a* mother. [1916–1917, p. 161]

> A woman rescuing someone else (a child) from the water acknowledges herself in this way as the mother who bore him . . . [1910d, p. 174]

> If in a dream a woman pulls (or tries to pull) a man out of the water, that may mean that she wants to be his mother (takes him for her son. . .). Or it may mean that she wants him to make her into a mother: she wants to have a son by him, who, as a likeness of him, can be his equivalent. [1922a, pp. 212–213]

> . . .the meaning of rescuing may vary, depending on whether the author of the phantasy is a man or a woman. It can equally mean (in a man) making a child, i.e. causing it to be born. . . . A man rescuing a woman from the water in a dream means that he makes her a mother . . . [it] amounts to making her his own mother. . . . At times there is also a tender meaning contained in rescue-phantasies directed . . . at expressing the subject's wish to have his father as a son—that is, to have a son who is like his father. [1910d, p. 174]

It must be remembered, however, that rescue dreams are capable of different interpretations. Freud notes that Rank (1912) "has shown from a series of dreams that birth-dreams make use of the same symbolism as dreams with a urinary stimulus. The erotic stimulus is represented in the latter as a urinary stimulus; and the stratification of meaning in these dreams corresponds to a change that has come over the meaning of the symbol since infancy" (1900, p. 402). As always, the therapist must consider a symbol as representing multiple possibilities; only the content of the rest of the dream and the associations will reveal its actual significance.

Fantasies of intrauterine life or of existence in the womb are often expressed by some device such as an underwater camera or tube through which one is looking into some cavity or darkness. Dreams with submarines or bathyspheres, of exploration with scuba diving equipment, etc. express the dreamer's fantasies of his own intrauterine existence with the added opportunity to view what is going on around him. Sometimes these fantasies refer to observation of the primal scene from inside the uterus.

By use of the mechanism of reversal and by substitution of the dreamer's whole body for the penis, dreams of birth may also express the wish to return to the mother (Lorand, 1950), or may symbolize having sexual relations with the mother (Ferenczi, 1926). The wish to be back in the womb may also fulfill an unconscious wish to "be copulated with there by [the dreamer's] father, [to] obtain sexual satisfaction from him, and [to] bear him a child" (1918, p. 101).

Freud adds some additional comments about the symbolism of fantasies

and unconscious thoughts about life in the womb. They contain an explanation of the remarkable dread that many people have of being buried alive; and they also afford the deepest unconscious basis for the belief in survival after death, which merely represents a projection into the future of this uncanny life before birth. *Moreover, the act of birth is the first ex-*

perience of anxiety, and thus the source and prototype of the affect of anxiety. [1900, p. 400–401n3]

Because of the facility with which fantasies about intrauterine existence can stand for thoughts about life after death, the therapist should always view the expression of birth fantasies in dreams as a possible indication of anxiety in the patient about his own death and/or his death wishes toward another person.

One is sometimes able to see intrauterine fantasies expressed in dreams of dying where a "story line" seems to go on after the original statement, "It is as though I died in the dream" or "I died in the dream" or "I was shot and killed" or "I was dead and found myself in Heaven" etc. In such instances the action in the manifest dream often refers to elaborate fantasies of intrauterine existence.

Freud's comment about dreams of birth expressing "a prototype of the affect of anxiety" provides us an important clue to their interpretation: look for expressions of anxiety in the patient's associations.

Death Symbols

" 'Departing' on a journey is one of the commonest and best authenticated symbols of death," Freud writes (1900, p. 385); "departure in dreams means dying" (1916–1917, p. 161). This is an idea well expressed in the line: "The undiscovered country from whose bourne/No traveler returns . . ." (*Hamlet*, III, i, 79–80). Freud elaborates: "Dying is replaced in dreams by *departure*, by a *train journey*, being dead by various obscure and, as it were, timid hints . . ." (1916–1917, p. 153). Sometimes the imagery of departing on a journey is expressed as going downhill, going out west, or going far away.

When dreams deal with departures, journeys, and trips, definite connections to the dream elements should, as always, be elicited. Frequently the symbolic significance of these elements is associated with specific events and their consequences, real or fantasied. Thus, the element in the manifest dream of going away on a journey may refer to being sent away, i.e., being abandoned or rejected. Sometimes this refers to a childhood trip—to the hospital, for example—associated with an anxiety producing situation. At times the trip may refer to a parent's leaving, as after a domestic argument or, because of sudden illness, by ambulance to a hospital.

A patient dreamed of someone on a hospital cart being wheeled into a black contrivance "like into the belly of a plane." She commented that in the dream she knew the plane was ready to take off. The dream referred to the dreamer's father, who many years before had suffered an acute abdomen (*belly* of a plane) and was taken from the house on a stretcher. She saw her father again when he was being wheeled on a hospital cart just before surgery. He developed complications following surgery and died of a massive myocardial infarction. Following the funeral service, his body was taken by a black hearse to the cemetery. Thus it was possible to see the specific determinants of the trip in her dream.

Dreams of departure on a journey may refer also to a honeymoon trip (going [away] together = co-itus). Because of the common association between death and sexuality in people's minds, either theme may be symbolized by the other. In this connection, the term "to go" may represent its opposite, "to come," thus referring to the popular term for orgasm.

If associations lead to the topic of death when the material is sexual, the therapist should consider the possibility that the patient is expressing his anxiety that the gratification of his sexual wishes will result in his own demise or that of his sexual partner.

Sometimes dreams dealing with departures on trips occur during therapy before a break in the regular schedule, as before the therapist goes away for a few days or for a vacation. The therapist must then distinguish whether the patient fears his own death or whether he is concerned, because of his aggressive feelings, that his therapist will either die or abandon him forever, i.e., never return.

As a journey or a trip in dreams is also symbolic of the analytic process (see chapter 8), the departure on a journey may refer to termination of the analysis, i.e., the fact that the patient is ready to "depart" (see chapter 12).

Freud indicates elsewhere that "dumbness in the dream [represents] death. Hiding and being unfindable . . . is another unmistakable symbol of death in dreams; so, too, is a marked pallor . . ." (1913d, p. 295). There are other symbols as well that may represent death. Beautiful dreams are often dreams of death (Grotjahn, 1980), particularly if the details in the description allude to cemeteries. One patient, for example, dreamed of being in a large, peaceful, grassy area where many daisies and other flowers were blooming. Her associations led to the slang expression "pushing daisies," which means death. When images of sunsets accompany these scenic dreams, such phrases as "going off into the sunset" or the "sunset years" of one's life (referring to thoughts about aging and death) are frequently given as associations. Dreams in which the color black appears, where there is reference to emptiness, darkness, ugliness, destruction, disorder, deterioration, dried-up fecal droppings, dirt or going into the dirt, may also symbolize death. Freud writes also that "white clothes [may be] an allusion to death" (1918, p. 43n). So, too, are cold metals like silver, and ashen gray colors.

All dreams in which there is a reference to death are extremely important and must be viewed with circumspection. The therapist must carefully evaluate whether such dreams refer to a concern about the actual possibility of someone's death, whether they express a death wish (conscious or repressed) against someone, possibly the therapist, or whether the patient is contemplating his own death.

If the reference to death is to someone other than the patient, the question must be raised whether it is due to a recent or anticipated reality (e.g., serious illness in a friend or relative), or to some event in the past (e.g., the departure, loss, or death of a close friend or relative). Thoughts, fantasies, and reactions to the death of a parent may be understood from the associations to such dreams (see Furman, 1974).

If the dream expresses a death wish (conscious or unconscious) toward some person, then the circumstances for such a wish and the reason for the intense feelings should be understood. For example: Is the patient angry because of a narcissistic injury or humiliation? Is he hurt because of some rejection, real or imagined? Is he angry because he has been frustrated or disappointed in attaining some wish? Or is he responding to a current conflict in terms of the past (e.g., an oedipal conflict)?

If the patient is having thoughts of his own death, then the reasons for this must be clearly understood. Are these thoughts based on some fantasy, or are they an identification with someone who has died, either some time ago or recently? People will often have thoughts and dreams alluding to their own death after attending the funeral of a contemporary. Sometimes people have thoughts about their own death when they have learned some reality about themselves, such as discovering they have a serious or life-threatening illness. Under these circumstances people will frequently bring up material out of their past that they associate with their present experience.

A man who had been in analysis for some time began to undergo physical deterioration as a result of renal failure from a chronic glomerulonephritis. He was hospitalized for what he felt would be a terminal illness. In the hospital he had many tests, received a good many injections, and eventually was subjected to dialysis. While in the hospital, he had a dream of a wire cage. He connected this element in his dream with an incident from his childhood. His father had caught a mouse or a rat in a wire trap. (The wire cage in the dream looked something like that wire trap.) His father then took an ice pick and jabbed it repeatedly into the animal, while it tried frantically to get away. The animal bled profusely and died. The patient remembered having watched the scene with horror and fascination, regarding his father as brutal and sadistic. Now that he was hospitalized and subjected to numerous traumatic and extremely painful medical procedures, he felt he was being tortured to death like the rodent in the trap.

Sometimes dreams containing elements symbolizing death herald a patient's depression or reveal suicidal thoughts before the patient is ready to mention them spontaneously to his therapist. It is therefore the therapist's responsibility to bring such thoughts out into the open as soon as possible. A significant clue to understanding these dreams is the nature of the patient's affect, either in the dream during its narration, or in the patient's associations to it. Another important clue is whether the individual is alone in the dream or, if not, who is with him.

There are a number of themes commonly present in the dreams of patients contemplating suicide. There is often some reference to desperation, to "no exit" or "no way out," that they have come to a "dead end" in a trip. There may be some people in the dream who the dreamer knows are dead. There are indications of some type of destruction or a kind of peaceful feeling (Litman, 1980). We have previously discussed the very depressed and suicidal patient who dreamed of taking her child with her on a long trip. A frank discussion of her suicidal intentions helped prevent her acting upon her impulses.

Chapter Eight

Means of Representation

The content and the form of the manifest dream are closely interrelated. Either can be used as a means of representation in dreams.

Dreams in treatment regularly represent the therapist and/or the therapeutic situation. The therapist is frequently represented by someone who has been engaged to perform a service for the patient. The allusion may be complimentary or derogatory. A male therapist, for example, may be represented by a respected professional, such as a financial analyst, or by a medical specialist other than a psychoanalyst or psychiatrist. He may be referred to as a radiologist, a surgeon (e.g., a neurosurgeon or urologist), a dentist, another kind of mental health professional (e.g., a psychologist or counselor) a religious figure (e.g., a rabbi or priest), or an attorney, judge, professor, or teacher. He may be downgraded by being represented as a carpenter, plumber, gardener, barber, garbage collector, day laborer, or hired hand. Sometimes he is represented as some unknown shadowy figure lurking in the background.

The analyst may also be represented as a tailor: German *Schneider*, from *schneiden*, to cut (1918, p. 87n). He may be referred to as "Snyder," "Taylor," or "Doc," a switch word ("dock": to cut off, as a tail).

A male therapist may sometimes be represented by a person of the opposite sex: a teacher, a maid, a female hairdresser, a manicurist, a pedicurist, etc. Quite often sexual stereotypes prevail in the dream imagery. At times the therapist is represented as a spectator or as a companion. The manner in which this individual is represented in the "story line" of the dream is a clue to the nature of the transference situation at the time. The figure in the dream may appear to be benevolent or hostile, friendly or critical, helpful or interfering. Yet, since any element in the dream may be considered in an opposite sense, positive attributes may screen negative ones and vice versa.

At times the analyst in the dream may be endowed with attributes (physical or characterological) that bear some actual resemblance to the analyst, while at other times these characteristics are obviously projected from other figures of the individual's past or represent aspects of the patient's own personality. These may include elements from the ego (e.g., reality testing), superego (e.g., conscience), or id (e.g., bisexual strivings).

Freud notes that

> it is not surprising that a person undergoing psycho-analytic treatment should often dream of it and be led to give expression in his dreams to the many thoughts and expectations to which the treatment gives rise. The imagery most frequently chosen to represent it is that of a journey, usually by motor-car, as being a modern and complicated vehicle. The speed of the car will then be used by the patient as an opportunity for giving vent to ironical comments. [1900, p. 410]

The patient may find himself embarked on a voyage of exploration through unfamiliar territory in his dream (1900, p. 453). It is important to learn whether the terrain of this journey is represented as rough or smooth, uphill or downhill, whether the dreamer is in friendly surroundings or perilous ones, whether he is making progress easily or with difficulty, whether he is making headway or is bogged down. Such allusions to the treatment can generally be read directly.

If the imagery in the patient's manifest dream refers to the analysis as a journey, then the means of transportation is important. The patient may be on foot, walking, jogging, climbing, etc. Vehicles other than the motorcar mentioned by Freud are also used in this imagery. The bus is an especially interesting symbol, as it carries many passengers: the analyst's other patients, the patient's work associates, members of his present or childhood family. One can change buses, just as one can change therapists, and the bus driver conveniently provides the rider with transfers (transference). If the bus is a school bus, the reference to the analysis as an educational process, alluding to childhood, is clear. Sometimes the dreamer finds himself in a streetcar which his associations connect with the "Streetcar Named Desire" or another one in New Orleans labeled "Cemeteries." As streetcars, trolleys, and interurban trains are no longer in use in many areas of the country, the reference may be to something from a bygone era. A reference to the past may also be expressed by a horse and buggy or a carriage, the latter often being connected with a baby carriage.

More modern contrivances such as jet airplanes, rockets, spaceships, or nuclear-powered submarines are frequently used as symbols of travel. One patient dreamed of floating in a hot air balloon. The metaphor depicted his feeling that his analyst "was full of hot air" but also that he himself was at times, and that the hot air referred to flatus. In a somewhat exotic dream, a patient found himself on a "flying carpet." The reference was to a picture the patient had seen of the oriental rug on Freud's analytic couch.

Sometimes the metaphor is of a factory where production is fast or slow, quality control good or bad, and where payments are made in terms of an hourly rate and labor-management disputes have to be negotiated.

"If 'the unconscious', as an element in the subject's waking thoughts, has to be represented in a dream," Freud writes, "it may be replaced very appropriately by subterranean regions" (1900, p. 410). Quite often the dreamer may find himself wandering through such subterranean passages.

Dream elements referring to the analytic situation are common and, if understood, reveal a great deal about the transference. The dialogue between patient and analyst may be represented as a conversation by telephone, two-way radio, or dictaphone (cold and impersonal). Sometimes the patient expresses his confusion about what is going on in this way: "I dreamed I was listening to the radio, but the announcer's voice was garbled," or "I couldn't hear clearly."

The location of the analyst's office, the street and number, the number of his office suite, the zip code of his address, the telephone exchange or telephone number may all appear in dreams, but inserted into a different context. The analyst's consultation room, disguised and altered in various ways, is a frequent setting in the manifest content of dreams in therapy.

One patient dreamed he was in a bathroom. His initial associations led to the analyst's office, but then he expressed his concern whether the analyst had a bathroom that would be available to him should he need to urinate or have a bowel movement. After a bit, he cautiously volunteered the information that he had anxiety about using public bathrooms, that he was, to use his term, "pee shy." This revelation led in turn to his relating that, during his childhood, he had once gone to use a public men's room and a homosexual had made some overtures toward him. The transference aspects of the situation expressed his fear that the analyst would make similar advances.

Dream elements such as furniture, *objets d'art,* bric-a-brac, books, pictures, and the like may be derived from the daily observations of these objects in the consultation room. Such objects may appear as themselves or be disguised in the manifest content, at times bearing only a token resemblance to the actual object. Often they serve as nodal points that link the analytic situation with things and events in the individual's past.

The analytic couch itself is represented in dreams by various metaphors that reveal the nature of the patient's transference. It may appear as a day bed or sofa, especially one that converts into a bed. It may have sides like a crib or be a doctor's examining table where all sorts of procedures are performed.

Nor do such references stop with material objects. The sphere of allusion extends to people directly connected with the analyst, either people the patient may actually know or have casual contact with or others the individual does not know at all. The list may include the analyst's wife, children, secretary, or receptionist, or some other member of the staff or establishment where the therapist sees the patient. Other patients, whom the individual has seen entering or leaving the therapist's office, or whom he knows are (or have been) in treatment with the same analyst, or with other analysts, may also appear in the manifest content and offer a ready vehicle for communication of the patient's concerns and anxieties. Prominent people who have been in analysis and have divulged this fact to the media may also come up as elements in the dream. One patient, for instance, who dreamed about a popular celebrity, quickly remarked that he had read that this individual had been in psychoanalytic treatment for a good many years. He promptly expressed his concern that his personal analysis might also last for a long time. Another dreamed of someone who reminded him of a prominent screen star who, he had learned, had been in analysis and who had committed suicide. The patient feared that the same fate might befall him. In both these dreams there was also a wish to be prominent.

A patient, who saw his therapist in a large office building, remarked in association to a sad-appearing figure in a dream, "All your patients are sad when they leave your office. You must be disturbing them." "What patients are you referring to?" asked the puzzled analyst. "Well, all those people I see coming out of the elevator while I'm waiting for one in the lobby." The patient had projected his own feelings upon a whole host of people he did not even know, who had been coming out of the elevators in a busy office building. Needless to say, they were not all seeing his analyst.

Dreams relating to the analytic situation regularly allude to the fee, the number of sessions, the schedule, interruptions for weekends, and vacations. References to the fee are particularly frequent early in an analysis, and also around the time the statement is due. Dreams are particularly high-handed about decimal points and zeros. Thus, fifty cents in the dream may refer to five cents, five dollars, fifty dollars, five hundred dollars, etc. It is important, however, to understand why, in the manifest dream, the decimal point should occur where it does.

Shortly before the end of the month, a patient had a dream in which the element "fifty cents" appeared. His associations clearly revealed that he was concerned about the coming analytic bill. By dreaming of fifty cents, he had successfully reduced the amount of the analytic fee per session to a very easily affordable figure. Apart from the obvious economic advantage of such a fee, which he desired, was his feeling that for all he was getting out of the treatment, he should only be paying fifty cents per session. His further associations confirmed this when he described how, as a boy, he made fifty cents for mowing a lawn. His disgruntlement about paying the therapist's fee was further substantiated by a parapraxis he made while discussing this particular element. He complained in high dudgeon about what he thought was an exorbitant fee: "I pay you fifty cents a week." As he was being seen five times a week, he had successfully reduced his fee to ten cents a session.

When the therapist goes on vacation or interrupts the treatment for some other reason, patients' dreams often contain elements that refer to interruptions of various kinds, to people leaving, to rejection, or to abandonment. A patient had a dream in which the maid left without finishing her work, leaving a pile of dirty dishes in the sink and refuse on the floor. The patient's analyst had told him that he was going away on a vacation, and the patient responded to the information by reducing him to the level of a maid who did not complete her job.

Sometimes patients respond to their analyst's leaving by dreams in which a variety of pleasurable activities symbolic of sexual activities emerge: sailing, swimming, riding, mountain climbing, skiing, golfing, playing tennis, and the like. The figure indulging in these activities refers to the pleasure-seeking analyst, who leaves, unconcerned about the patient's discomfort. At times the allusions may be to grossly sexual activities referring to the patient's past. Prior to her analyst's departure for a week's vacation, one patient dreamed of a drunk, who bore some resemblance to her analyst, reeling from bar to bar in some decrepit neighborhood in which there were a number of whorehouses. She readily connected the dream to her father's going out of town for a week or two at a time, during which he would go on drunken binges. She had reason to believe that during these times he would consort with prostitutes.

In the previous chapter we discussed how the patient's body and ego are symbolized in the dream. Regardless of its specific content, it is axiomatic that every dream, in one way or another, deals with the dreamer. "Dreams," Freud writes, "are completely egoistic. Whenever my own ego does not appear in the content of the dream, but only some extraneous person, I may safely assume that my own ego lies concealed, by identification, behind this other person. I can insert my ego into the context" (1900, pp. 322–323); "the person who plays the chief part in [the dream] scenes is always to be recognized as the dreamer" (1917b, p. 223). In these quotations Freud specifically refers to dreams in which the manifest content does not include the dreamer directly. Rather, the dreamer projects upon some figure in the dream an aspect of his own personality. The "story line" of the dream is an almost transparent expression of this, along the lines of "I have a friend who. . . ."

In some instances, a figure in the dream representing the patient's analyst may be invested with attributes that are actually part of the patient's own personality, e.g., dishonesty or lack of discretion. This means of representation in a dream is rather easy to follow, and it is equally easy for the patient to recognize that the dream deals with himself and his specific problem. Freud cautions, however, that we "should reject as a meaningless and unjustifiable piece of speculation the notion that *all* figures that appear in a dream are to be regarded as fragmentations and representatives of the dreamer's own ego" (1923a, p. 120).

Even important figures in the manifest content do not *always* deal with the dreamer. There are many instances in which such figures specifically refer to people who have been sources of conflict for the dreamer—various members of his family, as well as friends, business associates, etc. Thus, a patient involved in a business negotiation dreamed of a person who clearly stood for his adversary; the characteristics he attributed to the dream figure were those very attributes that he perceived in this actual person. Care should be taken to establish the significance of these figures in the dream, however. While the main emphasis of the patient's associations is upon an external figure, and should most certainly be acknowledged, the therapist should be mindful of whether the characteristics of the other person, about which the patient is so troubled, may not also be aspects of the patient's own personality which he is either unaware of or unwilling to recognize.

"On other occasions," Freud writes, "when my own ego *does* appear in the dream, the situation in which it occurs may teach me that some other person lies concealed, by identification, behind my ego. In that case the dream should warn me to transfer on to myself, when I am interpreting the dream, the concealed common element attached to this other person" (1900, p. 323). The content of these dreams in which the patient appears directly in the manifest content, bears a special relation to the *situation* in which the dreamer finds himself. Such dreams often involve a twin, a spouse, a companion, or a partner. A man dreamed that he was in an antique shop and was haggling with the salesman about the cost of some item. His associations led to his view of the analysis as an antique shop which dealt in old things, and to the salesperson as the analyst, with whom he had wanted to haggle about the fee. But then his thoughts led to his wife's frugality, which at times bordered on penuriousness. Actually, this was a character trait of his own; he often prided himself on being able to "Jew someone down" on the price of an item. What had been concealed here was his anti-Semitic attitude, which he had had to conceal from his Jewish analyst.

Freud continues:

> There are also dreams in which my ego appears along with other people who, when the identification is resolved, are revealed once again as my ego. These identifications should then make it possible for me to bring into contact with my ego certain ideas whose acceptance has been forbidden by the censorship. Thus my ego may be represented in a dream several times over, now directly and now through identification with extraneous persons. By means of a number of such identifications it becomes possible to condense an extraordinary amount of thought-material. [1900, p. 323]

Moreover, he writes, "It often happens, too, that the dreamer separates off his neurosis, his 'sick personality', from himself and depicts it as an independent person" (1900, p. 410). Thus, the sick part of the dreamer may be represented by a person in the dream who is sick, old, crazy, deformed, or crippled, or as a suffering martyr, saint, or Christlike figure. Some patients, especially those with a Catholic background who view any manifestation of their unconscious as "sick," may dream of the devil. Freud writes that the devil "is certainly nothing else than the personification of the repressed unconscious instinctual life" (Freud and Oppenheim, 1911, p. 188).

There are dreams in which the individual's pathological ego or self is represented as a burden, an object to be borne, a hump, or a growth (see Ferenczi, 1930). A disturbed, unhappy male homosexual dreamed of a large hollow head resembling the grotesque masks worn by performers in Mardi Gras. The patient puts his penis into the mask's mouth. Among the patient's associations to the mask was his comment that its composition of papier-mâché, wax, paste, etc. and its hollowness made it very fragile. "It could crumble easily, like an eggshell," he said. This hollow masklike head represented his sick ego. He felt hollow and empty as a person, one who could easily crumble and fall apart. By his driven homosexual behavior, he desperately tried to prevent his ego from fragmenting.

A variant of these dreams are dreams of self-dissection, fairly common among patients who have had courses in anatomy. The figure being dissected may represent themselves (Freud, 1900, p. 452; Little, 1971).

Sometimes patients dream of looking at themselves in a mirror. These dreams may refer to the individual's recognition that the analysis is a way of looking at himself and his conflicts (M. L. Miller, 1948). Eisnitz (1980) states that mirror dreams "usually are reactions to a narcissistic crisis in the life of the patient, often induced by the emergence of an unacceptable wish (often a transference wish) during the analysis. In practically every instance the self-scanning activity, which is represented by the mirror in the dream, is closely connected to superego qualities" (p. 378). But mirror dreams may have another significance. Kohut (1971) writes that "there also occur dreams during the analysis which portray a relationship (of the self) with someone who is seen as through a mirror (the analyst as the reflector of the grandiose self)"; these dreams, he continues, occur "in cases in which a major part of the instinctual investment of the grandiose self was in the process of becoming mobilized in relationship to the therapist" (p. 116).

The distribution of different aspects, facets, or states of the individual's ego among various characters in the dream allows the dreamer to represent contrasting or repressed parts of his personality (Weiss, 1952). These may be the patient's idealized self, a fantasied double, or an alter ego. In some instances, a companion in a dream may represent the other half of the bisexual ego; e.g., a female companion in a man's dream may represent the passive feminine part of his personality. Under certain circumstances, the presence of a woman with the dreamer may refer to an early child-mother unity.

Sometimes the companions in dreams refer to childhood or adolescent companions with whom the dreamer shared experiences he is ashamed to discuss directly with his therapist. The dream then presents the companions as instigators bearing complete reponsibility, thus exculpating the dreamer. A man dreamed that he was with a "bunch of guys who said they wanted to go to a whorehouse." The dream referred to an incident in his adolescence. He was with a group of his friends and they had all been talking about "having some sex." One of them suggested going to a prostitute. They all agreed and he was persuaded to go with them. He was ambivalent but was ashamed to refuse, so he went along. When it came his turn, he was frightened, disgusted, and completely impotent. After they left the prostitute, he was too embarrassed to tell his friends about his failure, so he bragged about his success, although in such a way that he doubted his friends believed him. In his dream, the patient exculpated himself by completely shifting the responsibility for going to the prostitute onto his friends, thereby avoiding the recognition of his own interest in doing this. He thus protected himself from what he felt would be criticism by his analyst, not only for going to the prostitute, but also for being impotent with her.

Sometimes the other people in dreams represent one or more imaginary companions that the dreamer had as a

child (Nagera, 1969). One patient, whose younger and preferred brother died when he was about five years old, often
dreamed of a companion, another man who seemed roughly
his own age. The patient was subsequently able to identify
this dream companion as his dead brother. The patient then
recalled that he had had an imaginary companion with whom
he shared all his thoughts and fantasies. This companion, who
came into existence some time after his brother died, had
"grown up" with him. At times, even in his adult life, the
patient found himself talking to him in his mind.

Sometimes, instead of using other people to represent
facets of the dreamer's personality, the dream uses animals.
"*Wild animals*," Freud writes, "mean people in an excited
sensual state, and further, evil instincts or passions" (1916–1917,
p. 158).

> Wild beasts are as a rule employed by the dream-work to
> represent passionate impulses of which the dreamer is afraid,
> whether they are his own or those of other people. (It then
> needs only a slight displacement for the wild beasts to come
> to represent the people who are possessed by these pas-
> sions.) . . . It might be said that the wild beasts are used to
> represent the libido, a force dreaded by the ego and combated
> by means of repression. [1900, p. 410]

The reference here is to the patient's fear of his id impulses
going out of control. Both aggressive and sexual impulses
must be carefully considered—his own as well as those of
other people. Specific attention should be paid to what the
dreamer believes the wild animals will do, often based upon
his own experiences and frightening stories he has heard. It
is important to note whether the patient fears he will lose
control over his id impulses as a consequence of his therapy.
The patient may also project his own anxieties upon the therapist and fear that the therapist will lose control.

A woman dreamed that she was walking with her pet
cat, but in the dream the cat on the leash was like a huge
panther. Her associations led to a play, *The Visit* by Friedrich

Durrenmatt, in which a woman returns with a panther to a town where she had once been grossly humiliated by a man who was now its mayor. The woman is now wealthy, buys out the town, turning the population against the mayor so that they give him up to her and she destroys him. The patient's "panther-cat" in the dream alluded to her own murderous vengeful fury against a man in her own background who had subjected her to gross humiliation.

On other occasions, aspects of the individual's personality are expressed in dreams by a reference to place. "Identifications in the case of proper names of *localities*," Freud writes, "are resolved even more easily than in the case of persons, since here there is no interference by the ego, which occupies such a dominating place in dreams" (1900, p. 323). One must bear in mind whether the locality itself is historically significant, either recently or remotely, or whether it is the *name* of the locality which is important. In one instance, a man dreamed of Falmouth, Massachusetts, which was a switch word referring to "foul mouth" and his disgust at the halitosis of a sexual companion who had accompanied him to Cape Cod. Behind this, however, his associations led to his almost obsessive concern with his own breath: his frequent gargling, his use of mouth washes and various preparations to insure that his breath did not offend. Further associations indicated that these concerns were displacements from his concern about passing flatus and his worry that people would think he had a bad body odor.

Affects in Dreams

Inasmuch as emotions are at the base of the individual's problems, all psychotherapeutic efforts involving the use of dreams must pay close attention to the expression of affects in dreams. In this connection Freud notes the following: "Thanks to the isolation of the single emotions in the unconscious, a slight annoyance during the day will express itself in a dream as a wish for the offending person's death, or a breath of temptation may give the impetus to the portrayal in the dream of a criminal action" (1921, p. 78n2).

Usually dream work "brings about a *suppression of affects*" (1900, p. 467) so that the manifest dream is frequently "indifferent" as to content and as to its emotional tone. Freud makes the point that "a dream is in general poorer in affect than the psychical material from the manipulation of which it has proceeded" (1900, p. 467). But while the affective tone in many dreams is rather colorless, the range of the affective reaction may vary from mild feelings of all kinds to the intense terror of a frightening nightmare that causes the individual to awaken. At times the absence or diminution of affect in a dream may constitute a defense against overwhelming feelings of which the dreamer is afraid (Nunberg, 1931). While the emotions in a dream may be suppressed altogether, they may appear immediately following the dream. Alternatively, the patient may awaken feeling anxious or depressed. Sometimes the affect, e.g., anxiety, is experienced by the patient on his way to his appointment or in the session itself, either before or during the recounting of his dream.

One patient dreamed of a pencil sharpener, the wall-mounted type in which the pencils are sharpened by turning a small crank. There was no affect at all connected with this manifest dream. When he arrived for his appointment, he was vaguely uneasy, and he commented on the traffic being more than usually irritating. As he reported the dream, he experienced so much anxiety that he had to sit up on the couch and bend over. He became pale and perspired visibly. "I am so awfully scared," he said softly, several times. Asked "Why, what was it?" he said that he did not know except that it had something to do with the pencil sharpener in the dream, but he did not know why it was so frightening, because "there was nothing about it in the dream that was so scary. It was just there, mounted on a box or something." Presently he calmed down, resumed the horizontal position on the couch, and tried, amid waves of severe anxiety, to verbalize his thoughts. The pencil sharpener reminded him of a pun made by the boys in grammar school when they filed by rows to sharpen their pencils. They would ask each other amid gales of laughter if they were going to get their "petzels" sharpened, referring to having sexual relations. He went on to speak of having been attracted to one of the secretaries in the office where he worked, and of having thought of taking her out on a date and having sexual relations with her. He was somewhat fearful, however, thinking of what the boys had said in grammar school, that the secretary might be so aggressive in sexual relations that she would grind his penis to bits.

What frightened him the most, however, and had caused him to sit up on the couch and assume a position that protected his genitals, was his extreme anxiety that his analyst would be so enraged with him for going out with the secretary that he would castrate him. He had seen sharp-pointed pencils lying on his analyst's desk, just as he had seen them on the secretary's. He had projected upon the analyst the punitive aspects of his own superego, characteristics derived in part from his excessively harsh father. The observation of what would ordinarily have been an indifferent stimulus served in this instance as a common denominator for highly affect-laden material.

In dreams where affects or even their most subtle nuances are present, some impulse has broken through the barriers of censorship. As we have indicated, beginning the exploration of a dream with the affect is frequently advisable, as it is important that the therapist understand what these emotions are connected to. Considerable caution must be exercised when explaining frightening affects in dreams, nightmares in particular, as it may be difficult for the patient to deal with the material that led up to the emotion. In these instances it is essential for the therapist to be certain of the patient's ability to tolerate the interpretation. The therapist must deal appropriately with the patient's defenses and present the interpretation from the side of the ego.

One man dreamed that he was attending his mother's funeral. He was struck by the details of the ritual but beyond that had no particular feelings. In another part of the dream he was involved in a bitter argument with someone whose identity was not clear. His rage at this person, however, was so intense that it awakened him. The patient's mother had died a number of years before, and he had attended her funeral. What he had not discussed prior to this dream was that a few days before her sudden death he had had a violent argument with her. He had succeeded in repressing all the details of this experience along with his fury with his mother at the time. Even when this was discussed, he had the greatest difficulty recognizing the connection between the argument with his mother and his feeling that he was somehow responsible for her death.

When attempting to understand an affect in the manifest content of a dream, the therapist must always consider the possibility that the affect may also stand for its opposite. Joy, humor, and tranquility will at times refer to sadness, grief, and turmoil. Sadness may in turn conceal some forbidden pleasure. A man, concerned that a nodule in his wife's breast might prove to be malignant, dreamed of attending a funeral and seeing all his male friends and their wives. He felt sad and lonely, depressed that his wife was not in attendance. He had not realized that it must have been her funeral he was attending in the dream. While he had been happy in his marriage, the patient had often longed to have an affair with a certain woman, a friend of the family. He had actively resisted this impulse, however, because he felt it would not be fair to his wife. Even though he was saddened by the prospect that his wife might have cancer and die, a part of him was joyful at the thought that her death might free him to pursue his sexual pleasures. He had had to repress this wish in the manifest dream.

Freud writes: "The person who in the dream feels an emotion which I myself experience in my sleep is the one who conceals my ego" (1900, p. 323nl). This rule provides the therapist an important clue to help him identify the patient's underlying problems. Quite frequently the elements or story line of the manifest dream associated with the emotion explains the basis for the feelings, though their form may be disguised or distorted. When using this rule, the therapist must make a very significant distinction between dreams in which the dreamer himself, or someone with whom he is clearly identified, experiences the feelings, and those in which he is the onlooker and someone he observes is having the emotion. The first instance is relatively easy to understand. A woman, whose daughter had taken ill with a respiratory illness, dreamed that this child was ill with a high fever. The child in the dream was afraid she would die. The dreamer experienced anxiety in the dream and identified herself with her daughter and her fears. The patient herself had been seriously ill when *she* was a child, and like the child in the dream had been afraid she would die. Thus, the dream, while expressing the woman's anxiety about her child, was also historical and revived an extremely troubled period in her own life.

Dreams in which the dreamer is the onlooker and someone else is having the emotion may be difficult to understand, as the dreamer may be identified with that person and displace the affect on to him, yet repress his own feelings. Thus, a man dreamed that his employer, a big, burly, heavy-set man, was angrily reprimanding someone. He observed the scene with no emotion. The dream referred to an incident, which had actually occurred the previous day, in which his employer had angrily "chewed him out" for some relatively minor error. The anger in the dream referred to his own fury with his employer for *his* unreasonable anger. His own emotion, however, had to be repressed because of his anxiety.

In other situations, the emotion in the dream may in fact belong to another person and not be appropriate to the dreamer. A man dreamed of an older woman sitting in a large overstuffed chair. She was very sad and tearful. He was the observer but recalled no particular feelings in the dream. This dream was historical. The patient's mother went through a period of depression when he was a child. He recalled her sitting in just such a chair, barely moving, weeping quietly to herself. He recalled being confused by her condition and feeling alternately abandoned and angry.

At times, according to Levitan (1980a), a split occurs: "a character other than the dreamer is depicted as experiencing the affect while the dreamer himself is actually expressing it. For example, . . . a dream character other than the dreamer is represented as crying during the dream but when the dreamer awakens he finds his pillow soaked, indicating that he himself has actually been crying" (p. 226). A similar observation may be made in the case of sexual dreams in which a figure in the dream is sexually aroused, but the dreamer has an ejaculation.

Quite frequently the figure in the dream expressing an emotion may refer to the transference situation; the dreamer experiences the analyst as some figure out of his past who had the emotion. In one such instance, a patient dreamed that a large man, dressed in a pair of trousers and a sleeveless undershirt, was brandishing a straight razor and angrily shouting at him in such a way that he was sure he would cut him in "some horrible way" or kill him. The dreamer was frightened and awoke. Two emotions were evident in this dream: the anger of the figure dressed only in pants and sleeveless undershirt, and the dreamer's intense anxiety.

The patient's associations led via a tortuous path to a childhood memory: he was about four years of age and was in a hotel room with his parents during a trip to the West Coast. He recalled that his father, dressed in his trousers and wearing a sleeveless undershirt, was shaving with a straight razor near a basin located in the same room. The patient had been watching his father shave, but then had moved over to his mother's side of the bed and was masturbating by rubbing himself, face down, on the mattress. He did not recall where his mother was at the time, but presumed that she had gone into the bathroom or some place. He vividly remembered his father, his face lathered and partially shaved, his razor in his hand, turning to him and angrily shouting, "What are you doing there?" His father's angry face and the brandished razor terrified him. He was convinced that his father would castrate him or kill him, not only for masturbating in his mother's bed, but for his oedipal wishes. While the dream referred to an historical event, the feeling of terror was revived in his analysis: he was convinced the analyst would be as furious with him as his father had been for wanting to masturbate and for the emerging oedipal thoughts in his analysis.

Sometimes the affect in a dream may be expressed by a description of some object in the manifest content: "The boiler was hot and looked as though it had been burned up" or "The boiler was hot and looked as though it would explode" or "His face was red like a boiled lobster" or "I was in the kitchen and noticed that the counter-top heating element had been turned on." Each of these may be viewed as a reference to anger, aggression, and/or sexual feelings.

Freud reports the dream of a woman in which "someone knocked and then she awoke." He indicates that it was an arousal dream in which "she felt the first sign of genital excitation. There had been a 'knock' in her clitoris" (1915a, p. 270).

Emission Dreams

Freud writes: "it not infrequently happens that a stimulus awakens a dreamer *after a vain attempt has been made to deal with it in a dream under a symbolic disguise*. This applies to dreams of emission or orgasm as well as to those provoked by a need to micturate or defaecate" (1900, p. 402). Quoting Rank (1912, p. 55), he continues: " 'The peculiar nature of emission dreams . . . enables us to convince ourselves that some apparently innocent situations in dreams are no more than a symbolic prelude to crudely sexual scenes. The latter are as a rule represented undisguisedly in the relatively rare emission dreams, whereas they culminate often enough in anxiety dreams, which have the same result of awakening the sleeper' " (1900, p. 402).

Emission dreams may occur with or without orgasm. Special care must be taken with these dreams to ascertain whether the emission is a result of sexual excitement in the dream (in which case it is often accompanied by an orgasm) or if the emission is a result of castration anxiety. Sometimes the anxiety is not apparent in the manifest dream and becomes evident only in the patient's associations.

A man dreamed he was with a beautiful woman; as the dream scene became progressively more erotic, the patient had an emission. He awoke, ascertained this fact, went to the bathroom, cleaned himself off, and changed his pajamas. In his associations the woman in the dream reminded him of a woman he had picked up in a bar in southern France. As a result of the brief affair, he had contracted pubic lice, gonorrhea, and syphilis. The emission in the dream, apart from expressing his anxiety, also referred to the painful gonorrheal discharge.

Emission dreams may reveal aspects of the transference situation. A man struggling with his passive homosexual transference dreamed he was in a car driving with another man. The man reached over, put his hand on the patient's thigh, and moved his hand toward the patient's penis. At that point the patient had an emission and awoke. This dream was partly an expression of the homosexual feelings emerging in the transference and partly an expression of the tremendous amount of castration anxiety stirred up by these feelings.

Another patient dreamed he was taking an oral examination. The examiner asked him a theoretical question based on a concept in basic physical science that he was unfamiliar with. He became flustered, stammered something, and awoke, realizing that he had had an emission unaccompanied by any sexual pleasure at all. In his associations the patient recalled that when he was a senior in high school he had had a somewhat similar experience during a written final examination (not oral, as in the dream). There were two long discussion questions on a subject that he had never been able to understand. He was afraid he would fail the examination and not be able to graduate. He became dizzy and black spots appeared before his eyes (a castration equivalent). He felt nauseated, thought he would die, and suddenly had an emission. The dream in his analysis was clearly an emission dream based on anxiety.

The Senation of Inhibited Movement in Dreams

Clearly associated with the expression of affects in dreams is the sensation of inhibited movement, often associated with anxiety. Freud offers two examples of this sensation in dreams: "One tries to move forward but finds oneself glued to the spot, or one tries to reach something but is held up by a series of obstacles" (1900, p. 336). Sometimes the dreamer finds himself moving forward but then "for some reason" is pulled back or slips back so that he ultimately returns to the original position.

At times there does not appear to be any emotion, but the inhibition of movement is "simply a part of the content of the dream" (Freud, 1900, p. 336). Freud indicates that in those dreams, "in which the 'not carrying out' of a movement occurs as a *sensation* and not simply as a *situation,* the sensation of the inhibition of a movement gives a more forcible expression to the same contradiction—it expresses a volition which is opposed by a counter-volition. Thus the sensation of the inhibition of a movement represents a *conflict of will*" (1900, p. 337). In other words, "the 'not being able to do something' " in the manifest content of a dream is "a way of expressing a contradiction—a 'no' " (1900, p. 337), or expresses "a contradiction between two impulses, a *conflict of will*" (1901a, p. 661). It often represents a conflict between some wished-for gratification and its prohibition by the superego.

In the dreamer's associations to such dreams, the therapist will often find repeated references to the patient's inability to come to some decision or to make up his mind about a given problem. The inhibition of movement in the dream indicates the degree of conflict and expresses the notion that none of the alternative solutions is entirely satisfactory. In one instance, a man dreamed that he was driving his car and came to a crossroad. The car suddenly stalled: "I couldn't make it go at all: forward, backward, right or left." His associations led to his fear of becoming involved in an extramarital heterosexual situation and, coincidentally, his fear that he might be tempted to experiment with homosexual activity. Neither solution was acceptable to him. The dream graphically demonstrated the "no" to either solution or action, and expressed his feeling that he was stalled and could not go in any direction.

Sometimes the degree of conflict and the attendant anxiety are dramatically expressed in the manifest dream. A passive man who had an extremely bad marriage dreamed that he was looking out of a window and saw his wife being pursued by a group of menacing men armed with guns and knives. He is sure they will attack her, rape her, and kill her. He is frightened for her safety but feels rooted to the spot, unable to help her and unable to call for help. He thinks, "If I go out there, they'll kill me, too." Just as the men grabbed his wife, he awoke with anxiety. The dream expressed his fury with his wife, his wish that he could be rid of her, as well as his intense guilt about his feelings. This patient had struggled for many years with obsessive thoughts about women who were raped and attacked in various ways. His passivity was in part a defense against his own aggressive impulses toward them. As this dream indicated, his inability to act (here, his inability to move) was the expression of his defense against his own aggressive sexual fantasies. Moreover, it was clear from his associations that he was also identified with his wife, who was going to be attacked by the menacing men.

Dreams of inhibition of movement may also have historical significance in reference to situations in which the patient was forced into a position of immobility, as for example, when held down and given an enema, held down on an operating table, tied to a potty chair, etc.

There are situations in which immobility in a dream refers to an identification with a *dead* love object. One patient, whose mother had died after a prolonged illness during which she was immobilized alternately in a bed or a chair and was then "laid out" for several days before interment, had repeated dreams in which she herself was unable to move. She was identified with her sick and dying mother who could not move, as well as with her dead mother.

Chapter Nine

Specific Representation of Content

Temporal Relations

In general, temporal relations in dreams are represented by spatial ones. "In a dream," Freud writes, ". . . one
may see a scene between two people who look very small and
a long way off, as though one were seeing them through the
wrong end of a pair of opera-glasses. Here, both the smallness
and the remoteness in space have the same significance: what
is meant is remoteness in *time* and we are to understand that
the scene is from the remote past" (1933, p. 26).

In dreams referring to childhood, Freud says, "the characters and scenes are seen as though they were at a great
distance, at the end of a long road" (1900, p. 408). References
to the individual's childhood also may be represented spatially
by the dreamer's finding himself in a large room or in a place
where objects or people about him are very large. The representation of objects in a dream as extremely small may also
be the result of aggression, a "cutting them down to size,"
so to speak (Bartemeier, 1941b).

A woman dreamed of seeing a man with huge genitals.
"His penis was larger than that of an elephant's and his testicles were the size of large grapefruits." Her associations led
to her having seen her father's erect penis when she was a
small child and her later thought, after she learned about

sexual intercourse, that if a man inserted his penis into her, it would be into her rectum and she would be ripped apart.

At times, elements in the manifest dream dealing with antique or antiquated buildings, museums, or old manuscripts, books, or localities may refer to childhood. For example: "I was in a medieval village." "I was standing near a Gothic cathedral." "I was in a prehistoric cave." While this means of representation serves to "date" the allusion historically, the therapist must also discover what is being referred to and, if possible, which period of the patient's life is being dealt with. In the case of the examples just cited, "the medieval village" referred to a period in one patient's life that he considered his own "dark ages." The patient who dreamed he was standing near a Gothic cathedral had gone to a Jesuit school as a boy and was particularly fond of a very inspiring priest. The prehistoric cave referred to events that occurred in the prehistory of the third patient, i.e., before he could remember anything.

Sometimes the allusion to things from the past serves as a defense against what is happening in the patient's life in the present, or what is going on in the transference situation at the time. A patient dreamed he was traveling along an old winding dirt road and saw some men in the distance who appeared to be having an argument. His associations led to an argument he had recently had with a colleague and to some quasi-argumentative conversations he had had with his therapist. He finally revealed that as a boy he had often witnessed violent arguments between his older brother and his father. These were always frightening to him, as he alternately identified himself with his brother and with his father. He had sought to master his early anxiety by replaying the arguments with various people in his circle of associates, as well as in his relationship with his analyst.

Freud indicates that in dreams, as in associations, "propinquity in time" is to be interpreted as "representing connection in subject-matter. Two thoughts which occur in immediate sequence without any apparent connection are in fact part of a single unity which has to be discovered" (1900, p. 246).

A woman dreamed of a man and a woman in bed together. In another part of the dream there was an infant in a crib. The dream referred to the patient's being in a crib in her parents' bedroom and being exposed to multiple observations of the primal scene. When she was about four years of age, her mother gave birth to a baby girl and the patient was placed in another room in a junior bed of her own. The dream element of the infant in the crib thus referred not only to herself but to her younger sister who had inherited her crib.

"The time of day in dreams," Freud notes, "very often stands for the age of the dreamer at some particular period in his childhood" (1900, p. 409). A man dreamed that an event occurred at five o'clock. This referred to the birth of a younger brother when he was five years of age. He remembered that as a child, even in grammar school, when asked how old he was, he would respond by giving his age as the time of day: instead of saying he was five years old, for instance, he would say he was five o'clock.

Quite frequently the time of the day in dreams is a direct or modified allusion to the time of the analytic appointment. It may express the wish for a longer or shorter time, for a more convenient time, or it may express some other conflict about the schedule. The time in a dream may also represent a condensation of other feelings and wishes. An interesting use of a specific time in a dream occurred in a patient's dream of eight o'clock at night. The time did not refer to any event at the age of eight in her life, nor to the time of her appointment. It referred instead to the play, *Dinner at Eight,* and her wish that instead of having an analytic appointment she would be invited out for dinner followed by an evening of entertainment culminating in sexual activity.

Certain "acts" are especially prone to be expressed by a "numerical repetition" of an object, because they have been prominent in the dreamer's life. One man, who had been married three times, always dreamed of objects in three's. "There were three books, three rings, and even three beds. I sound like the 'three bears,' " he quipped. A woman who had three children had been pregnant six times. She had had one abortion and two miscarriages. Quite frequently she dreamed of objects in sixes. On one occasion, she dreamed of looking in a box of tampons and seeing that there were "half a dozen in the box." The dream condensed the number of her pregnancies and her thoughts about menstruation: if she were pregnant, as she had been six times previously, she would not need to use any tampons.

The multiplication of an object, especially if it is to be considered in a symbolic sense, very often refers to the opposite, that is, the fear of the loss of that object. A man dreamed he had several pocket knives. In reality, he had many of them plus a large collection of similar objects. He frequently acquired pens, pipes, guns, cameras, etc., not so much because he used them or needed them but, in his own words, "to gratify some inner compulsion." It became apparent to him that he desperately feared he would become impotent, i.e., castrated, and he sought continually to replenish what he feared would be lost or missing.

In another connection, Freud writes that "dreams reproduce *logical connection by simultaneity in time*" (1900, p. 314) or "by *approximation in time and space*" (1901a, p. 661). "Dreams," he continues, "carry this method of reproduction down to details. Whenever they show us two elements close together, this guarantees that there is some specially intimate connection between what corresponds to them among the dream-thoughts" (1900, p. 314).

In the manifest content of a dream, a patient, a professional man with many cultural interests, saw four skulls lying in a row on a shelf. He was horrified and awoke. His first association was to a painting by Cezanne. His thoughts then led to his older brother, an artist, who was going into the hospital to have some brain studies because of a suspected brain tumor. The patient's uncle and father had both had brain tumors, and both had died from them. The patient was fearful that his brother might have a similar disease and that he would die also. The obvious concern of the dream was that he himself (the patient) would be next. Hence, four skulls.

Similarities and Parallels

In order to express the idea of "just as," the manifest content of the dream frequently makes liberal use of "similarity, consonance or the possession of common attributes" (1900, p. 320). It will be readily seen that this means of representation is to some extent a variant of representation by simultaneity in time and space. The allusions here may be to situations or people sharing one or more points of congruity (1900, pp. 319–320). The reference may be to specific situations or persons, to situations with a similar or equivalent emotional value, or to people with some underlying common denominator (e.g., the dream of the four skulls).

The therapist's understanding of the patient's allusions and metaphors is highly useful in recognizing what is going on in the transference situation. He can then explain what is happening to the patient by utilizing the same parallel or metaphor in his interpretation.

Thus, the patient who dreamed of taking his car to be repaired by the greasy, unscrupulous mechanic, who would overcharge him and do a poor job, discussed several situations in his associations where something similar had, in fact, happened. The therapist, recognizing that the allusion was to therapy and the therapist, was able to make this connection for the patient.

To express the idea of a similarity, the dream may make use of a mechanism Freud calls "identification": "one of the persons who are linked by a common element succeeds in being represented in the manifest content of the dream, while the second or remaining persons seem to be suppressed in it. But this single covering figure appears in the dream in all the relations and situations which apply either to him or to the figures which he covers" (1900, p. 320).

Recognition of this mechanism permits the therapist to pay special attention to the reasons behind the suppression of the identity of the other person or persons to whom the "single covering figure" refers in the manifest content of the dream. Caution should prevail, however, in ascertaining whether the "suppressed" figure or figures in the dream are to be identified with the dreamer, with some other figure in the dreamer's life, or with the therapist. The latter possibility is especially clear if the dream-figure resembles the therapist in some way, while having other attributes characteristic of someone else. Behind this covering figure resembling the analyst one then usually finds allusions to the original object, whose identity had been concealed in the covering figure.

A man with a mild drinking problem (an obsessive need for two martinis before dinner when he came home from the office) had a lengthy dream about a business associate, an alcoholic who went from bar to bar and became progressively more intoxicated. His associations led briefly to his concern about his own drinking (although he had never had any desire to go to bars). Then, after a short silence, he confessed that he had often thought, but had not said, that his analyst was an alcoholic (he was not) and that he believed the analyst kept a bottle of whiskey in the bottom drawer of his desk (he did not). When confronted with his ideas, the patient realized that he had projected his father's pattern of going to bars and keeping a bottle of whiskey in *his* desk upon his analyst. What remained concealed for a time, however, was his conviction that his mother drank, too, as she kept a bottle of Scotch hidden behind the lingerie in her dresser. He recalled having looked at it from time to time and noticing that the contents of the bottle rapidly diminished and that the bottles were replaced. He had not been certain that his mother drank and therefore had never discussed it, because he thought that perhaps it was his father who drank the Scotch and not his mother.

Another device that dreams use to express parallels is "composition." Freud writes:

> In composition, where this is extended to persons, the dream-image contains features which are peculiar to one or other of the persons concerned but not common to them; so that the combination of these features leads to the appearance of a new unity, a composite figure. [1900, p. 320]

> I may build up a figure by giving it the features of two people; or I may give it the *form* of one person but think of it in the dream as having the *name* of another person; or I may have a visual picture of one person, but put it in a situation which is appropriate to another. In all these cases the combination of different persons into a single representative in the content of the dream has a meaning; it is intended to indicate an 'and' or 'just as', or to compare the original persons with each other in some particular respect, which may even be specified in the dream itself. [1901a, p. 651]

> Another rule in dream-interpretation would tell us that when one person is replaced by another or when two people are mixed up together (for instance, by one of them being shown in a situation that is characteristic of the other), it means that the two people are being equated, that there is a similarity between them. [1907, p. 74]

Sometimes parallels are expressed by similarity of position, e.g., "You were sitting in a chair and alongside you was sitting X" (Sharpe, 1937, p. 27).

A man dreamed he was having sexual intercourse with a very beautiful young woman he had met at a party the evening before the dream. Her dream name, he suddenly recalled, was not her real name and was "unusual" in that it was identical to his sister's name, although the woman did not bear the slightest resemblance to his sister. His associations revealed that he had at one time engaged in some genital sex play with his sister. He realized that contained in his wish to have sexual relations with the woman he met at the party, was his wish to reexperience the same forbidden erotic pleasure he had had when he engaged in the activity with his sister.

Localities in dreams follow the same principles as names and people. A locality may have one name but be like some other place. A patient dreamed he was in New York City, but the Eiffel Tower was there somehow in Times Square, and then he thought the area looked more like Picadilly Circus. The therapist must always bear in mind the dreamer's reason for choosing specific localities, as each may be the starting point of a chain of associations which are ultimately connected by common denominators not readily apparent. In the case of the man's dream about Times Square, the Eiffel Tower, and Picadilly Circus, his associations led to his having looked for prostitutes in New York, Paris, and London. On exploration, the setting of the dream in a particular situation or locale often provides the therapist easy entry into a discussion of events that may previously have been shrouded by repression.

Sometimes the allusion to a location refers not so much to the location itself, but to a person connected with the location. The person and the characteristics that identify him are repressed, however.

The location may also allude to some traumatic incident that took place in that location or was related to it. In one instance, a woman dreamed of a sink with a string stretched above it on which were hung some objects of clothing. The locale referred to the sink over which bathing suits were hung to dry in her mother-in-law's ocean house and to an episode which occurred there. The patient had been in psychotherapy with a prominent person who was a friend of the family. She had invited him to be a house guest at her mother-in-law's house for a few days. One night they went swimming in the nude and then had sexual relations. When they returned to the city, she continued treatment with him, but the nature of the relationship had obviously changed. The patient had needed to suppress this incident, not only because she felt guilty about the affair, but also because it had obvious implications as far as the transference to the present therapist was concerned.

Freud describes various means of composition, some of which have already been described. The therapist's awareness of these possibilities enhances his ability to understand the patient's dream and associations.

> The actual process of composition can be carried out in various ways. On the one hand, the dream-figure may bear the name of one of the persons related to it—in which case we simply know directly, in a manner analogous to our waking knowledge, that this or that person is intended—while its visual features may belong to the other person. Or, on the other hand, the dream-image itself may be composed of visual features belonging in reality partly to the one person and partly to the other. Or again the second person's share in the dream-image may lie, not in its visual features, but in the gestures that we attribute to it, the words that we make it speak, or the situation in which we place it. In this last case the distinction between identification and the construction of a composite figure begins to lose its sharpness. But it may also happen that the formation of a composite figure of this kind is unsuccessful. If so, the scene in the dream is attributed to *one* of the persons concerned, while the other (and usually the more important one) appears as an attendant figure without any other function. The dreamer may describe the position in such a phrase as: 'My mother was there as well' (Stekel). [1900, pp. 320–321]

In one dream, a woman dreamed that a man she had met at a social gathering was making love to her. Somewhere in "the background of that dream," or of another dream during the night, was the shadowy figure of her analyst. The dream referred to similar libidinal wishes that she had entertained toward her analyst.

At times the presence of a scene with a splitting of the figures serves to express the idea that the feelings involved concerned multiple figures. In interpreting such a dream, it is helpful to the patient if the therapist points out how the various figures or situations are parallel or similar.

Freud continues:

> The common element which justifies, or rather causes, the combination of the two persons may be represented in the dream or may be omitted from it. As a rule the identification or construction of a composite person takes place for the very purpose of avoiding the representation of the common element. Instead of saying: 'A has hostile feelings towards me and so has B', I make a composite figure out of A and B in the dream, or I imagine A performing an act of some other kind which is characteristic of B. The dream-figure thus constructed appears in the dream in some quite new connection, and the circumstance that it represents both A and B justifies me in inserting at the appropriate point in the dream the element which is common to both of them, namely a hostile attitude towards me. [1900, p. 321]

It is important for the therapist to keep in mind the possibility that a dream element (a locale or person) may be a composite figure and that he must therefore search for one or more common denominators in the dreamer's associations. What often happens is that the characteristic to which the individual alludes, such as hostility in the example Freud uses, is characteristic of not just A and B but rather of a whole host of people. The therapist is then in a position to explore with the patient the problem with which he is struggling—his deep feelings that people are hostile and aggressive toward him. Again using Freud's example, why are A and B hostile toward him? And, by implication from the associations, are other people hostile toward him as well, and, if so, why? The specific composite figure thus becomes a means of representing a *general* theme rather than a specific allusion.

Moreover, in dealing with this type of material the therapist must keep in mind the possibility that the individual is actually expressing his own aggressive feelings by projecting them upon various individuals. It would then be important to ascertain why the dreamer is aggressive toward these people. One often finds that when the dreamer is expressing his own feelings (here, anger or aggression) toward a *number* of people, there is actually *one* person who is the focus of his aggression, and he has temporarily suppressed or repressed his anger against that person.

This type of situation will be seen frequently when the patient has had the need to repress transference feelings. A patient dreamed that he had taken his car to a car wash. It was run by blacks who were performing many functions: hosing the wheels, using long brushes to remove mud from around the bumpers, crawling into cars to clean the interiors, etc. The man in charge was a large black man with a heavy beard. The patient went to claim his car and, finding that it was still dirty, complained about its condition to the black man. At that point the man menacingly said: "Get the hell out of here!" Many of the patient's associations dealt with his negative feelings toward blacks: that they are incompetent, lazy, and aggressive. He had actually had his car washed the previous day, but not at a car wash run by blacks. He had not been satisfied with the job but had not complained about it. The black man reminded him of his uncle, who was similarly built and had such a beard. He lashed out at length about his uncle, castigating him for his boorish insensitivity.

It was almost the end of the session before the patient finally realized that he was actually furious with his analyst for cancelling an appointment when he needed to talk with him about a problem that had come up. The aggression against the analyst had been displaced to the composite figure in the dream and had been reversed. In the dream the black man was angry with him. Yet it was the patient who was furious with his analyst (who had no beard) for the cancelled appointment, angry that the analyst had not been doing a good job, and that he still had symptoms (the car was still dirty). He was also fearful that if he complained about the professional service his analyst would throw him out, just as he had been hesitant to complain about the unsatisfactory car wash for fear he would be thrown out. The intensity of the patient's anger and his fear of his analyst proved to be derived from the patient's feelings about his father, represented in his associations to the dream by his uncle.

Freud gives the following rule:

> When a common element between two persons is represented in a dream, it is usually a hint for us to look for another, concealed common element whose representation has been made impossible by the censorship. A displacement in regard to the common element has been made in order, as it were, to facilitate its representation. The fact that the composite figure appears in the dream with an indifferent common element leads us to conclude that there is another far from indifferent common element present in the dream-thoughts. [1900, p. 322]

A man dreamed of two of his male employees. He described them as particularly well dressed. "They were both sharp-looking, clean-cut young men." They were both good salespeople, aggressive in their dealings. After extolling their virtues and their importance to his corporation, he said, after some digression, that he had suspected that they both had homosexual leanings, a matter that he had not wanted to get into in his analysis because it might "prove disadvantageous" to him.

Because of the fact that all elements in a manifest dream must be considered in a positive or negative sense, it is important to determine whether the patient is expressing a *parallel* or a *contrast*. Freud writes: "The dream-work is particularly fond of representing two *contrary* ideas by the same composite structure" (1901a, p. 652). At times both may

be present in the associations, especially when there is ambivalence toward an object.

Sometimes contraries are expressed by means of identification, "cases, that is, in which the idea of an exchange or
substitution can be brought into connection with the contrast"
(1900, p. 326). This is particularly applicable to transference
material. Thus, a woman who had been in analysis for some
time dreamed that she was on an expedition to the Himalayas,
which she could see clearly in the distance. The patient had
been in therapy before with an incredibly incompetent person
who was cold, austere, and distant. With pontifical certainty,
he had predicted the ultimate success of her treatment, promising her such freedom from her incapacitating anxieties that
she "would be able to go to the Himalaya Mountains." Her
dream gratified this promise the former therapist had given
her and simultaneously, in the metaphor of the mountains,
alluded to his coldness and lofty distance. She was also drawing parallels with her present situation, expecting her present
analyst to be like the former one, promising her much and
yet being no more helpful than the initial therapist.

Yet, having seen that the present therapy and therapist
were completely different, she was also able to express the
contrast in her dream: that it was not at all like her previous
experience; that her symptoms of being extremely inhibited
had markedly diminished; and that perhaps now she would
actually be able to attain the goal set by her former therapist
and be able to go to the Himalaya Mountains (though not in
reality, of course, as she had not the slightest interest along
those lines). On a deeper level, she was also expressing certain
early transference aspects in her dream, as her mother was
also singularly austere and remote. The symbolic expression
of the snow-covered mountain peaks was an accurate pictorial
representation of her perception of her mother and her
mother's breasts. Here once again was the anticipated parallel, that the analyst would be like her mother, but also the
known contrast. After discussing these aspects of her dream

and her associations, she said tearfully to her analyst, a man, "You are the best mother I ever had."

Alternatives: Either-Or

Freud writes:

> The alternative 'either-or' cannot be expressed in dreams in any way whatever. Both of the alternatives are usually inserted in the text of the dream as though they were equally valid. [1900, p. 316]

> If . . . in reproducing a dream, its narrator feels inclined to make use of an 'either-or'—e.g. 'it was either a garden or a sittingroom'—what was present in the dream-thoughts was not an alternative but an 'and', a simple addition. An 'either-or' is mostly used to describe a dream-element that has a quality of vagueness—which, however, is capable of being resolved. In such cases the rule for interpretation is: treat the two apparent alternatives as of equal validity and link them together with an 'and'. [1900, p. 317]

> take each of the apparent alternatives as an independent starting-point for a series of associations. [1901a, p. 650]

In one dream, a man viewed the dream scene as being in either one office or another. His associations led to his specific problems with his employees in each of his offices (each was a different business). The problems were different, each leading to its own idiosyncratic complexities, but there was also a common denominator in his approach to these problems. In each instance he had hired people to work for him on the basis of their physical attractiveness rather than on the basis of their competence. In each instance, the choice proved disadvantageous to his business.

Sometimes the "either-or" may represent two (or more) alternative solutions. One bisexual man, for example, had a dream in which he was driving his car in a notorious "pick-up" area. He wanted to pick up someone: "either a man or a woman to give me a blow job. I wasn't sure which I wanted to pick up and I guess it didn't really make a difference. After all, a mouth is a mouth. The sex it belongs to doesn't matter." The attitude expressed in the dream was an accurate presentation of his practices of picking up either male or female prostitutes.

At other times the "either-or" will express a conflict of ambivalence or indecision with which the dreamer is struggling. A young unmarried woman dreamed that she was in church getting married. She went on to say: "I was so happy. The groom was either Tom or John." She had been going with both of these men and liked both of them. Both had indicated that they wanted to marry her. She was undecided and ambivalent about both of them. "I think I could be happily married to either one of them. I don't know what to do."

On other occasions the "either-or" is used to express a vagueness or uncertainty referable to some situation such as a confusion in childhood.

The use of "either-or" in the manifest content of dreams may also be considered in the nature of a comment or gloss on some element in the dream.

Inversion

In this category are those dreams or dream elements that express ideas or feelings by their opposite or by reversal (1900, pp. 326–327). It may be noted that children reverse the sound of words (metathesis, e.g., God, dog) which Freud indicates "is perhaps even more intimately related to the dream-work than are contradictory meanings (antithesis)" (1910a, p. 161n1). While such specific reversals of sounds or letters do not occur frequently, their presence, when they do occur, suggests some reference to childhood. The use of opposites in the manifest content of dreams may produce so much distortion that at times the therapist may be totally frustrated in his attempts to unravel the dream.

Dreams about people who are unknown to the dreamer or whose names have been forgotten exemplify this use of reversal. These people are usually those who are "mostly . . . very near to one" (1916–1917, p. 196). More than likely, the strangers in the dream are members of the dreamer's own family (1900, pp. 245–246). Why they are represented in precisely the way they are, however, must be understood. Sometimes it occurs because the dream figure has characteristics that the dreamer may not like to recognize as belonging to particular family members. At other times, the significance of strangers refers to certain character traits that the dreamer regards as strange. In one instance, a patient made clear the significance of the stranger in his dream when he stated: "Sure, it was a stranger who stood for my father in the dream. I know why. I never knew my father. He was never home. He was like a stranger."

Sometimes the reversal may deal not only with one or more specific elements but may also deal with the entire sequence of elements so that "to make sense in interpreting [the dream] we must take the last one first and the first one last" (1916–1917, p. 180). In other dreams the sequence is not so orderly, especially in instances in which there are several dreams or fragments to be considered. In such instances, one can only understand them if one begins in the middle and then considers how the other parts fit. A series of dreams often deals with the progression of an impulse (it becomes more overt, e.g., a sexual wish) or describes some causal or historical connection.

With regard to dream interpretation in the light of the mechanism of reversal, Freud provides the following suggestion: "In some instances . . . it is only possible to arrive at the meaning of a dream after one has carried out quite a number of reversals of its content in various respects" (1900, p. 328). Here we must repeat our earlier statement that, generally, if there is an indication that one element (noun, verb, modifier) in the manifest content of a dream has been reversed, other reversals will be present. This does not mean, however, that everything in the dream is reversed.

Quite frequently, the elements to be understood in a direct or positive sense and those that are reversed are both derived from the latent dream thoughts. This makes it possible for the therapist to see the expression of the patient's ambivalence, the various polarities (e.g., active and passive strivings), and the intrapsychic conflicts that result from such contradictory feelings.

Sometimes inversion serves "to give expression to the fulfilment of a wish in reference to some particular element of the dream-thoughts. 'If only it had been the other way round!' This is often the best way of expressing the ego's reaction to a disagreeable fragment of memory" (1900, p. 327). For instance, a male patient who had been placed on probation for his pedophilic homosexual behavior, though with the stipulation that he receive psychotherapy, dreamed that he was in a car with a woman and was fondling her breasts. The dream represented in part his wish that he was heterosexual, because then he would not need to be in treatment.

Freud indicates another reason for the use of reversal in dreams. "I think," he writes, " . . . that all these dreams of turning things round the other way include a reference to the contemptuous implications of the idea of 'turning one's back on something' " (1900, p. 327). To this remark Strachey appends the following footnote: "The German '*Kehrseite*' can mean both 'reverse' and 'backside'. Cf. the vulgar English phrase 'arse upwards' for 'upside down', 'the wrong way round' " (1900, p. 327n1; note also such Americanisms as "ass backwards" or "back asswards"). Freud also points out that "reversal is employed precisely in dreams arising from repressed homosexual impulses" (1900, p. 327). This application of reversal is discussed in chapter 4.

A specific form of inversion is *temporal inversion*. On this subject Freud has the following to say: "Quite a common technique of dream-distortion consists in representing the outcome of an event or the conclusion of a train of thought at the beginning of a dream and of placing at its end the premises on which the conclusion was based or the causes which led to the event" (1900, p. 328). Sometimes such dreams represent the patient's symptomatology at the beginning of the dream. Then, at the end of the dream, the elements allude to circumstances that have led historically to the development of this symptomatology.

A man dreamed that he was going to have intercourse with a woman, but just as he was about to penetrate her, he became impotent. As the dream continued, he found himself being chased by a man. The patient did in fact suffer from impotence, which was very disturbing to him, and many determinants of his difficulty emerged in the course of his analysis. This dream, however, alluded to a specific incident in his childhood, when he and a little girl were inspecting each others' genitals in a woodshed belonging to the girl's family. Her father had unexpectedly walked in upon them, carrying an axe, apparently with the thought of chopping some firewood. His entry frightened the patient. Thinking that the man would attack him with the axe and chop off his penis, he ran away. The man chased after him, however, with the axe still in his hand.

Temporal inversion is especially evident in dreams that are divided into parts representing a series of events. In such dreams, one part of the series may refer to events of long ago. Temporal inversion may also occur in dreams in pairs. Current or relatively recent material in dreams may screen events or reactions from early childhood.

Directions

Another common means of representation in dreams is the use of directions. These must be considered from a direct or positive standpoint and also as representing their opposite.

"Up" and "down" or "under." Sometimes these expressions refer to the location of the genitals or to some specific

sexual activity. Thus, one patient dreamed that he was in an elevator and the elevator operator said, "Going down." The reference was to fellatio.

Dreams of "up above" or "over" may refer to the heavens, to someone who has died, or to reaching the pinnacle of success. More commonly, the "up above" may be used to symbolize the superego or a voice from on high, some judicial or religious figure or God himself. Genetically, the voice from on high often refers directly to the parents, who originally towered above the little child. A woman whose religious background was extremely strict dreamed she was being judged by a tribunal. Seated on a high judge's seat or throne that extended almost to the sky was a large man with a snow-white beard. He looked somewhat like her grandfather and somewhat like a picture of Moses she had seen in Sunday school. Then, in a thundering voice so loud it woke her, he proclaimed, "You are guilty." The proclamation in the dream expressed her guilt over her sexual involvement with her brother-in-law.

Right and left. Freud, citing Stekel (1909) writes that " 'right' and 'left' in dreams have an ethical sense. 'The right-hand path always means the path of righteousness and the left-hand one that of crime. Thus "left" may represent homosexuality, incest or perversion, and "right" may represent marriage, intercourse with a prostitute and so on, always looked at from the subject's individual moral standpoint' (1900, pp. 357–358).

Dreams in which right or left are present are very common, often expressing many of the individual's fundamental conflicts in a symbolic way—for example, the problems of bisexuality. A male patient, while struggling with the idea of whether to go into analysis, had a dream in which he was driving a car and suddenly made a left turn. He awoke with great anxiety. After some time he went into analysis. When he discussed this dream in the course of his analysis, he related that he had been having conflicts with his business partner at that time and had developed *pruritis ani*. A few days before the dream he had gone on a hunting trip with a group of men and was particularly disturbed when some of them spent the evening drinking and telling homosexual jokes. From his associations it was evident that the dream of going to the left expressed his anxiety that he might go to the left, i.e., get homosexually involved with someone. His mention of his *pruritis ani* in connection with the dream expressed his fear and unconscious wish that he would be anally penetrated by another man (in this instance, his business partner). He confirmed this point by recalling one of the homosexual jokes. Later in his analysis, he returned once more to this anxiety dream, adding the detail that he was in his father's car. By supplying this detail, he revealed that his fear of passive submission to his father was a genetic determinant of the dream. A number of the members of the hunting party who were telling the homosexual jokes were older men whom he regarded as father figures. The patient returned to this dream several times in the course of his analysis. In each instance the dream occurred when he was struggling with a similar problem in the transference.

People who are socially or politically minded may use the reference to right and left in a metaphoric sense, alluding to conservatism or liberalism with appropriate implications as to the degree of involvement. At times such references in dreams succeed in providing access to a great deal of material about an important aspect of the individual's life that may not come up otherwise.

Often one sees dreams of going to the right heralding changes in the patient's personality and his readiness to assume adult responsibilities and mature positions. These dreams may presage the patient's entry into the termination phase of his therapy.

Condensation

Every element in the manifest content of a dream is overdetermined and is the result of the condensation of two or more ideas, impressions, or experiences. "These elements," Freud writes, "need not necessarily be closely related to each other in the dream-thoughts themselves; they may belong to the most widely separated regions of the fabric of those thoughts" (1901a, p. 652).

By understanding the particular elements in the dream, the therapist is thus provided ready access to what is going on in the patient's mind. In actual clinical practice, however, one rarely has the opportunity to explore all the determinants of every element in a dream.

Freud writes: "The work of condensation in dreams is seen at its clearest when it handles words and names. It is true in general that words are frequently treated in dreams as though they were things, and for that reason they are apt to be combined in just the same way as are presentations of things. Dreams of this sort offer the most amusing and curious neologisms" (1900, pp. 295–296). The analysis of such "nonsensical verbal forms" offers one of the easiest starting points from which to unravel a dream. A patient of mine had a dream in which there was a man named Lipstein. The name was a neologism, as he knew no one by that name. He immediately recognized that the "stein" part referred to the second syllable of my name. He went on talking about other people with names ending in "stein," names beginning with "stein," and various Steins he had known over the years. Then, after a pause, he went on to tell me about the first part of the neologism. "Lip," he said, reminded him of a Dr. Louis Lipschutz, a senior training analyst in the area who had had a myocardial infarction, retired from his analytic practice, and, after a number of years, died. The patient had identified me with Dr. Lipschutz. He feared that I would also have a sudden heart attack, retire from practice, and eventually die, abandoning him as he felt Dr. Lipschutz had abandoned his patients.

The mechanism of condensation is particularly evident in short, compact dreams, especially those in which there seems to be a "ready" connection in the manifest dream with the day residues. Often both patient and analyst are satisfied when they have been able to establish this connection and fail to explore the other determinants condensed in the particular element. In the case of transference dreams, patients may be inclined to interpret the dream as a whole, viewing it from the manifest content rather than pursuing the latent dream thoughts behind it (Sharpe, 1937).

Sometimes in condensation it is "possible clearly to distinguish . . . two trains of thought [one consoling and one self-reproachful]—trains of thought which [are] diametrically opposed to each other but whose similar though contrary elements [are] represented by the same elements in the manifest dream" (Freud, 1900, p. 319).

Other dreams employing condensation may refer to coexisting positive and negative attitudes toward the same figure. A man dreamed about a physician who had a splendid reputation in the community. He admired him greatly and extolled his virtues as a diagnostician, teacher, and therapist. But then he went on to relate some negative aspects about him: he was insensitive to patients' needs, kept them waiting unnecessarily, charged too much, and, he had heard, was involved in an affair with a very low-class woman. The transference aspects of the communication were clearly evident.

Vividness, Lucidity, Vagueness, and Confusion

The therapist should look for condensation whenever *vivid* elements are described in the manifest dream. Freud observes "that the most vivid elements of a dream are the starting-point of the most numerous trains of thought—that the most vivid elements are also those with the most numerous determinants. . . . the greatest intensity is shown by those elements of a dream on whose formation the greatest amount of condensation has been expended" (1900, p. 330). "It by no means rarely happens," he writes elsewhere, "that in the course of a comparatively long, complicated and on the whole confused dream one particularly clear portion stands out, which contains an unmistakable wish-fulfilment, but which is bound up with some other, unintelligible material" (1901a, p. 646).

In the case of adults, "behind the obvious wish-fulfilment some other meaning may lie concealed" (1901a, p. 646). Often in these instances, a shift or displacement of the material has taken place so that a more forbidden impulse is not readily apparent. This may occur, for example, when the dream seems to express a rather obvious heterosexual wish, but conceals homosexual material.

Sometimes the reverse is true: the most indistinct element is the one in which the greatest number of associations have converged: "We assume as a matter of course," Freud writes, "that the most distinct element in the manifest content of a dream is the most important one; but in fact [owing to the displacement that has occurred] it is often an *indistinct* element which turns out to be the most direct derivative of the essential dream-thought" (1901a, p. 654).

Keeping these principles in mind, the therapist can thus easily focus attention on the most vivid and lucid or, conversely, the most indistinct or confused elements in a dream. Although this matter was taken up earlier, it is appropriate to renew the discussion here to emphasize a number of points. The therapist, aware that dream elements selected by the dream-work are generally the result of the condensation of two or more trains of thought represented by the particular element, should not be satisfied if the patient provides only one connection to the element. Frequently, some persistence in the inquiry about the choice of the particular element will reveal associations which the patient had some resistance to revealing.

In some instances a particularly vivid or indistinct element in a dream may be specifically connected with an especially vivid or traumatic event in the individual's past, around which many reactions may have been condensed. The event may be an observation or an experience, or it may be something the dreamer heard, felt, tasted, or smelled that made a distinct impression on him.

At other times the sensory quality of the element, the impression of its distinctness or indistinctness, or its powerful affect may in itself be the essential element in the communication. It may refer, for example, to the dreamer's affect at the time of the experience, i.e., that it was overpowering or that he was confused and did not understand what was going on, that it was not clear to him, that it was vague or even incomprehensible. Some primal scene dreams are like this and refer to a time when the dreamer did not clearly understand what was involved.

Freud noted that *"there is an intimate and regular relation between the unintelligible and confused nature of dreams and the difficulty of reporting the thoughts behind them"* (1901a, p. 643).

In the narration of some dreams, the patient may interpolate a remark, often with some hesitation, introducing it by an "as though." Freud indicates that these interpolations in content are

> not in themselves particularly vivid and are always introduced at points at which they can serve as links between two portions of the dream-content or to bridge a gap between two parts of the dream. . . . In a complete analysis these interpolations are sometimes betrayed by the fact that no material connected with them is to be found in the dream-thoughts. . . . as a rule the connecting thoughts lead back nevertheless to material in the dream-thoughts, but to material which could have no claim to acceptance in the dream either on its own account or owing to its being over-determined. [1900, p. 489]

It has been my experience with material that has been interpolated into the dream content, that the hesitation and the vagueness, prefaced by comments such as "as if " or "as though" or "somewhat like," etc., often lead to specific associations. In some instances the individual may be comparing one situation with another that has been subjected to repression. Or, the "as though" may be an allusion to some other incident which may be less pertinent than the one presented but which has an equivalent significance for the dreamer. In this respect it may allude to an "either-or" but without specifying the alternative. On other occasions the vagueness may refer to an episode that happened a long time ago, as in the preverbal period, about which the dreamer's memory is understandably hazy. Sometimes dreams during fever or toxic delirium may evoke such memory traces.

In one instance, a man dreamed that he was in some kind of car. He was not in the driver's seat and added, "It was as though the vehicle was being propelled by some external force." While the reference to the car referred to certain specific incidents that had occurred during the dream day, his comment, "It was 'as though' the vehicle had been propelled by some external force," related to his early childhood when he sat in a baby carriage which was being pushed. His associations led to memories of a somewhat later period, of which he vaguely recalled being in a baby carriage with his year-and-a-half-old younger brother and his feelings of antagonism toward him.

Finally, with regard to the various possibilities we have discussed, Freud cautions "that the elements which stand out as the principal components of the manifest content of the dream are far from playing the same part in the dream-thoughts. And, as a corollary, the converse of this assertion can be affirmed: what is clearly the essence of the dream-thoughts need not be represented in the dream at all" (1900, p. 305).

Color

When a specific color is mentioned in connection with a particular element or group of elements in relating the manifest content of the dream, the descriptive detail must be regarded as an element in its own right and subject to analytic investigation, just as any other modifier (size, configuration, etc.) would be. Generally, the choice of color occurs because a number of trains of thought have converged upon it or because the color in and of itself has special significance.

In many instances the element color follows rather traditional usage: yellow = cowardice; green = jealousy; red = passion or blood; blue = depression; brown = feces; purple = royalty. Black, in dreams, often alludes to death, but it may also allude to crude sexual or aggressive impulses. White may signify death, but also may refer to purity or innocence. There may be some parallels in associations to color to the responses to the Rorschach cards.

In addition to the specific choice of color being related to experiences in the dream day, the latent content may refer "to the scoptophilic-exhibitionistic impulses of the dreamer [and its relation to] primal scene material" (Calef, 1954, p. 459).

Sometimes the color in dreams is not confined to one or a few specific elements, but is pervasive throughout the dream (technicolor dreams). Color may be present in the dreams of people who are artistic or trained in the use of color, or it may occur when people are upset or have severe personality disturbances. In the latter instance, the colors are unusually vivid. Kohut (1971) writes that technicolor dreams often appear "to signify the intrusion of unmodified material into the ego in the guise of realism, and the ego's inability to integrate it completely. One might say that the technicolor expresses the ego's subliminally experienced anxious hypomanic excitement over certain intrusions of the grandiosity and the exhibitionism of the grandiose self" (p. 172). He adds that "the fact that the dream was in color (especially in the unnatural technicolor . . .) is an expression of the fact that the dreamer's ego was unable to achieve the complete integration of the new experiences; that it was able fully to absorb neither the intensity nor the content of the drive demands" (p. 322n9).

Numbers and Calculations

Freud indicates that numbers, combinations of numbers, or calculations in dreams are "torn out of their true context and inserted in a new one" (1905a, p. 97n2).

Generally they refer to specific material in the day residues which must be obtained from the patient's associations. For example, a bisexual man dreamed that he was driving on the expressway and came to the interchange between Interstate 696 and 96. He was uncertain which way to go. The dream referred to his conflict between staying with the woman he was involved with or giving up heterosexuality altogether and living with his male lover. While the interchange in the dream expressed the idea of change, the particular location referred to the "69" that he practiced with both lovers. Another patient dreamed of 34 1/2, which had to do with his wanting a woman that he had taken out to perform fellatio on him. "It was one half of 69," he said. The dream referred to what he wanted done to him and not what he wanted to do with her.

Sometimes dreams of numbers refer to the age of the patient at the time of some event, especially if it was traumatic. We have already mentioned the patient who dreamed of an event that occurred at five o'clock. The dream referred to the birth of his brother when he was five. Sometimes numbers may represent a time interval between two events, e.g., the patient's birth and the birth of a sibling (1913b, p. 195).

Certain numbers frequently have a specific significance. The number nine, for example, often refers to the months of gestation (Freud, 1923a, p. 89). A woman, who was not particularly interested or gifted in mathematics, dreamed of some complicated mathematical formulas. In her associations, she recalled that in grammar school the children, with much amusement, had passed around a note upon which was written the following formula: $M/W + 9 = B$. The formula meant: a man over a woman plus 9 months equals a baby.

The number eight refers to the openings of the vagina and rectum in close relation to each other, as in the figure 8. Sometimes the reference to the number is made via a pun, e.g., "ate." The number five may refer to the fingers in masturbation (Sharpe, 1937) or to the hand in general. The number four may stand for "for." A man dreamed of a portable outhouse, a "Porto-John," on which was a sign "4U2P." He said that he had actually seen such a sign near a construction site the previous day.

Freud indicates that dreams take "liberties" with numbers:

> The number is kept, but its denominator is changed according to the requirements of condensation and displacement. Nine years in a dream could thus easily correspond to 9 months in real life. The dream-work plays about with numbers of waking life in another way, too, for it shows a sovereign disregard for noughts and does not treat them as numbers at all. Five dollars in a dream can stand for fifty or five hundred or five thousand dollars in reality. [1923b, p. 89; see also Freud and Oppenheim, 1911, p. 186n3]

We have already given examples of this in connection with the analytic fee. Freud writes that calculations in dreams are "sham calculations which are quite senseless *qua* calculations and are once again only copies of calculations in the latent dream thoughts" (1916–1917, p. 182). And again:

> it merely throws into the *form* of a calculation numbers which are present in the dream-thoughts and can serve as allusions to matter that cannot be represented in any other way. . . . [The dream uses] numbers as a medium for the expression of its purpose in precisely the same way as it treats any other idea, including proper names and speeches that occur recognizably as verbal presentations. [1900, p. 418; see also 1907, p. 74; 1909a, p. 21]

References to calculations in dreams may be to the organization of material, statistics, rules, regulations, and specific calculations in the dreamer's profession or to money matters in his thoughts. The figures and calculations may have to do with thoughts about business dealings and finances. In these instances, while the manifest dream deals with the "numbers," the underlying dream-thoughts deal with the patient's real concern about finances. The dream may thus be expressing the wish to be out of a difficult financial situation as well as the wish that the difficult situation was only a dream.

Sometimes dreams of numbers in sequence and calculations express the ruminations of a compulsion. One compulsive patient who had some background in accounting had repetitive dreams in which he was trying to add up and balance columns of figures whenever he was confronted with a decision. The dreams seemed to go on interminably as he went back and forth over the calculations, never quite able to come to a satisfactory conclusion. At other times calculations in dreams refer to early times in the patient's life and the individual's attempt to "figure things out" regarding age differences, anatomy, and sexual functions.

Speeches

In chapter 1 we indicated that one may begin working with a dream by inquiring about the patient's associations to a speech in the dream. Regarding the use of spoken words in a dream, Freud writes:

> Where spoken sentences occur in dreams and are expressly distinguished as such from thoughts, it is an invariable rule that the words spoken in the dream are derived from spoken words remembered in the dream-material. The text of the speech is either retained unaltered or expressed with some slight displacement. A speech in a dream is often put together from various recollected speeches, the text remaining the same but being given, if possible, several meanings, or one different from the original one. A spoken remark in a dream is not infrequently no more than an allusion to an occasion on which the remark in question was made. [1900, p. 304]

Freud indicates that "another copious source of undifferentiated speeches . . . seems to be provided by material that has been *read*" (1900, p. 420).

Speeches may refer to what the patient has heard, read, or seen in an advertisement, book, newspaper, magazine, journal, movie, or radio or television program. The allusion may be to the pertinence of the speech for the material being dealt with in the therapy, to the topic, situation, or title of the particular reference, or to the person making the speech. Like speeches derived from what has been said or heard, quotations from an actual text may be grossly distorted. Therapists who are analytic patients will sometimes misread or misquote professional material that clearly reveals the nature of their own problems.

Freud emphasizes that "whatever stands out markedly in dreams as a speech can be traced back to real speeches which have been spoken or heard by the dreamer" (1900, p. 420). He indicates that the dream deals arbitrarily with fragments from various recollected speeches, those actually made or heard. Sometimes the dream-work exchanges "one word for another till it finds the expression which is most handy for plastic representation" (1917b, p. 228).

He states that the dream not only drags speeches out of their context and cuts them in pieces, "incorporating some portions and rejecting others, but it often puts them together in a new order, so that a speech which appears in the dream to be a connected whole turns out to be composed of three or four detached fragments. In producing this new version, a dream will often abandon the meaning that the words originally had in the dream-thoughts and give them a fresh one" (1900, p. 418).

Freud carefully distinguishes between two categories of speeches in dreams. First we have "such speeches in dreams as possess something of the sensory quality of speech, and which are described by the dreamer himself as being speeches" (1900, p. 419).

A man dreamed that he was seated at the dinner table

with members of his family, including his parents. He was telling them that he was in analysis and his parents said that he didn't need it. The dream was a replay of an actual scene that had occurred a few days before. The speech also represented his own conflict about being in analysis and verbalized his own thoughts, partially derived from his parents' attitude, about his problems. Further, the dream contained his conviction that his parents did not understand him nor were they really concerned about him.

The second category comprises speeches in dreams which are not felt by the dreamer "as having been heard or spoken (that is, which have no acoustic or motor accompaniments in the dream), are merely thoughts such as occur in our waking thought-activity and are often carried over unmodified into our dreams" (1900, p. 420).

Sometimes a speech in the dream is a distortion or a reversal of an actual thought during the dream day. A woman dreamed that she was at a lunch counter with a woman friend and thought to herself: "I will not pay anyone to plant peanuts in my garden." The speech in the dream was a reversal of an actual thought that she had had after her previous session: that she would pay someone (her analyst) to plant his penis (and nuts) in(to) her garden and make a baby. The dream had followed the beginning of her menstrual period that day and also coincided with her receiving her bill for analytic services.

A speech from current reality may serve as a stimulus for the revival of the memory of an earlier speech in the past, often one made in a different context (see Sharpe, 1937). A woman suffering from sexual anesthesia dreamed of being in a bathroom. A large, heavy-set woman, like a prison matron, was shouting at her, "Don't you ever do that!" The patient had visited her sister in another city for a weekend. Her little nephew was poking his sister at the dinner table and her brother-in-law, the children's father, had yelled at them to stop. The speech in the dream, however, reminded her of her own childhood, when their maid, a heavy-set woman like the prison matron, had caught her masturbating in the bathroom and shouted those very words at her in a very frightening manner.

An exception to the rule of the source of spoken words is to be found in obsessional formations. Freud writes that "an obsessional command (or whatever it may be), which in waking life is known only in a truncated and distorted form, like a mutilated telegraph message, may have its actual text brought to light in a dream. Such texts appear in dreams in the shape of speeches" (1909b, p. 223).

Sometimes the obsessional command with which the patient is struggling is displaced onto the analyst and then he, or his voice, provides the speech in the dream. A homosexual patient who suffered from a severe obsessive-compulsive neurosis lost his mother when he was a child. In the course of his lengthy analysis he dreamed that someone was saying to him, "You are a homosexual because your mother died." He realized upon awakening that the voice in the dream had the same quality and inflection as the voice of his analyst. His analyst, however, had not said anything like that to him at any time. The spoken words had come from himself and were his own interpretation of his basic symptomatology.

The patient's mother had died while giving birth to his sister when he was about two years old. He had grown up hating his sister because he felt that she had caused his mother's death. He was bitterly angry with his mother for dying and for leaving him. He hated all women and avoided intimate contact with them, as he felt that they were responsible for wrecking his life. He also hated his father because he felt his mother's death was his fault: he had made her pregnant and not provided her proper obstetrical care at the time of her delivery. The patient's anger was extended from his father to all men.

The "interpretation" he heard in his dream, that he was a homosexual because his mother died, was actually a condensed and distorted command from his superego to be a homosexual. It eliminated, however, the complex determinants which were, in part: "You must be a homosexual because if you are intimate with a woman, have sexual relations with her, and impregnate her as your father impregnated your mother, she will die as a result. You will be responsible for her death, just as your father is responsible for your mother's death." Since he hated men, he felt profoundly driven to pursue them for homosexual purposes, sometimes even in situations involving great personal danger, so that he could defile them.

Chapter Ten

Comments on a Dream

As part of the total picture when dealing with any dream, the therapist must pay special attention to the dreamer's comments about the dream as a totality or to parts of it during his account of the dream. These comments constitute invaluable associations to the dream.

Sometimes such comments serve to connect the dream with reality and with the patient's life situation. Freud wrote that "all . . . judgements on a dream and comments upon it [e.g., what the patient really did during the dream day], though they have made themselves a place in waking thought, invariably form in fact part of the latent content of the dream . . . (1900, p. 187).

A patient, who had not been seen since Friday, said at his Monday appointment: "I had a dream on Friday night." His comment alerted the analyst that one of the dream's determinants was the day residues belonging to Friday and hence probably had to do with material from Friday's session. Another man, also seen on a Monday, related that he had had a dream the night before (i.e., Sunday night). He, too, had not been seen since Friday, but his dream not only referred to the events of the weekend, but also to his anticipation of the analyst's reaction to his activities.

At times, patients will indicate that a dream occurred

just before awakening, before the alarm clock woke them, in the middle of the night, while they were taking a nap, etc. In these instances it may be difficult to ascertain the significance of their comments about the time of the dream.

Comments and Glosses

Freud indicates that "glosses on a dream, or apparently innocent comments on it, often serve to disguise a portion of what has been dreamt in the subtlest fashion, though in fact betraying it" (1900, p. 332). Sometimes patients will comment about various dream elements while relating the dream, thus providing ongoing associations to the dream content. Glosses, whether referring to an individual's ideas about the individual elements of the dream or about the dream as a whole, are also associations to the dream. The dream and the gloss in such instances must therefore be regarded together.

A man reported that he had had a dream the night before. Then he said, "Nothing sticks out in my dream. I think the whole thing is obvious. No, the whole thing is not obvious. I only remember a snatch of it. But the whole idea makes me anxious." In the previous session, he had been discussing material that had to with his observations of the female genital (hole), his mother's and his sister's. The dream itself referred to his looking at something, "an animal or a book or something." He was not sure what it meant. His comments *about* the dream clearly referred to his observations of the female genital and his reaction of anxiety to the observation.

A woman patient reported the following dream. "I had a long dream which I think was made up of three parts. One of these parts, I think it was the middle part, was a real long part. When I woke up the whole dream was gone." In this instance, we do not have any manifest dream content, but the patient's comments are a communication which is to be regarded symbolically, as it contains a piece of infantile history. When the dreamer was a child she believed she had male genitals, but then she discovered they were "gone." Another woman dreamed of a plate and then added, "I think it was cracked, I think it had a hole in it." The interpolated thoughts about the dream element "plate" referred to her ideas about herself and her genital. She had equated herself with the cracked plate which had a hole in it.

Sometimes the patient's comment about a dream is his projection of what he believes the analyst's reaction to it will be, e.g., the dream was disgusting or the dream was interesting. In these instances the patient fears the analyst's disgust with him or his dream, or hopes that the analyst will be interested in him as well as in his dream. There are times when comments about dreams or dream contents clearly refer to the attitude of the patient's parents. If dreams referring to fecal matter or the odor of bowel movements are associated with disgust, they often reflect the attitude of parents or educators toward excretory functions. The patient may also be expressing his own reaction formation toward his excretory product. In instances where there is no disgust about bowel movements or fecal odor in the dream, the dreamer may be expressing his own view about his productions, i.e., that they are not offensive to him.

Patients' comments about their dreams reveal a great deal about their attitude toward themselves and their approach to dealing with life's problems. Some people are enthusiastic about their dreams. ("I had a fascinating dream last night") and proceed to work with them with vigor. Others take a highly indifferent attitude or give up from the start, saying, "I can never do anything with my dreams." Characterologically, these people may display a passive stance to all of their problems, hoping that someone else will solve them and tell them what to do. In one instance, a man who had this kind of negative attitude about his dreams and hoped that his analyst would initiate work with them was found to have a similar approach in his relations with women. He often hoped that the woman would make the overtures (see Altman, 1969).

Sometimes the patient's comments on a dream may be in the negative: "You were not in this dream" or "You will probably think this dream has to do with you, well, it doesn't." Usually when a patient makes such a remark, the reverse is true and the comment must be considered a negation (Freud, 1925a).

Frequently, general descriptions of the dream—"It was a sad dream," "a funny dream," "a confused dream," etc.—refer to the underlying affect in the dream. While such comments may allude to a variety of specific material with which the dream deals, they may also allude to the period of time in the dreamer's life when he experienced such emotions.

Sometimes a patient may say that he had a "strange" dream. This comment may be due in part to a displacement of accent that affects the dreamer's view of the dream (1916–1917, p. 140). The dreamer may use the feeling of strangeness to distance himself from the emotions generated by the dream. At other times, dreams indicating a feeling of strangeness or confusion are connected with the observation of the female genital. One patient dreamed of seeing a forest in the distance. "It was kind of strange looking. It seemed that there was a swamp or a cave of some kind in the woods. I was not sure which." The allusion was to his confusion as a child when he observed his mother's genitals while she was sitting on the toilet. The woods in the distance referred to the pubic hair as well as to the observation having been made a long time ago.

In some dreams, the dreamer experiences a feeling of familiarity, of having been there before. Freud explains this *déjà vu* phenomenon as follows: "whenever a man dreams of a place or a country and says to himself, while he is still dreaming: 'this place is familiar to me, I've been here before', we may interpret the place as being his mother's genitals or her body" (1919b, p. 245). This has been discussed at greater length in chapter 7.

There are also dreams which by their very nature generate such a feeling of reality that the dreamer finds it difficult to be certain whether or not what happened in the dream really did happen. Freud provides a rule for use in such instances:

if a belief in the reality of the dream-images persists unusually long, so that one cannot tear oneself out of the dream, this is not a mistaken judgement provoked by the vividness of the dream-images, but is a psychical act on its own: it is an as-surance, relating to the content of the dream, that something in it is really as one has dreamt it; and it is right to have faith in this assurance. [1907, p. 57]

It assures us that some part of the latent material of the dream is claiming in the dreamer's memory to possess the quality of reality, that is, that the dream relates to an occurrence that really took place and was not merely imagined. [1918, p. 33]

Sharpe (1937) indicates that

when a strong positive or negative transference is in full swing a dream may so gather up the infantile longings and so strongly picture them with regard to the analyst that the manifest dream content is taken almost as a reality. The reason for this is often due to the fact that in the dream there is embedded a bit of childhood reality not remembered in consciousness, and unknown to the patient this submerged experience is being relived. [p. 77]

The reference to realness in such a dream may be to the dreamer's actual thoughts or wishes. A man dreamed that his mother had died. He awoke and was so certain that she had died in reality that he telephoned her house. She cheerfully answered the phone and he felt foolish about having called her. The dream referred to a time in his childhood when his mother left home during the night to go to the hospital to have a baby. At the time, he was convinced that she would die and he would never see her again.

Sometimes the patient will interrupt the report of the dream with many "asides" and ongoing associations to its various elements. The result may be very confusing to the therapist, as he may have great difficulty in following the patient and distinguishing the manifest dream from the commentary on it. He may, of course, interrupt the patient and ask for clarification. When confronted with such a situation, some therapists pointedly ask the patient to finish relating the dream first and then to give his associations. While such a suggestion may be justified under certain circumstances, this technique may miss the point that in some instances the confusion brought about by the patient's method of presentation may be the essential point of his communication. It may be a reenactment in the therapeutic situation of some period in the patient's life when he was confused, or he may be trying to confuse the therapist as he himself was confused. He may be expressing the feeling that in his mind there are times when the distinction between his dream life and reality does not seem to be clear-cut. Sometimes the patient may provide a running commentary under the pressure of resistance or when he feels under particular pressure to cover a great deal of material, as after a break in the therapy (e.g., after a weekend). Under these circumstances the patient would experience the therapist's injunction to finish telling the dream as a criticism, one geared to the interests of the therapist's sense of order rather than to his own needs.

Doubts and Uncertainties

These are a specific form of comment or gloss, about which Freud makes the following remarks:

> In the course of our work of interpretation we learn what it is that corresponds to the doubts and uncertainties which the dreamer so often expresses as to whether a particular element occurred in the dream, whether it was this or whether, on the contrary, it was something else. There is as a rule nothing in the latent dream-thoughts corresponding to these doubts and uncertainties; they are entirely due to the activity of the dream-censorship and are to be equated with an attempt at

elimination which has not quite succeeded. [1916–1917, p. 178]

When patients express "doubt whether a dream or certain of its details have been correctly reported" (1900, pp. 515–516), Freud recommends the "technical rule of disregarding doubt and uncertainty in the narrative of the dream, and of treating every element of the manifest dream as being quite certain" (1921, p. 78n1). He indicates that the doubt and uncertainty is "a derivative of the dream-censorship, of resistance to the penetration of the dream-thoughts into consciousness" (1900, p. 516). In addition, he writes, "we assume that the primary dream-thoughts are not acquainted with doubt and uncertainty as critical processes. They may of course be present, like anything else, as part of the content of the day's residues which lead to the dream" (1921, p. 78n1). In line with this, Freud offers another technical suggestion: "If the narrative wavers between two versions, we should incline to regard the first one as correct and the second as a product of repression" (1905a, p. 17n2).

In analyzing dreams, then, one ignores any doubt and uncertainty expressed with regard to the dream elements and deals instead with the initial rendering. A man dreamed that something occurred on the ninth floor, then indicated that he was uncertain whether it really was the ninth floor and changed it to "the eighth floor or something like that." It was decided to work with the first version. Subsequently, it became evident from his associations that the element "nine" referred to his thoughts about the possibility that his mistress may have become pregnant. The uncertainty and doubt about the number was an attempt to divert the therapist from pursuing this material. Moreover, the doubt and the uncertainty about the location of the floor contained an allusion to the patient's uncertainty about what to do about the pregnancy and his doubt that it was a reality at all.

In another passage, Freud calls attention to a special situation: "If . . . an indistinct element of a dream's content is in addition attacked by doubt, we have a sure indication that we are dealing with a comparatively direct derivative of one of the proscribed dream-thoughts" (1900, p. 516). It is important also to keep in mind that the doubt about a dream element is itself an important element of the dream and is connected with specific reactions to the latent dream thoughts.

Sometimes the doubt is connected with a general or global characteristic of the dreamer's personality and is an expression of his tendency to doubt many things about himself. At other times, it is an indication that the dreamer has gone through a stage in which he doubted the truthfulness of statements which were made to him, as, for instance, with regard to material concerning sex, the origin of babies, and certain facts about his family history. In one instance, doubt about a dream element led to a discussion of the patient's not believing his mother's reasons for going off during the day for long periods of time. The dreamer had reason to suspect that his mother was involved in an extramarital affair.

Doubt about a dream element may represent a parent's attitude that has been internalized and then expressed in the comments on a dream element. "They never believed anything I told them, they always doubted everything I said," a patient related after telling a dream and doubting the accuracy of every element.

As doubt and uncertainty about a dream element are often manifestations of some resistance, the therapist should try to understand the reasons behind the resistance. It is difficult to specify the degree to which the therapist should attempt to deal with the dreamer's specific doubts about a given element or to state categorically that the therapist should disregard it for the time being and proceed with other matters, such as the general question of what is going on in the transference. Quite often, Freud's injunction about "not bothering too much" (1923a, p. 110), cited earlier with regard to dreams where the pressure of resistance is high, will determine the therapist's decision.

Judgments

Another type of comment on a dream (glosses, doubts, etc.) expressed by the dreamer is a judgment about the dream as a whole, or about a part of it (1900, pp. 445, 449, 450, 459). A judgment may be rendered either during the dream or upon awakening. A special but common judgment about a dream is the dreamer's recognition of its importance and his determination to relate it to his analyst. In this connection Freud makes the following remark: "If in the actual course of a dream dreamt during psycho-analytic treatment the dreamer says to himself: *'I must tell the doctor that'*, it invariably implies the presence of a strong resistance against confessing the dream—which is not infrequently thereupon forgotten" (1900, p. 446n2).

A variant of this occurs when the dreamer awakens from the dream or immediately following it, reviews it, resolves to tell it to his analyst, goes back to sleep, and upon awakening finds that he has forgotten the dream either partially or completely. Sometimes the patient understood the dream at the time and even provided himself an interpretation he believed correct, only to forget both the dream and his interpretation.

While this type of resolution and forgetting are manifestations of resistance, there is another aspect to be considered. Actually, patients remember only a small percentage of their dream material and the latent dream thoughts. What a patient brings in to discuss during his sessions is also a small fragment of all that is going on in his life. Both patient and therapist are able to make headway on the basis of the available material. Resistances expressed by not remembering a particular dream must be dealt with just as all other forms of resistance. It is also possible that in some instances of this kind of forgetting the patient has already achieved some understanding of what is involved and is ready to go on to other material.

According to Freud, when the phrase "after all, this is only a dream" appears in the dream, its significance is "to detract from the importance of what is being dreamt" (1900, p. 338). "In my view," Freud writes, "the contemptuous critical judgement, 'it's only a dream', appears in a dream when the censorship, which is never quite asleep, feels that it has been taken unawares by a dream which has already been allowed through. It is too late to suppress it, and accordingly the censorship uses these words to meet the anxiety or the distressing feeling aroused by it" (1900, p. 489).

The thought in the dream that "it's only a dream" succeeds in reassuring the dreamer's superego that the wishes, whether sexual or aggressive, that are emerging in the dream are not going to be fulfilled in reality and that it is therefore permissible for the dream to continue them to the point of gratification. In the therapeutic situation it is important to recognize what these impulses are, and to discover the basis for the patient's anxiety about them. Transference material of a forbidden nature is especially prone to be dealt with in this manner. A man dreamed that his analyst was lying on top of him and kissing him. He thinks to himself, "It's all right, it's only a dream." As the dream continues, he grasps the analyst's penis. The patient then awakens with an emission. The patient, not a manifest homosexual, had been struggling with the emerging intense homosexual transference in his analysis. The dream occurred just as this material was coming closer to consciousness.

The judgment about the dream upon awakening also serves the critical aspects of the superego, but in a *post hoc* manner. The patient has remembered the dream, is distressed by it, and so repudiates it (i.e., the wish behind it). The very act of judgment, quite apart from its specific content, may itself portray the characteristics of the individual's superego. Such judgments, by their very nature, are very harsh and criticial: e.g., "It was a stupid dream," "The dream was crazy," etc. In one instance, the comment that the dream was stupid was made by a man whose parents often told him he was stupid when they disapproved of something he wanted to do. In his judgment of the dream, the patient took over his parents' critical attitude by adopting it toward his dream. In clinical practice it is important for the therapist to encourage the patient to express his feelings about such criticism.

There are times when the judgment, "it is only a dream," whether made in the dream itself or on awakening, refers specifically to a traumatic event in the life of the patient that has entered his dream. The judgment, in these instances, is the patient's wish that the traumatic event did not really occur, but was only a dream (Levitan, 1980a).

Absurdity

Among the specific comments and judgments made about a dream are those in which the dreamer judges the contents as *absurd*. These judgments can be present in the dream or on awakening. Freud indicates that "a dream is made absurd . . . if a judgement that something 'is absurd' is among the elements included in the dream-thoughts—that is to say, if any one of the dreamer's unconscious trains of thought has criticism or ridicule as its motive" (1900, pp. 434–435; see also 1916–1917, p. 178). Nonsensical or absurd dreams, and dreams containing nonsensical or absurd elements, are a means of representing "embittered criticism and contemptuous contradiction" (1905b, p. 175) or "derision which may be present in the dream-thoughts" (1900, p. 445; see also 1901a, p. 662).

Frequently in these instances some ridicule of an important figure or situation in the patient's past or present life is expressed. A patient who was going to attend his parents' wedding anniversary celebration in a different city dreamed he was attending a coronation. The king and queen, wearing robes with long purple trains, were proceeding down the aisle of a big cathedral amid a great deal of pomp and circumstance. What struck the dreamer as particularly absurd and made him break out laughing in the dream was the sight of two little mice, who were walking or dancing on their hind legs, each holding up the train of one of the royal personages. The contrast between the solemnity of the occasion and the funny mice struck him as totally incongruous.

The patient's associations led to his parents. He had often described his father as a very pompous, arrogant man who demanded that his sons obey and respect him. "I am your father and you must obey me." "I am your father and you must respect and honor me as it says in the Ten Commandments." He had intoned this countless times. His mother, the patient felt, was very stuffy. She prided herself on her collection of jewelry and wore it all (rings on all her fingers, many necklaces) when she went to parties. He laughed at his dream that had made his parents into a royal couple and had converted the anniversary celebration into a coronation. "My parents would really have loved being crowned king and queen. They always acted as though they were, anyway." He realized that he and his brother were the two mice in the dream, who by their antics were really making fun of their parents' pomposity and pretentiousness. The absurdity of the scene in the dream thus expressed his ridicule and criticism of his parents' personalities.

Absurd dreams often occur when patients are struggling to express some criticism of the analyst's interpretation or some negative feeling toward the analyst in the transference situation. One patient dreamed of a figure who obviously stood for his analyst. The man in the dream was dressed in a kind of ridiculous clown outfit with large floppy shoes, a big tie with large polka dots, a big, ill-fitting coat, etc. At first his associations led to his vague dissatisfaction with the decor in the analyst's office and his disapproval of his analyst's taste. Then, after some hesitation, he launched into a lengthy discourse about the analyst's taste in clothes. "You must be color-blind. You wear black shoes with brown socks, that is, when you wear shoes. Most of the time you wear those godawful Western boots with high heels so you look like some cowboy out of a Marlboro ad. And those ties with the big wild splotches on them make you look like a circus character [i.e., a clown]." Much of the diatribe was in reaction to the analyst's having pointed out some passive traits in the patient's character during the previous session.

Night Fantasies

Freud writes that "there are dreams which are to be distinguished from the usual type by certain special qualities, which are, properly speaking, nothing but night-phantasies, not having undergone additions or alterations of any kind and being in all other ways similar to the familiar daydreams" (1922a, p. 208). In these instances the manifest content appears to be an accurate rendition of the daytime fantasy. Certain erotic fantasies such as those occurring in the transference situation may appear in these dreams.

Character Traits and Symptoms

Patients' character traits are often represented in their dreams or in the way they handle their dreams. The manifest content of the dream may reveal a patient's preoccupation with minutiae or with doubts, or his chronic passivity or state of confusion. Some patients' dreams deal almost entirely with references to current events. In these instances one may be dealing with an obsessional personality, a passive personality, a grossly confused person, or with someone who can relate to material only on a superficial basis. We have already mentioned dreams in which the manifest content strongly suggests that the patient may be suffering from some rift in his ego. Dreams in which there are *repeated* references to collapsing buildings, dissolution, fears of merging or fusion, "being lost in space or becoming progressively smaller against a backdrop of darkness or afloat in a vast sea" (Socarides, 1980, p. 239), or crumbling figures or structures are to be regarded seriously by the therapist.

The patient's method of handling the manifest content

is also significant. Some patients either avoid associations or obsessively perseverate over minituae and never quite get to the point. The pattern of their associations to their dreams is one of continual divergence. In some instances the patient may not associate directly to the elements of the manifest dream, but may instead provide the analyst with a litany of his symptoms.

In all these situations the therapist must demonstrate to the patient the relationship between his general symptomatology on the one hand, and the content of his dreams, as well as his general approach to dealing with dreams, on the other. But here, as in other instances, it is important for the therapist to assess and to deal with the patient's character traits on the basis of the entire therapeutic situation and to use his method of dealing with dreams as an example of these traits.

Chapter Eleven

The Form of a Dream

Another means of representation used by the dream is the *form* of the dream itself. Freud indicates that "the form of dreams is far from being without significance and itself calls for interpretation" (1916–1917, p. 177). *"The form of a dream or the form in which it is dreamt is used with quite surprising frequency for representing its concealed subject-matter"* (1900, p. 332).

Bearing this in mind, we note that there are dreams that require the therapist to pay much more heed to the form than to the content. Long, involved, rambling dreams that take up a good part of the session to relate are of this type, as we have indicated previously. These dreams often express the patient's ego as being confused or in danger of disintegration. These dreams may occur at a point in the therapy when the individual is expressing a period of confusion in his past: e.g., in childhood when he was bewildered and in search of sexual enlightenment, or at a later stage, when he did not know what to do with his life (Freud, 1914, p. 150). "Greatly distorted dreams give expression mainly (though not exclusively) to sexual wishes" (1916–1917, p. 192).

As we have indicated before, the vividness, clarity, and intensity of a dream element "coincides with [its] psychical *value*: the most intense elements are also the most important ones—those which form the centre-point of the dream-thoughts"; and yet we know that frequently "the intensity of the elements in the one has no relation to the intensity of the elements in the other. . . . A direct derivative of what occupies a dominating position in the dream-thoughts can often only be discovered precisely in some transitory element of the dream which is quite overshadowed by more powerful images" (Freud, 1900, p. 330).

Logical Relations

When viewing the form of any dream, the therapist should not be put off by its sensible, logical, or intellectual character. Freud stresses the fact that even if a dream "has an apparently sensible exterior, we know that this has only come about through dream-distortion and can have . . . little organic relation to the internal content of the dream" (1916–1917, p. 181). "Logical relations between the dream-thoughts," he writes,

> are not given any separate representation in dreams. For instance, if a contradiction occurs in a dream, it is either a contradiction of the dream itself or a contradiction derived from the subject-matter of one of the dream-thoughts. A contradiction in a dream can only correspond in an exceedingly indirect manner to a contradiction *between* the dream-thoughts. [1900, p. 313]

> Dreams have no means at their disposal for representing these logical relations between the dream-thoughts. For the most part dreams disregard all these conjunctions [if, because, as, though, either-or, etc.]. [1900, p. 312]

These relationships, however, are expressed in various ways by the form of the dream or of the dream fragment. Freud writes that "the number of part-dreams into which a dream is divided usually corresponds to the number of main topics or groups of thoughts in the latent dream" (1916–1917, p. 177).

A patient had a dream in two parts. In the first she is going to the cemetery to visit her parents' gravesite, while in the second part she is a little girl (no pubic hair) and is masturbating by pushing a pencil into her vagina. The two dreams referred to two traumatic events in her life. The first alluded to the death of both of her parents in a horrible automobile accident in her early adolescence. The other part of the dream referred to her masturbation in childhood, which she clearly remembered. As a child she had habitually inserted objects into her vagina: pencils, crayons, toothbrushes, etc. On one occasion she was masturbating with the cork of a wine bottle and "lost it" in her vagina. She could not retrieve it and was too embarrassed to tell anyone about it. After a period of time, she developed a very smelly discharge which eventually became so bad that she was taken to a doctor who removed the cork, much to her humiliation. For a time her analysis was taken up with the two themes of death and sexuality and the complicated interrelationship between them.

Freud continues: "A short introductory dream will often stand in the relation of a prelude to a following, more detailed, main dream or may give the motive for it; a subordinate clause in the dream-thoughts will be replaced by the interpolation of a change of scene into the manifest dream, and so on" (1916–1917, p. 177). At other times, two alternatives are represented "by dividing the dream into two pieces of equal length" (1900, p. 318).

Causal Relations

Freud writes: "A *causal relation* between two thoughts is either left unrepresented or is replaced by a *sequence* of two pieces of dream of different lengths. Here the representation is often reversed, the beginning of the dream standing for the consequence and its conclusion for the premise" (1901a, p. 661).

One way in which dreams express causal relationships is the following: the introductory dream represents the dependent clause, i.e., the "since," and the main dream the principal clause, i.e., the "therefore" or the consequences. Temporally, the dream may be reversed. "But," Freud writes, "the more extensive part of the dream always corresponds to the principal clause" (1900, p. 315). He goes on to say that "in a certain number of dreams a division into a shorter preliminary dream and a longer sequel . . . signif[ies] that there is a causal relation between the two pieces" (p. 316).

In this connection, Freud writes: "The symptoms of the illness (anxiety, etc.), when they appear in a dream, seem generally speaking to mean: 'I fell ill because of this (i.e. in connection with the earlier elements of the dream). Such dreams, accordingly, correspond to a continuation of the analysis in the dream" (1913b, p. 198). The two or more parts of the dream may express current or historical cause and consequences or a forbidden wish or impulse with the resultant fear of punishment and/or the formation of a defense against the wish or impulse.

In one situation, for example, an historical connection could be observed between the two parts of the dream. A woman who was a manifest homosexual dreamed, in the first part of a lengthy dream, that she was attending a funeral in the fall of the year. Many details of the funeral and the interment of the casket were present in her dream. The second part of the dream had to do with spring and spring flowers. In it two girls were playing with each other's breasts. The dreamer's mother had died in the fall of one year and she had become involved in her first homosexual practices with a contemporary in the spring of the following year. The dream indicated a causal relationship between the two events in her life.

In one dream of a male patient, the genetic determinants of his general characterological passivity were demonstrated. In the first section of a lengthy dream he was dealing in an elaborate fashion with arguments between various members of a business group he was associated with. The scene culminated in open warfare, with tanks and planes bombing and strafing the enemy and people being killed and destroyed. In the second part of the dream, which was very brief, he found himself in the locker room of a club to which he belonged, and there was some allusion to homosexual activity. He awakened from the dream with a feeling that he had to have a bowel movement. From his associations it was evident that his defense against his intense aggression and hostility toward many men was to assume a passive anal position (the feeling of a full rectum). At the same time, his defense against his passive homosexual wishes was to be argumentative and aggressive.

Alexander (1925) indicates that a dynamic relation usually exists between pairs or series of dreams:

> The two dreams are then complementary to one another and permit, as it were, a complete gratification of the wish in two stages, by which it escapes the notice of the censor. . . . Both the symbolically disguised sexual intercourse with an incestuous object and the manifest sexual act with an indifferent person are, if taken alone, capable of entering consciousness; they express the real wish, however, only incompletely. But taken in connection with each other, the second dream having reference to the first, they constitute a complete representation of the repressed tendency. [p. 372]

There are instances where the dream contains a reference to the patient's symptomatology and also to other elements, the associations to which lead to an understanding of some of the dynamics responsible for the symptoms. In these dreams the causal relation becomes clear only when the associations are added to the dream itself.

A male patient, who had a perversion in which he tied himself up and masturbated, reported that he had had two dreams during the night. In the first, an elaborate dream, he was in a wheelchair going down a long corridor. In the second he was tying himself up to masturbate. The wheelchair reminded him of his lengthy hospitalization when he was a child. He recalled being subjected to many frightening diagnostic tests and medical examinations during which he had to remain passive. The second dream referred to his symptom, which was evidently related to the hospitalization.

Another man dreamed that he was seeing his internist, a man dressed in a long white lab coat. He complained about a headache that in reality had been one of his symptoms. The dream continued in a long complicated fashion and at one point he found himself in a kitchen where all sorts of food preparations were going on. His associations contained many references to his headaches and his treatment by various physicians. Sometimes he felt he was being helped in his analysis; other times he was not so sure.

After a while he returned to the dream and talked about the food preparation and his memory of his mother in a long white apron standing by the stove or by the sink. He recalled his mother's temper and her uncontrolled rages. On many occasions she would be so angry with him she would grab him by his shirt and beat him on the head with an empty frying pan. He had not realized before this recollection that one of the determinants of his headaches was his mother's hitting him on the head. Moreover, some of the transference implications of his complaints in his analysis were also clarified. He had expected that if he succeeded in provoking his analyst, as he had his mother, his analyst too would beat him on the head.

Freud indicates, however, that

the division of a dream into two unequal parts does not invariably . . . signify that there is a causal relation between the thoughts behind the two parts. It often seems as though the same material were being represented in the two dreams from different points of view. (This is certainly the case where a series of dreams during one night end in an emission or orgasm—a series in which the somatic need finds its way to progressively clearer expression.) Or the two dreams may have sprung from separate centres in the dream-material, and their content may overlap, so that what is the centre in one dream is present as a mere hint in the other, and *vice versa.* [1900, pp. 315–316]

We have already discussed dreams that begin with a urinary stimulus and end with a sexual stimulus. Freud indicates that

sometimes, in a dream in which the same situation and setting have persisted for some time, an interruption will occur which is described in these words: 'But then it was as though at the same time it was another place, and there such and such a thing happened.' After a while the main thread of the dream may be resumed, and what interrupted it turns out to be a subordinate clause in the dream-material—an interpolated thought. A conditional in the dream-thoughts has been represented in the dream by simultaneity: 'if ' has become 'when'. [1900, p. 335]

Tausk noted that a change of scenery in a dream "means a reminiscence of an event that contains an essential element belonging to the most important part of the dream" (Nunberg and Federn, 1962–1974, vol. 4, pp. 156–157). Freud gives another "method of representing a causal relation," one which

consists in one image in the dream, whether of a person or thing, being transformed into another. The existence of a causal relation is only to be taken seriously if the transformation actually occurs before our eyes and not if we merely notice that one thing has appeared in the place of another. [1900, p. 316]

an immediate *transformation* of one thing into another in a dream seems to represent the relation of *cause and effect.* [1901a, p. 661]

In the course of a difficult analysis, impeded by a great deal of resistance, a woman patient finally revealed that she had had a sexual relationship with her former therapist, also a male. She had succeeded in suppressing this information for a long time. Shortly after this revelation, which came about through the analysis of a dream, the patient had another dream in which she saw her former therapist and her present therapist actually changing into one another: first it would be her former therapist, then the present one, then the former one, etc. The dream expressed her anxiety that her feelings toward her first therapist were being transferred to the second therapist, and also expressed her belief that because of what happened in her relationship with the first therapist, the same thing would happen during her present treatment. This belief was so intense that it had been the source of a great deal of her resistance.

Freud summarizes the representation of causal relationships in dreams:

> I have said that the two methods of representing a causal relation were in essence the same. In both cases causation is represented by temporal sequence: in one instance by a sequence of dreams and in the other by the direct transformation of one image into another. In the great majority of cases, it must be confessed, the causal relation is not represented at all but is lost in the confusion of elements which inevitably occurs in the process of dreaming. [1900, p. 316]

Care should be exercised when interpreting these causal dreams by taking into consideration the associations and the affect following the dream. As mentioned earlier, sometimes the cause is expressed in the dream, while the consequence is expressed in the associations. In two-part dreams it is essential to understand the relation between the parts.

A man dreamed that his thumb had been damaged. "It is bruised but the bone is not broken." In another part of the dream, he was having an argument with his father. The patient related that on the morning before the dream he had had a telephone call from his father. Even though it was Sunday morning, his father had called early and awakened him with an insistent interrogation: was he going to church and, if so, when? He was furious with his father for awakening him, for not letting him sleep late as he had wanted to do, and for his insistence that he go to church. He felt that his father was meddling in his life and would not let him be independent. He went to the bathroom, urinated, and went back to bed. After that he tried to have intercourse with his wife but was impotent. The dream, while assuring him that his penis was bruised but not broken, also indicated that the cause of his sexual problem was the anger and fear he felt toward his father, and his resulting castration anxiety.

The Dream Within a Dream

Freud indicates that the intention of dreams of this type is

> to detract from the importance of what is 'dreamt' in the dream, to rob it of its reality. What is dreamt in a dream after waking from the 'dream within a dream' is what the dream-wish seeks to put in the place of an obliterated reality. It is safe to suppose, therefore, that what has been 'dreamt' in the dream is a representation of the reality, the true recollection, while the continuation of the dream, on the contrary, merely represents what the dreamer wishes. To include something in a 'dream within a dream' is thus equivalent to wishing that the thing described as a dream had never happened. In other words, if a particular event is inserted into a dream as a dream by the dream-work itself, this implies the most decided confirmation of the reality of the event—the strongest *affirmation* of it. The dream-work makes use of dreaming as a form of repudiation, and so confirms the discovery that dreams are wish-fulfilments. [1900, p. 338]

Freud's explanation is helpful technically, as it provides the therapist the useful suggestion that he begin the exploration of such a dream with the dream within the dream. This does not mean, of course, that the therapist should exclude any of the other suggestions about working with dreams that have been discussed. In some respects, Freud's technical suggestion is similar to selecting a portion of the dream that had been repressed and is now suddenly recalled.

Sometimes the dream within the dream refers to a recent incident. A homosexual man with a tendency to act out from time to time dreamed that he was having an analytic session. He was on the couch telling his analyst, who did not resemble his analyst in reality, that he had had a dream. In this dream (the dream within the dream), he had gone to a "gay bar" and picked up a man with whom he went to a motel room where they had a "wild party." "We went down on each other," he added. In the main dream, the patient stated, his analyst gave him some explanation but he could not understand it. He wondered, in the main dream, whether his analyst was disgusted with him.

The dream within the dream referred to an actual reality: the patient had gone to a "gay bar" after his previous session and had done exactly what he had dreamed about. The wish that the thing described as a dream had never happened referred here mainly to his wish that it hadn't happened so that he would not have to tell his analyst what he had done. He thought the analyst would be disgusted with him, especially since he had also allowed himself to be anally penetrated. The "explanation" which the analyst in the dream gave him, and which he "did not understand," referred to the patient's homosexual transference; this had been discussed in a number of previous sessions, and he had acted it out after the session just prior to the dream.

There are variants of the dream within the dream. Sometimes the patient will report that in the dream he is reading a book, magazine, or paper, or that he is watching a play, movie, or television program, and proceeds to tell the plot of what he has read or seen. In these instances the focus of analytic attention should begin with this part. The reality expressed in this variant of a dream within a dream is, of course, the fact that the patient actually read or saw what is in the dream within the dream. But of greater significance is the fact that the material alludes either to some real experiences of the patient or to some current or past fantasies which the patient has really had and wished to repudiate.

In another variant, a patient dreamed that he was with his analyst in a posh hotel room. In the dream the analyst recounted an incident from his own childhood to the patient. The dream story culminated with the analyst being sent away from home for several months. The "story" part in the dream was projected upon the analyst from an event in the patient's own childhood: he had been sent to live with his grandparents when his mother had a baby. It was a very traumatic period for him, and he often wished that none of it had happened: that his mother had not had a baby, that he had not been sent away, and that he had not had to live with his grandparents at that time.

In still another variant of the dream within the dream, a man dreamed he was telling his therapist a dream but forgot it while telling it. The following night he had another dream, in which his adolescent daughter was telling him that she wanted him to have sexual intercourse with her. Both dreams were reported in the same session. The added dream stood in the position of the dream within the dream that had been forgotten. In his associations to the second dream, the patient related that he had "accidentally" walked into his daughter's bedroom and saw her in her brassiere and panties as she was getting dressed. He excused himself and promptly left, thinking that she had indeed developed into a very attractive young woman, one who would appeal to him sexually. He clearly recognized his incestuous wishes. He then recalled that when he was an adolescent he had had intense erotic feelings toward his somewhat younger sister, whom his daughter now resembled. He remembered that he often thought of having sexual relations with his sister, but he never did. The patient's "added" dream provided the reality he wished, via his "forgetting," to repudiate: his current incestuous wishes toward his daughter and his earlier incestuous wishes toward his sister.

The Form of a Dream

At times the dream within the dream refers to a piece of historical reality that has been repressed and is not accessible as a memory. A patient dreamed she was telling her analyst a dream in which she was lying down with her hands tied down. Someone behind her was putting a strainer of some kind over her nose and mouth and was telling her to count backwards beginning with the number one hundred. She was frightened. The analyst in the dream told her that the dream was important. The dream within the dream referred to her tonsillectomy when she was six or seven years old. Her mother had fooled her and had not told her where she was going. The episode described in the dream within the dream was her first description of some of the preoperative events. She had not recalled them consciously before, but knew how important they were. They helped explain some of her anxiety in the analytic situation, as she was fearful her analyst would trick her, not tell her the truth, and would put an ether mask over her nose and mouth and subject her to a frightening experience. In this instance of a dream within a dream, it is very clear that the dream expressed the wish that the incident of the tonsillectomy had never occurred, that it had only been a bad dream.

Chapter Twelve

ical Dreams with Constant Meaning

In the course of doing analytic work, the therapist is often in the position of understanding a patient's dream without many associations. This is the case when the therapist is familiar with his patient's particular style and language, and knows his problems and conflicts and the current themes with which the patient is concerned (Blum, 1976; Brenner, 1976; Greenberg and Pearlman, 1980). This is an area, however, in which Freud cautions the therapist: "Even if, owing to one's own experience [with the patient], one is in a position to understand many dreams to the interpretation of which the dreamer has contributed little, one must always remember that the certainty of such interpretations remains in doubt and one hesitates to press one's conjectures upon the patient" (1925b, p. 129).

There may be times in the course of therapy when a patient seems unable to do anything with a dream, no associations come to any of the elements, and the therapist has dealt appropriately with whatever resistances and transference manifestations are present. Under these circumstances it may be helpful if the therapist offers a suggestion or a possible interpretation of what he thinks the dream may be about (Fromm-Reichmann, 1950). In these instances the therapist's remarks may merely help maintain a working alliance.

The patient can accept or reject the proposed interpretation. Ultimately, the correctness of the interpretation
will be confirmed only by the patient's overall response. He
may agree and yet his subsequent associations and dreams
will disprove the interpretation. He may disagree and yet the
material may prove that the interpretation was correct nonetheless.

Sometimes the correctness of such an interpretation,
as with any interpretation, will be confirmed by the patient's
bringing up further material, by the recollection of memories,
or by a feeling of conviction: "It rings a bell," "It clicks," or
"It feels right." Sometimes the response is an "aha" or "Oh,
I see," or laughter with an accompanying alleviation of tension. At other times there may be an outburst of tears or
anger (Sloane, 1979).

Apart from these general considerations, however, the
understanding of certain typical dreams will provide the therapist important guidelines in his work with patients. Freud
divides typical dreams "roughly into two classes: those which
always have the same meaning, and those which, in spite of
having the same or a similar content, must nevertheless be
interpreted in the greatest variety of ways" (1900, p. 385).
We will discuss the dreams in the first category in this chapter
and those in the second in the next.

The dreams in the first category are quite universal and
their general format may be regarded as almost "standard."
According to Freud, "If we attempt to interpret [such] a
typical dream, the dreamer fails as a rule to produce the
associations which would in other cases have led us to understand it, or else his associations become obscure and insufficient so that we cannot solve our problem with their help"
(1900, p. 241). In this respect, these typical dreams are like
symbols: their meaning is quite universal. But just as with
certain symbols which usually have a constant meaning, the
interpretation of these typical dreams is always subject to
modification by the general context of the patient's material,

even if he does not produce direct associations. The therapist must keep in mind the possibility that these typical dreams should be viewed according to their wording, their use in a positive or negative sense, and their reference to current or past experiences. Thus, even though the dreams in this category do have a "universal meaning," they frequently have many other meanings as well. To venture an interpretation based solely on their typical content would be hazardous, arbitrary, and speculative. The therapist, by keeping their typical significance in mind, can use it as an "auxiliary method" in formulating his interpretations.

It should be noted that while the dreams in this category do occur in patients in analysis, they are by no means as frequent as dreams in the second category. The dreams in the first category are apt to be related by the patient as having occurred at some time before coming into treatment, or they may occur as part of a sequence of dreams. When these dreams are reported in the course of psychotherapeutic work as having occurred at some previous time, their significance must be assessed. They must be viewed not only from the standpoint of their being typical dreams, but also from a point of view that asks why this particular dream was dreamt when it was and why it was reported at that precise time.

We will now discuss typical dreams which have a single invariable meaning.

Embarrassing Dreams of Being Naked

Freud indicates that in typical dreams of this type

one *does* feel shame and embarrassment and tries to escape or hide, and is then overcome by a strange inhibition which prevents one from moving and makes one feel incapable of altering one's distressing situation. . . .

The nature of the undress involved is customarily far from clear. . . . As a rule the defect in the dreamer's toilet is not so grave as to appear to justify the shame to which it gives rise. . . .

The people in whose presence one feels ashamed are almost always strangers, with their features left indeterminate. In the typical dream it never happens that the clothing which causes one so much embarrassment is objected to or so much as noticed by the onlookers. On the contrary, they adopt indifferent or (as I observed in one particularly clear dream) solemn and stiff expressions of face. [1900, pp. 242–243]

He further indicates that dreams of nakedness are exhibition dreams. The "strangers" who take no notice are "nothing more nor less than the wishful contrary of the single familiar individual before whom the dreamer exposed himself" (1900, p. 245).

When children are in the genital phase the wish for exhibition can often be seen to be a defense against castration anxiety. The typical dreams of nakedness which refer to this period contain allusions to the wish for exhibition, often connected both with a feeling of shame and with castration anxiety.

It is important for the therapist to explore the patient's experiences, thoughts, and feelings on the subject of his own nakedness and that of other people. As these dreams contain an underlying reference to a wish to exhibit oneself, one of the questions which must be addressed is the identity of the person or persons the dreamer is exhibiting himself to.

Quite frequently these dreams refer to experiences in which the dreamer participated with other children in viewing and exposing their private parts, and to his reactions as well as those of his companions. The embarrassment in the typical dream may refer to the dreamer's reactions at that time, to that of his companions who participated in the activity, or to their having been discovered by a parent or other adult who shamed or humiliated them. As Freud notes, the element of the people in the dream appearing to be "indifferent" is the wished-for contrary of what was actually the situation when the child exhibited himself or, we may add, was discovered by grown-ups who reacted with intense emotion: "They scolded me and said 'shame on you.' " "Her mother sent me home." "I was afraid I would be beaten." "I didn't know what to do, so I hid." "He grabbed me by the ear, told me to get dressed, and if I ever did anything like that again, he would send me away to reform school."

There are other instances where the element of exhibition may be completely reversed. Thus, while the dream picture may be cast in terms of the typical dream, the scene to which it actually refers may have been some incident in which the child observed the parent in the nude and experienced curiosity, excitement, and a wish to touch.

The typical dream may refer to other specific historical situations in the life of the dreamer. In one instance, for example, a man dreamed that he was giving a lecture and noticed that the zipper on his trousers was not properly fastened. He was embarrassed, tried in some way to close the zipper, but was unable to do so. He felt there was no way he could do it gracefully or casually. He felt unable to move and his embarrassment increased. He watched his audience looking at him coldly and indifferently with no expression on their faces and he awoke with some anxiety.

The man's associations led to an incident in high school when he was called upon to recite in front of the class and worried, as he went to the front of the room, that he might have an erection while reciting. He was frightened, moreover, that should he have an erection it would be apparent to his classmates and they would make fun of him. In the dream, the audience did the very opposite: they were cold and expressionless.

In the actual experience, in order to avoid the humiliating possibility he had put his hand in his pants pocket, which served only to call attention to a bulge. Throughout that recitation he remembered being fearful that somehow he had succeeded in pulling his zipper open when he had put his hand in his pocket, or that perhaps he had not fastened the zipper at all that day, so that his penis was exposed. He recalled being so embarrassed that he fumbled his recitation and stammered during his speech to such a degree (which he had never done previously) that his classmates did indeed laugh at him. The incident was horribly humiliating and embarrassing to him. His fumbling of the recitation and being unable to speak properly, as well as his protective gesture with his hand, were a displacement of his unconscious wish to exhibit himself. The inhibition of motion in the dream expressed a "no" from his superego against this wish. The dream also referred to the tremendous amount of castration anxiety which was present in the whole episode.

Historical material which emerges as associations to embarrassing dreams of being naked frequently refers to episodes dealing with doctors and medical examinations (see the section on Examination Dreams, below). Here the persons before whom one is ashamed are indeed strangers and their faces have to some extent become indistinct, as time may blur the specific memory of the doctors in question. Sometimes the patient may have had experiences with a number of physicians, whose figures are merged together as a group of solemn, dispassionate people before whom the dreamer is naked and embarrassed. This is in sharp contrast to those instances in which the patient states that he remembers a particular doctor distinctly: "I will never forget him as long as I live for what he did to me."

The displacement of these memories to the transference situation is readily apparent. Patients on the couch will feel embarrassed at times, feel that they are exposed and, because of their physical position, that the therapist is able to view them "almost as if they were naked." Here again, as in the typical dream of nakedness, the patient wishes to escape or hide but is "overcome by a strange inhibition" and feels somehow rooted to the couch and unable to move. While the wish for exhibition may be one determinant of the feeling of being naked, the fear of having one's self and one's body looked at, examined, and criticized is equally important. Therapists who have seen patients initially in a sitting-up, face-to-face arrangement, and who have then put them on the couch for various reasons, have been impressed that their patients' dreams and associations express how exposed they feel in the new position as compared to how protected they had felt before.

We can also consider dreams of nakedness from the standpoint of their connection with memories from earliest childhood. As Freud observes, "It is only in our childhood that we are seen in inadequate clothing both by members of our family and by strangers—nurses, maid-servants, and visitors; and it is only then that we feel no shame at our nakedness" (1900, p. 244). The dream may thus express the wish to return to that idyllic period of earliest childhood, with its sense of joy and freedom.

Dreams of the Death of Persons of Whom the Dreamer Is Fond

Here Freud distinguishes two types of dreams, "those in which the dreamer is unaffected by grief, so that on awakening he is astonished at his lack of feeling, and those in which the dreamer feels deeply pained by the death and may even weep bitterly in his sleep" (1900, p. 248). Freud does not consider dreams of the first kind "typical," as on analysis they are found "to conceal some other wish" which "gave no occasion for grief" (1900, p. 248). He gives an example of a dream of this kind. What appeared to be a lack of feeling about a nephew's death in the manifest dream was, in the latent dream thoughts, connected to the dreamer's wish to meet again a man (of whom she was very fond) who had been present at the funeral of another nephew. Thus the underlying wish had nothing to do with the recent death of the nephew and the affect of grief would have been completely inappropriate to the patient's latent dream thoughts. Clearly, the affect in the manifest content thus belongs to its latent content (1900, p. 248).

Dreams of the first type are treated as any other dream and the associations to the specific elements are submitted to scrutiny and interpretation. Attention should be carefully paid to the emergence of affect in the associations, an affect which is not present in the manifest dream itself. Quite often, because of the dreamer's ambivalence to the person who appears dead in the dream, the affect has been repressed and may only emerge during the session. One may then see that the dreamer's surprising lack of feeling in the manifest dream actually conceals a great deal of underlying emotion.

One patient dreamed that he and his wife were on the deck of an ocean liner, leaning over the rail watching the water and the sea gulls following the boat. Suddenly he saw that his wife had fallen overboard and was drowning. He was watching the scene in a matter-of-fact manner as she sank beneath the waves. In the dream he was completely unaffected by the event, but vaguely wondered whether he would be considered responsible. He assured himself that, after all, there were witnesses to her carelessness.

In his associations he discussed his recent conversation with his mistress, who was pushing him to divorce his wife. The dream conveniently resolved his conflict: if his wife were drowned, or died by some other means not his fault, he would not need to divorce her, nor would he be responsible for any aggressive action toward her. He would be free to do what he wished. The ocean voyage reminded him of their honeymoon, when they had, in fact, gone on a cruise. The trip then was enjoyable. He wondered, if he and his wife were divorced and he married his mistress, whether they would go on a cruise. His general affect was reflective and rather coldly dispassionate about the problems of his marriage and his affair.

After a while he stopped talking and it became evident he was uncomfortable. He related then that he had gone tuna fishing on one occasion and a tuna had been sighted, harpooned, and hoisted aboard the ship. He remembered that he had watched the scene with a great deal of fascination. Suddenly he returned to the subject of leaving his wife and began to weep at the idea of hurting her by asking for a divorce. "She hasn't done anything to deserve such treatment," he sobbed. The dream had concealed his feelings of remorse about hurting his wife. His pushing her for a divorce was like the tuna fishermen harpooning the fish. His wife was in the water like the tuna and he was watching her drown, just as he and the tuna fishermen had watched the fish gasping and struggling as it was being brought into the boat. His wish was not to be responsible for hurting her, just as he was not responsible for harpooning the tuna.

Sometimes dreams in which there is no particular affect about the death of a loved person occur at a time in analytic work when negative feelings are being expressed toward that person. Often in these instances the affectionate feelings have been repressed. The dreams continue the theme of aggression against the person by expressing an indifference to the person's demise. A man whose father had made homosexual overtures toward him when he was a young pubescent dreamed that his father had died (in reality, he was still living). He was standing over his open grave making a gesture with his hands signifying that he was now finally rid of him. He did this coldly and dispassionately. The dream expressed his resentment at his father for his behavior and his responsibility for his symptomatology. It was only after a great deal of analytic work that the patient was able to bring back early memories of a close, tender, and loving relationship with his father.

The second group of dreams dealing with the death of persons of whom the dreamer is fond consists of those in which the dreamer is "painfully affected." Freud considers these to be typical dreams. "The meaning of such dreams, as their content indicates, is a wish that the person in question may die" (1900, p. 249). Freud indicates, however, that in such dreams the wish for the person's death may refer not to the present but to some time in the dreamer's past such as early childhood (p. 249).

When a patient brings up such dreams in therapy, the therapist must ascertain whether the material deals with the present feelings or clearly refers to something from earlier times. There is little doubt that in many instances past negative feelings toward love objects persist into the present, and death wishes exist toward these figures in current life as well as having come from the past.

It is important for the therapist to discern whether the pain and grief in the dream are directed toward a living person represented as dead in the dream, or toward someone who is in fact dead. In instances of the latter, the painful affect present in the dream may herald the work of active mourning. There are times when people have experienced the death of a close relative and have remained quite "philosophical" about it until they reach a certain point in their analysis when painful material about this figure appears. Then the feelings about this person's death become associated with a good deal of sadness, feelings of loss and remorse, so typical of active mourning.

In one instance, a rather blustering, aggressive young man began the first hour of his analysis with an "autobiography" in which he said: "My old man kicked the bucket a couple of years ago." As he made this statement, he suddenly threw his arm over his eyes. When asked about this gesture, he complained that the daylight in the room was too strong. (It was not; nor had he felt any need to shield his eyes before that.) The use of the words "old man" and "kicked the bucket" was striking because the patient was a rather cultured individual and such expressions were out of character for him.

After many months in analysis, during which he talked derogatively about his father on many occasions, he had a dream in which he was going to the crematorium to pick up an urn that contained his father's ashes. As the attendant was giving him the urn, the patient suddenly burst out sobbing, bitterly, and awakened from the dream. Now he no longer talked of his father as the "old man" who "kicked the bucket" but spoke of him as his "dear father," his "beloved dad" who had died and left him. He knew that he would never see him again and wished that he could have told him how much he meant to him, how much he loved him. Following this session, many warm, tender, loving memories associated with his father emerged. The patient's action of covering his eyes in the first session was a defense against his urge to weep over the loss of his father.

In general, the greatest reactions occur when significant figures out of the individual's past were actually lost to him through permanent separation or death, or when they had to be given up in the process of maturation. Thus, preoedipal conflicts, conflicts about ambivalent feelings toward the parents or parent substitutes (which reach a peak during the oedipal phase and again in puberty), and conflicts with siblings over rivalry for parental affection are often the subject matter behind dreams of death. Freud writes: "The situation is often obscured by the emergence of a self-punitive impulse, which threatens the dreamer, by way of a moral reaction, with the loss of the parent whom he loves" (1900, p. 256n1). The element of punishment is introduced in these dreams quite often as a result of the superego's attitude toward the individual for his aggressive wishes.

Dreams of the death of persons of whom the individual is fond often involve the therapist, particularly when there is an interruption in the regularity of appointments, or when a vacation or termination is anticipated. In any of these instances, it is important to assess what role the therapist is serving in the transference. While frequently the therapist represents a figure out of the past that may have been idealized by the patient, the separation or break in the continuity of the therapy may stir up feelings of dissolution of the patient's ego, as though a part of himself is now dead and gone. In these instances the feelings of grief are not so much connected with object loss as they are to a loss of self.

We may now consider dreams about *deceased persons*,

i.e., those who are actually dead at the time of the dream, although these dreams are not typical dreams. The deceased persons may be people of whom the dreamer is fond, or toward whom he has been ambivalent. In these dreams the dreamer may or may not be affected by grief.

During a phase of her analysis, a woman dreamed repeatedly about her aunt, whom she had loved very much and who had taken care of her during childhood. The aunt had died while the patient was away at college. Some of the patient's dreams and associations dealt with her numerous experiences with her aunt, trips they had taken together, etc. In some of these dreams she was sad. While other dreams appeared to be somewhat colorless, she found herself tearful when she related them and talked about her aunt. She felt sad that she had not seen her before she died and had not been able to take care of her aunt, as she had taken care of her. More than that, now that she had children of her own she was sorry that her aunt had never seen them.

Then one day she dreamed that her aunt was being laid out in a box. With the exception of the detail of the box, the scene in the dream was a direct representation of a scene that had made an indelible impression upon her. She had come in from college to attend her aunt's funeral and had noticed that something was wrong with the way her aunt looked in the coffin. The embalming process had so distorted her aunt's face that it seemed grotesque. She was so upset by this, she revealed in her analysis, that she had secretly doubted that it was really her aunt and wondered if it might be someone else. This obsessive thought, it turned out, stemmed from some thought that her aunt had actually died because of the patient's angry thoughts about her when she was a child. The aunt had discovered the patient playing doctor with a neighbor boy in a large packing box in the garage and had threatened to tell her father. She had been furious with her aunt for scolding her and because she, of all people, had threatened to betray her.

237

Freud writes:

> It very commonly happens that in dreams of this kind the
> dead person is treated to begin with as though he were alive,
> that he suddenly turns out to be dead and that in a subsequent
> part of the dream he is alive once more. This has a confusing
> effect. It eventually occurred to me that this alternation be-
> tween death and life is intended to represent *indifference* on
> the part of the dreamer. ('It's all the same to me whether he's
> alive or dead.') This indifference is, of course, not real but
> merely desired; it is intended to help the dreamer to repudiate
> his very intense and often contradictory emotional attitudes
> and it thus becomes a dream-representation of his *ambiva-*
> *lence*. [1900, p. 431]

In some of these instances the confusing effect on the
dreamer, that the dead person is both alive and dead, may
be based upon memories of experiences with the deceased
person during his lifetime. This "alternation between death
and life," as Freud described it, may be an expression of the
process of mourning, in which the individual conjures up the
person as alive once more, deals with his experiences with
this person when he was alive, and then says, "But he is now
dead and I have to give him up."

A variant of dreams of deceased people is described by
Freud in the following:

> In . . . dreams in which the dreamer associates with dead
> people, the following rule often helps to give us our bearings.
> If there is no mention in the dream of the fact that the dead
> man is dead, the dreamer is equating himself with him: he
> is dreaming of his own death. If, in the course of the dream,
> the dreamer suddenly says to himself in astonishment, 'why,
> he died ever so long ago', he is repudiating this equation and
> is denying that the dream signifies his own death. [1900, p.
> 431; see also 1913b, p. 197]

Such dreams may occur during an illness, when the
patient is fearful he will die and join the company of those
who are already dead. These dreams are not frequent in

analytic work but may be recounted by people who have at some time in the past been seriously ill.

When Oscar Wilde was terminally ill with severe meningitis following surgery, he was convinced that his death was imminent. He had a horrible dream which he related to his friends. He told them that in the dream "he had been supping with the dead" (Hart-Davis, 1962, p. 849). In accordance with Freud's suggestion we may understand this dream to mean that Wilde repudiated the equation of himself with the dead people and was denying the thought that he was really going to die.

A woman, whose mother had committed suicide by an overdose of sleeping pills when the patient was approximately eight years old, dreamed she was attending a large cocktail party at which her mother was present. She looked youthful, radiant, and beautiful in a dress the patient remembered her wearing. In the dream the patient was happy to see her mother and had begun to tell her all the news about herself just as the dream ended. There was no indication in the dream that her mother was dead. The patient had been depressed for some time and was drinking excessively and taking large doses of tranquilizers. She was preoccupied with taking her own life, either by an overdose of pills, as her mother had done, or by driving her car into an abutment. In her fantasies she thought of how happy she would be if she could be reunited with her mother. The dream clearly expressed this wish.

This type of dream may also occur when someone who is not suicidal has thought of a person during the dream day who is dead and has wished this person was alive so that he could tell him about important things in his life. The dream gratifies this wish and in no way signifies that the dreamer is equating himself with the dead. In one instance, a woman who was raised by her grandfather, who died when she was a child, remembered him telling her that one day she would be married and have a beautiful child. She loved her grandfather dearly and remembered how heartbroken she was when he died. Years later, when she gave birth to her first child, she dreamed, while still in the hospital, of her beloved grandfather. He was alive and well, just as she had remembered him. In the dream she was showing him her baby and telling him he was right in his prediction. The highly pleasurable dream continued, with her grandfather, who had been a religious man, extending his hand to bless the baby.

These illustrations of dreams of deceased persons, with the exception of Oscar Wilde's dream, involve members of the dreamer's family. Sometimes the deceased persons in the dream were never known to the dreamer at all, as in the case of historical or political figures. After the death of Franklin D. Roosevelt and the assassinations of John F. Kennedy and his brother Robert, patients reported dreams about these people. In every instance they represented important figures (father, grandfather, etc.) out of the dreamer's past and the feelings associated with them (see R. Sterba, 1946a).

Examination Dreams

The essence of these dreams is that the dreamer finds himself unprepared for some examination, discovers that he has failed a course, or learns that he has not been promoted or allowed to graduate. There are many variants of this typical dream. While the *Matura* examinations to which Freud refers have no precise equivalent in our country, many other examinations or academic exercises lend themselves to the same basic theme: licensing or certifying examinations, musical or declamatory recitals, bar mitzvahs or confirmations. The dreamer protests in the dream that he knows the subject, that he has already graduated or been licensed (i.e. that he is already a doctor, lawyer, engineer, etc.), that he has already been "bar mitzvahed," etc.

Questions are asked in the dream that the dreamer struggles to answer but cannot. He has forgotten his part, a chemical formula, a legal procedure, his bar mitzvah Torah or Haftorah portion, the answers to basic catechism questions, etc. Sometimes the material in the examination is material the dreamer had difficulty with when he was actually studying the particular subject. Often these dreams are accompanied by anxiety so intense that it awakens the dreamer, at which point the waking ego confirms what he has been telling himself in his sleep—that he has already passed that particular examination, he has already graduated, etc.

Freud observes that

> it would seem . . . that anxious examination dreams (which, as has been confirmed over and over again, appear when the dreamer has some responsible activity ahead of him the next day and is afraid there may be a fiasco) search for some occasion in the past in which great anxiety has turned out to be un-justified and has been contradicted by the event. . . . What is regarded as an indignant protest against the dream: 'But I'm a doctor, etc., already!' would in reality be the consolation put forward by the dream, and would accordingly run: 'Don't be afraid of tomorrow! Just think how anxious you were before your Matriculation, and yet nothing happened to you. You're a doctor, etc., already.' And the anxiety which is attributed to the dream would really have arisen from the day's residues. [1900, p. 274]

Freud came to the conclusion that the latent content of these dreams conceals a reproach as well as a consolation. He believes that "it would not be surprising if the self-re-proaches for being 'stupid' and 'childish' . . . referred to the repetition of reprehensible sexual acts" (1900, p. 276).

There is a good deal of condensation present in these dreams. The realization in the dream that one has already passed the course, graduated, etc., when viewed as a con-solation, assures the dreamer that he is no longer a child, that he has a right to his sexual knowledge, that he is already married and even has children of his own. But even though he knows this, the old anxieties are revived: he is still the child who will be criticized, condemned, and punished for his forbidden wishes.

Actually, examination dreams are a form of anxiety dream. Their specific content readily refers to puberty rites reenacted on a more adult level: preliminary exams, licensing exams, specialty board examinations, bar examinations, recitals, public addresses, etc. The reference to the professional or work aspect of the individual's life is often a displacement from problems with sexuality or aggression. The ignorance or lack of knowledge which the dreamer experiences may repeat his own lack of knowledge about sexual matters in childhood. The anxiety may be a repetition of anxieties from childhood, e.g., the fear of punishment for forbidden wishes.

A Jewish man dreamed that he was standing on the "bima" (a dais) about to recite his "mafter" (a portion from the Prophets). Various elders of the synagogue were around him in their prayer shawls. Some of the men were very old and wore beards. Everyone looked at him and he suddenly realized that he had forgotten the chant. He anxiously looked at the Hebrew script and found that he could not even read it. The men looked at him with critical "fishy eyes." In the dream he said to himself, and to the men about him, "I know it. I really know it." He thought, "But this is crazy. I was bar mitzvahed years ago." The dream "faded out" and he awakened.

In his waking life, the patient was going to New York City the next morning to meet some financial advisors, "those cold fishy-eyed men with green eyeshades," with whom he had to review a complicated business transaction. He was apprehensive, fearing they might not approve what he was doing, although his proposal was completely "kosher." His concern over their possible disapproval referred also to his plan to see a certain call girl while in New York. He had phoned her and they had arranged to meet, but he felt that his analyst (one of the elders in the dream and the financial advisor in his earlier associations) would disapprove.

Examination dreams, like many other dreams, must always be considered from the standpoint of whether they

242

are to be "read" directly (i.e., the dreamer is the one being examined who is unprepared and fails) or whether they are to be reversed (i.e., it is the dreamer who is asking the questions or doing the examining). In the latter instance, he turns the tables on the adults who did not enlighten him about sexual matters, for he is now the knowledgeable examiner and they are ignorant and childish. At times the dream combines both aspects.

A physician in analysis recalled a vivid dream in which he was in medical school again and was taking the practical part of a final examination. The examiner, a portly, bald-headed man, showed him a catheter and asked him what it is used for. In the dream the patient fumbled for an answer, experienced anxiety, and somehow felt he could not answer the question, even though he was a doctor and knew what a catheter is used for. Finally, he left the room. The dream referred to an event that had occurred when he was about five years of age. His father was a doctor in general practice. On some occasions he would take his son to his office and let him play in his consultation room while he saw a few patients. The patient would spend his time drawing pictures or reading at his father's desk. One day, while looking through one of the desk drawers, he found a catheter. When his father returned he asked him what it was and what it was used for. His father, who was somewhat portly and bald-headed, like the examiner in the dream, did not answer him but in a stiff, pompous manner said, "When you're a doctor you will know," and left the room.

The patient's manifest dream follows the features of the typical dream: being examined in medicine, not being able to answer the question, and having anxiety all the while knowing that he has already passed this examination and is already a doctor. The reference to the catheter clearly refers to sexual function and to passivity. There is also evidence of reversal in this dream. From his associations we can see that it is he who asked his father a question pertaining to sexuality, which his father wouldn't answer out of his own anxiety. And it was his father as well who *left the room*.

At times, the examination in the typical dream has to do with a physical or anatomical examination. In such instances the examination is one in which the individual actively participated, such as a doctor game in childhood, or to which he was subjected, as a medical or physical examination. In the latter instance there is often a good deal of anxiety about what the doctor will discover. Often this refers to the dread that by the examination the doctor will discover that the patient had masturbated, and will divine from this his particular fantasies and punish him severely: castration, humiliation, rejection, abandonment, etc. (see R. Sterba, 1928; Arlow, 1951; Kavka, 1979; Renik, 1981.)

Dreams of Missing a Train

Dreams of missing a train deserve to be put alongside examination dreams on account of the similarity of their affect. . . . They are dreams of consolation for another kind of anxiety felt in sleep—the fear of dying. 'Departing' on a journey is one of the commonest and best authenticated symbols of death. These dreams say in a consoling way: 'Don't worry, you won't die (depart)', just as examination dreams say soothingly: 'Don't be afraid, no harm will come to you this time either.' The difficulty of understanding both these kinds of dreams is due to the fact that the feeling of anxiety is attached precisely to the expression of consolation. [Freud, 1900, p. 385]

Dreams of missing a boat, a bus, an airplane, or any other contrivance that leaves on schedule express the same feelings as dreams of missing a train.

When these dreams deal with death or the patient's fear of death, it is important for the therapist to ascertain the specific determinants in the latent dream thoughts behind the dream. Frequently, the stimulus for such a dream is the news of someone's death, one with whom the dreamer can identify because of age, occupation, recreational activity, etc. The typical dream described by Freud reassures the dreamer that he need not identify himself with the person who died.

The element "to depart" or "to go off on a journey" signifying death in such dreams is extremely important, as it may provide not only a starting point for many associations leading to the patient's concern whether he is going to die suddenly of some natural cause, but also a clue to the presence of suicidal thoughts. The expression, "I'm going to go on a long trip, far, far away and never come back," whether spoken in waking life or woven into a dream, must alert the therapist to the patient's feelings of depression and despair. Under such circumstances, the reassurance that Freud speaks about may refer to a wished-for reassurance and consolation the patient may want from his therapist. While it is useful to know this, it is also essential that the patient be helped to understand the reasons behind his feelings of hopelessness, a reason that may be apparent from the content of the dream and the associations to it.

Actually, the fear of death as such is rarely the real source of the patient's anxiety (Freud, 1915b). While the material may refer to death, as Freud indicates, it is subject to many other meanings and interpretations. The underlying anxieties usually deal with such subjects as castration, loss, abandonment, rejection, etc.

Sometimes dreams in therapy of missing a train, etc. refer to the therapeutic sessions. The patient thereby indicates he might miss them or come in late. Rather than being a consolation for the fear of dying, these dreams may in such instances be an indication of resistance, an unwillingness to discuss some painful or embarrassing material or to deal with certain elements in the transference situation. Sometimes the dream anticipates missing an appointment or being late, which the patient subsequently acts out. From the content of the dream and the patient's associations, it is often possible to ascertain the nature of the resistance. Helping the patient recognize that his resistance is expressed in the dream facilitates exploration of its underlying basis. In instances where the patient rationalizes having missed an appointment for some extraneous reason, the presence before the missed appointment of a dream in which the patient misses a train or whatever tends to convince the patient of the power of his unconscious in "planning" such eventualities.

At times, dreams of missing a train or other conveyance are to be understood by their literal wording and may refer to "missing" the therapist or the therapeutic sessions when the therapist cancels an appointment for whatever reason. On other occasions, dreams of missing the conveyance refer to thoughts about the ultimate termination of therapy. Another significance of the wording in these dreams is in the sense of "missing the boat," a verbal expression indicating that someone, generally the therapist, has said something that was wrong: he is "missing the point." In the dream the criticism is reversed and it is the patient who is missing the boat rather than the therapist.

At other times the metaphor may refer to a conflict the patient cannot resolve. A woman dreamed of being at an airport waiting for her plane to take off. She found herself doing many things—shopping for magazines and books to read on her trip, etc.—and then discovered that her plane had already departed. The dream referred to her conflict about her marriage. She had been thinking of leaving her husband and was planning to take a vacation without him. At the same time she was concerned that he might leave her. The dream expressed her concern that she might procrastinate too long and he would leave her first.

One significance of dreams of missing a train has to do with the word "train." Used as a switch word, it may designate some aspect of the individual's training (i.e., education or sexual enlightenment) or, more specifically, toilet training. Missing the "train" or "training" in these cases may refer to some episode of incontinence or lack of sphincter control: missing the train thus becomes equivalent to having an accident. The cars of the train in such instances may refer to feces. At other times a train or boat is designated as a freight train or a freighter. Here the choice of wording may constitute a pun, i.e., "afraid," based on the patient's fear that he may have an accident.

Chapter Thirteen

Typical Dreams with a Variety of Meanings

Thus far we have discussed Freud's first category of typical dreams, dreams which generally have the same meaning. As we have pointed out, even a dream in this category requires that the therapist deal with the individual and specific determinants that carry its meaning beyond the narrow framework of a "standard" interpretation.

We come now to Freud's second category: dreams which, "in spite of having the same or similar content, must nevertheless be interpreted in the greatest variety of ways" (1900, p. 385). These dreams are the most common. In this category Freud includes dreams "in which the dreamer flies or floats in the air, falls, swims, etc." (1900, p. 392). He indicates further that "it would be possible to mention a whole number of . . . 'typical' dreams if we take the term to mean that the same manifest dream-content is frequently to be found in dreams of different dreamers" (1900, p. 395). Among these, Freud mentions dreams of passing through narrow streets, walking through suites of rooms, being pursued by wild animals, and being threatened with knives, daggers, or lances.

Flying Dreams

Initially Freud classifies dreams of "flying through the air to the accompaniment of agreeable feelings or falling with feelings of anxiety" as typical dreams in the first category, i.e., those which always have the same meaning (1900, p. 271). Actually these dreams may also be considered as properly belonging under symbolism (see 1900, p. 271n3). Yet in a remark added to the 1909 edition of the *Interpretation of Dreams* he indicates that these dreams "mean something different in every instance; it is only the raw material of sensations contained in them which is always derived from the same source" (1900, p. 393).

Freud believes these dreams are based essentially on two determinants. The first of these is the reproduction of the sensations felt during childhood games of movement (as well as during play on swings and seesaws) or when being tossed about by fond adults (1900, pp. 271–272). Such determinants in dreams always raise such questions as to why they are dreamt at the particular time they are, and, if they refer to games played, with whom they were played, etc. Kohut (1971) describes "the unmodified grandiose self" as urging "the ego to jump into the void in order to soar or sail through space" (p. 145n1). "The flying fantasy [or dream] . . . appears to be a frequent feature of unmodified infantile grandiosity. Its early stages are common to both sexes and are probably reinforced by ecstatic sensations while the small child is being carried by the omnipotent idealized self-object. . ." (p. 144).

Freud observes that "it not uncommonly happens that these games of movement, though innocent in themselves, give rise to sexual feelings" (1900, p. 393). The association of these games with such sensations leads to Freud's consideration of the other determinant of flying dreams, namely erection. He writes: "The close connection of flying with the idea of birds explains how it is that in men flying dreams usually have a grossly sensual meaning; and we shall not be surprised when we hear that some dreamer or other is very proud of his powers of flight" (1900, p. 394; see also 1910c, pp. 125–126). Citing Federn, Freud indicates that "a good number of these flying dreams are dreams of erection" and that frequently such dreams are "connected with erections or emissions" (1900, p. 394). By the same token, according to Freud, flying dreams in women indicate the conscious or unconscious wish to be a man (1916–1917, p. 155).

As the most frequent interpretation of flying dreams is sexual, what has been discussed under symbolism generally applies here. It is important, however, for the therapist to recognize and to deal with the reason for the choice of the particular symbolic expression. Obviously not all dreams involving sexual wishes are expressed as dreams of flying. Nor for that matter are regular nocturnal penile erections accompanied by dreams of flying (Fisher, 1974).

Other determinants of flying dreams are past experiences dealing with aviation—airplane trips taken or planned, etc. (Bond, 1952). In recent years patients have used the word "flying" to refer to Erica Jong's book, *Fear of Flying* (1973), and its reference to the sexual life of an analyst or his wife.

Sometimes dreams of flying may be considered a metaphoric expression of separation anxiety, i.e., the fear someone may fly away. At other times they may be an expression of ego wishes such as the wish for freedom or for increased or expanded ego boundaries. Ambition, "flying high," mania or hypomanic excitement, exhilaration, ecstasy, soaring "like a bird" are all determinants for this type of dream.

A man described a dream in which he was "soaring like a bird" over the landscape. He commented that birds have remarkable vision and are able to spot small objects and their movement at great distances. His associations led to his memory of being taken by his parents to visit some friends or relatives who lived in an apartment building. While there he was able to look into a room several floors below and watch a man with an erection make sexual advances toward a nude woman from the rear. He recalls being aroused and having an erection himself. The flying in the dream condensed his own vantage point in the memory, the man's erection, and his own sexual arousal.

Another patient, who flew his own plane, often had dreams of flying. His associations revealed his anxieties about flying and his fear that he would "accidentally" do something to injure himself in the plane. Men who have had experience with planes in wartime sometimes attempt to master these traumatic experiences in their dreams.

A few years ago, dreams of flying often referred to the book, *Jonathan Livingston Seagull,* by Richard Bach (1970), and its themes of individuality, high-mindedness, and dedication to causes. Some people interpreted it as dealing with religion, others with Freud and psychoanalysis.

Dreams of Falling

For these dreams, as with dreams of flying, Freud suggests a genetic determinant: "Almost every child has fallen down at one time or other and afterwards been picked up and petted; or if he has fallen out of his cot at night, has been taken into bed with his mother or nurse" (1900, p. 395). Moreover, he writes, "dreams of falling are . . . often characterized by anxiety" (p. 394).

Sometimes dreams of falling are a symbolic expression of childbirth: "to be delivered of a child" (Freud, 1920b, p. 162n1). Strachey comments in a footnote that "there is in English . . . a colloquial use of the verb 'to fall,' meaning pregnancy or childbirth" (p. 162n1). The expression that a woman "has dropped a baby" may also refer to childbirth. Freud indicates that "to throw oneself from a height = to be delivered of a child" (p. 162n1). Such dreams may therefore occur when pregnancy is being contemplated or anticipated.

Freud indicates that in women dreams of falling may have another symbolic significance: they are "a way of describing a surrender to an erotic temptation" (1900, pp. 394–395). "If a woman dreams of falling, it almost invariably has a sexual sense: she is imagining herself as a '*fallen woman*'" (p. 202). Freud's suggestion that these dreams, when dreamt by a woman, are to be understood by their wording, is also helpful generally, as they often have the same meaning for both sexes. The clue is that they often refer to any fall or lowering of self-esteem along Biblical lines: "How are the mighty fallen . . ." (2 Samuel 1:25).

These dreams occur in situations when the dreamer is forced to realize that his own conduct has or is about to run counter to his idealized view of himself or to the dictates of his superego. A man, whose high moralistic sense of ethics had been instilled in him by his parents, had a dream in which he had slipped from the edge of a cliff and was plummeting downwards. The dream occurred around the time he was about to get into a business deal that seemed somewhat shady; one of the principals was not the kind of individual with whom he was proud to be associated. A "fall" by an idealized figure with whom the person has identified may also give rise to such dreams. A woman learned that her father, whom she adored, had been indicted for a crime, another that her son had been arrested on a drug charge. In both instances the imagery in the manifest content of their dreams was that of a fall. In talking about her son, the woman remarked that he had "fallen from grace."

Dreams of falling may occur in response to dangers the individual perceives will be his lot as a consequence of success, even though achieved by merit and as a just reward. One patient, who had achieved acclaim as a result of a highly successful venture, dreamed that he was in an elevator that suddenly went out of control and plunged rapidly downward. He tried in vain to stop its fall by frantically pushing the various control buttons, including the emergency intercom button. As the elevator was slowly stopping, he awoke with anxiety. The patient was very apprehensive that his recent success would be met with great personal criticism by his competitors, that he would be hated and repudiated, that the fruits of his glory would be short-lived, and that now that he had achieved his triumph he would die or be killed. He feared he might succumb to a depression (a fall), and appealed for help in his therapy. One learned from his associations, as well as from what he had revealed before the dream, that he had frequently reacted to success by a fear that he would somehow "have to pay for it," as his superego did not allow him to rejoice in his accomplishment.

Frequently dreams of falling are associated with a good deal of anxiety and with the sensation of hitting the ground or the bed, from which the dreamer awakens with a start. These dreams are often related to the emergence of a forbidden aggressive wish and the need to punish oneself for it. One patient, who had many repetitive dreams of falling himself, or of watching people fall, was fascinated in his waking life by such activities as skydiving, by people climbing to dizzy heights, by men doing construction work on girders of skyscrapers. He eagerly watched movies or television programs in which stuntmen walked on the wings of airplanes. Behind this fascination was a horror that he himself would jump from a high building or from a window and be killed. He attempted to master his anxiety by going to the top of high buildings, by climbing out on precipices, by skiing recklessly down the most difficult and dangerous slopes. He remembered climbing on the roofs of garages and other low buildings as a boy and, whenever possible, jumping to the ground when the distance was not too dangerously high. He was particularly fascinated by pictures of the explosion of the *Hindenburg* at Lakehurst, New Jersey, on May 6, 1937, that showed people falling to their deaths from the dirigible.

It became evident in his analysis that behind his dreams and his fascination for heights this patient struggled with intense feelings of aggression. He was very sensitive and overtly not aggressive, although he was inclined to be sarcastic and to make humorous remarks that were more cutting than they were funny. As a boy he had often visited his father in his office on one of the top floors of a high building. His father was a very aloof man who, though loving to the patient, had little time for him. When the patient came to his office, the father busied himself with phone calls, meetings, and paperwork. The patient was hurt and angry and often had the thought that he would like to push his father out the window.

Dreams of falling may also refer to the expression "falling apart" and have to do with a patient's fears of ego disintegration and fragmentation. The therapist should be attentive to the patient's plea for help in dreams of this kind. In addition, Kohut (1971) calls attention to the "fear of uncontrollable regression which is expressed in falling dreams" while the transference establishes itself (p. 134).

Rescue Dreams

Rescue dreams in connection with birth and parturition have been discussed in a previous chapter. In our clinical work we often find them associated also with an individual's attempts to control his aggression. What may be initially overlooked by the dreamer in reporting a rescue dream is that he has put the person into a position from which he must be rescued, which implies that he harbors aggressive or hostile wishes toward that person or toward whomever that person represents (R. Sterba, 1940). In these dreams it is important to note the danger situation from which the person is being rescued. In most instances such dreams contain the ambivalence which the individual feels toward the object so that the dream expresses both the aggression and the defense against it. Careful note should also be taken of whether the person rescued is a child or an adult. If the person is a child, the therapist should ascertain who or what the child stands for. Quite often the combination of birth significance and aggressive wish in these dreams suggests a reference to a younger sibling or to the dreamer's own child. At other times the child rescued in the dream may refer to the dreamer's penis.

The theme of rescue may also refer to the dreamer's wish to be rescued by the therapist from some situation in which he currently finds himself. One man dreamed of climbing a mountain and slipping so that he dangled precipitously on a rope. He was waiting to be rescued in the dream when he awoke. The patient had in reality done some mountain climbing, but nothing like that had ever happened to him or to any of his companions. He had heard a discussion of such accidents, however, and had recently read an account of one in a magazine. The dream related to his fear that he might be slipping into an abysmal depression and to his wish that his therapist rescue him. There were also allusions to the umbilical cord, to his being like a newborn baby still attached to its mother.

In another instance a woman dreamed that she was rescuing her son from a wild dog that was about to attack and devour him. She caught her son in her arms, was relieved that she had succeeded in saving him from being bitten by the ferocious dog, and awoke. Her associations led to her feelings about her younger brother, who had definitely been preferred by her mother. The allusion to his birth is implied in the rescue theme, but so is her own aggression, as expressed by the ferocious dog. She remembered that as a child she wanted many times to get rid of her younger brother. She recalled how she enjoyed fairy tales in which children were to be gobbled up by some horrible witch. Her favorite story was *Hansel and Gretel*. She particularly loved the part about how the evil witch was going to eat up Hansel and how Gretel finally rescued him by pushing the witch into the oven. When she was a child, her mother often left her in charge of her baby brother. This was a constant source of conflict for her, as it placed her in the position of having aggressive thoughts toward him while having to take care of him and keep him out of danger. The intensity of her conflict was displaced upon her son in the dream. Contained in it, too, was her aggression toward her mother (the evil witch) for giving birth to her brother.

Observation Dreams

Dreams are primarily visual. Because of the power of the scoptophilic instinct, however, and the fact that observations of all kinds have such an important effect on the individual's development, dreams whose content clearly alludes to something seen are of great significance. Frequently they refer to a childhood observation of the genitals of a playmate, sibling, or adult of the opposite sex. A child's observation of his parents' genitals have a special importance for him. In all such instances it is important that the therapist learn the details of the incidents in which such observations were made, as well as the patient's reactions to them (Greenacre, 1950).

While Freud did not include dreams dealing with primal scene material in either of his two categories of typical dreams, there are many dreams in the course of an analysis that refer to the dreamer's observation of the primal scene as a child and his reactions to this observation. These dreams typically have the same meaning, subject of course to numerous idiosyncratic variations. The observations referred to may actually have been made or may have been fantasied.

These dreams regularly contain certin specific elements. The dreamer finds himself in a locale in which an observation can be made. He views (or hears) some activity. Frequently there are indications of an interruption of the activity and references to the dreamer's reaction to the observation, either in the dream itself or later, in an association to it.

In the typical dream the locale is often a theater, auditorium, stadium, classroom, amphitheater, church, etc. in which the dreamer is watching a performance. At times the locale incorporates a vantage point from which the dreamer can see the activity. He may be on a mountaintop, in a high building, a high tree, an observatory, or a "look-out." He may be surrounded by some barrier through which he can see: a window, a peephole, a one-way screen, a balcony with a guardrail.

On occasion the scene is more conducive to the perception of sound than to visual observation. Here references are made to thin walls and to radios or sound equipment of various types. At times the two sensory modalities are combined—e.g., "I was looking through a pane of glass and heard a great noisy commotion." This particular dream combined looking and hearing and expressed the dreamer's childhood conception that his mother was in pain because he heard her moaning.

In some instances the mention of a locale in the manifest content is completely omitted and the patient simply reports, "I was watching a movie or a television program," etc.

Primal scene dreams often use elements in their manifest content that specifically pertain to seeing better, or closer. "Snooperscopes," telescopes, binoculars, and observation satellites with surveillance equipment are common elements by which this idea is expressed. Cameras of various types frequently refer to recording or capturing in memory what has been observed. Movie cameras serve to record the movement. Candid cameras with flash or strobe equipment serve to take snapshots of what was going on, especially if there is an allusion to the speed of the shutter that can "stop the motion." The camera lens, particularly if it is a telephoto or zoom lens, may refer to the child's wish to get closer to the action and to see better what is going on. The references of people familiar with cameras to the "f-opening" and the ability of a "fast lens" to capture the scene under subdued illumination are of considerable importance. Also, the film used may be described—for example, as being "very fast," having the capability of recording the scene under subdued illumination, or as being infrared film, sensitive to heat.

The type of activity viewed in the dream, or in the patient's associations to it, reveals a great deal about the child's conception and interpretation of the primal scene. Frequently the reference is to a violent activity. It may be to an athletic contest of some kind, either team sports (e.g., football) or games with single competitors (tennis, golf). At other times the dream may be about a more artistic form of activity, such as dancing or ballet. Often in such instances there is a good deal of emphasis on the physical activity, with descriptions of the moving bodies and limbs. On other occasions the references are somewhat more subtle, as to a musical performance, a concert, or a chamber orchestra. A male patient dreamed he was watching a brass band and was particularly fascinated by a woman playing a trombone. The dream referred to his having observed fellatio when he was a child.

A man who was occasionally impotent dreamed that he was about to have intercourse with his wife when he noticed the bedroom door was open. He could not see out but heard his mother in the next room say, "It's okay." His mother's words were a complete reversal of her attitude of repeatedly and actively forbidding his sexuality when he was an adolescent and her specific warnings that girls would get him in trouble. His associations led beyond this to an incident in childhood when he had apparently gone past his parents' partially open door and heard his mother say to his father, "It's okay." Later he heard the sound of their bed shaking. The oedipal significance of the dream is rather obvious.

Another man dreamed of being in the Colosseum in Rome, seated among a throng of people dressed in tunics and togas and wearing sandals. In the arena he saw what appeared to be a crowd of people—early Christians, he assumed. Gladiators carrying short swords then appeared, followed by animals like lions. The gladiators then seemed to stab and hack at the people with their swords. There was blood and gore everywhere. He seemed unable to tear himself away from the sight and finally awakened. The dream referred to his having observed parental coitus as a child and his later assumption that the bloodstains in his parents' bed were the consequences of a sadistic bloody assault.

Sometimes primal scene dreams contain an allusion to the dreamer's reaction at the time he witnessed parental coitus. This may be anxiety, anger, frustration, a profound feeling of being left out, a flooding of the ego with sexual excitement, an identification with one or the other parent in an active or passive position, or some gross visceral or physiological response.

One patient reported a dream in which he was sitting in a grandstand constructed in a peculiar way. It seemed collapsible and yet could expand to seat more people. The idea of collapsibility and expansibility referred to his erection while watching intercourse. Another man dreamed that he was watching a tennis match and suddenly it began to rain. The reference here was to his urination at the time of the primal scene observation, as well as to his having felt that his parents' bed was wet on one occasion when he got up and climbed into bed with them when he was a small boy.

A woman patient reported the following dream: "I was in a prison and was looking through the bars." The dream referred to a time when she slept in a crib in her parents' bedroom. She recalled that her parents had covered the crib with a large sheet while they were having intercourse. From her associations it became evident that she had learned to push the sheet aside and peek through the bars to see what her parents were doing. In describing this scene, to which she returned many times, she cried, "They treated me like some kind of dumb, I mean damn, parrot."

References to primal scene material may at times be presaged by some innocuous reference in the manifest content—for example, to a sandwich. This may refer to a time when the child lay or slept between its parents (Sharpe, 1937). A dream of a "clever baby" who is "able to talk or write fluently, treat one to deep sayings, carry on intelligent conversations" may allude to "the *actual* knowledge of the child on sexuality" (Ferenczi, 1923a, p. 349n1). Dreams of this kind may be stimulated by primal scene observations.

Frequently dreams in which there is some interruption of an activity, conversation, or intimate exchange refer to the dreamer's having interrupted his parents in their sexual activity. Feldman (1945) describes a series of variations of such dreams in which the privacy of the patient's analytic session is interrupted by intrusions into the consulting room by the analyst's wife, his family, strangers, other analysts, etc. It is my impression that generally such dreams are to be understood as reversals: it is the patient who, as a child, wanted to or actually did interrupt his parents.

Izner (1959) points out that often a series of dreams with primal scene content occurs when there is a threatened separation between analyst and patient, as when the analyst has announced his plans for a vacation or trip. Dreams under such circumstances may occur early in an analysis, and unlike primal scene dreams brought in after a good deal of analytic work has been done, these seem almost totally unrelated to the general thrust of the material. The reference to primal scene material, moreover, often does not appear to be sustained after resumption of the therapy. These dreams express prototypical feelings of oral deprivation, rejection, and abandonment, just like those the patient felt when he was excluded by his parents while they were having intercourse.

Dreams with a Dental Stimulus
Basing his explanation on the principle of displacement from below upward (1900, p. 387), or transposition from the lower to the upper part of the body, Freud states categorically that, in males, dreams with a dental stimulus are derived from "the masturbatory desires of the pubertal period" (1900, p. 385) and "the dreaded punishment for it" (1916–1917, p. 190).

There are many modifications of this typical dream. The patient may dream of a toothache, of a tooth or teeth falling out painlessly, or of someone (e.g., a dentist) extracting a tooth (Thompson, 1932; Lorand and Feldman, 1955). Extraction dreams are "to be interpreted as castration" (1900, p. 387n1). A "dead tooth" in a dream often refers to impotence (Coriat, 1913). Freud indicates that "a distinction must in general be made between dreams with a dental stimulus and dentist dreams" (1900, p. 387n1).

In a footnote dated 1909, Freud refers to a communication by Jung to the effect that dreams "with a dental stimulus occurring in women have the meaning of birth dreams"; an addition to this note made in 1919 cites a 1914 paper by Ernest Jones, which in Freud's opinion confirmed Jung's interpretation. Freud notes that "the element in common between [the castration and birth interpretations] . . . lies in the fact that in both cases . . . what is in question is the separation of a part of the body from the whole" (1900, pp. 387–388n3). Sometimes the reference to "eyeteeth" may be a means of representing the ego—the "I" of the dreamer.

In a very comprehensive study of dental dreams, Lorand and Feldman (1955) demonstrate, on the basis of clinical material as well as myths and folklore, that dreams of teeth may have reference to all stages of libidinal development. As references to the oral stages, they may allude to any loss, separation, or deprivation. "The deep oral regression gratifies the wish for primitive narcissism—being back at the mother's breast" (p. 160). The removal of a tooth in such dreams can easily represent loss of the nursing nipple. Dreams of teeth not only have phallic and childbirth significance but may also refer to the vagina dentata, abortion, death, and psychosis. The toothless state of both the infant and the aged are also important considerations. Moreover, dreams of teeth may refer directly to aggression, to biting or chewing. Such references are particularly significant when used by depressed patients who have a good deal of oral aggression.

The wealth of material that can be symbolized by typical dreams with a dental stimulus should be a constant reminder to the therapist to explore the patient's associations fully and carefully before making any hasty interpretation. Among the various possibilities are "dentist dreams" occurring in patients where one or the other parent has been a dentist or dental hygienist and has provided professional services to the child. In one such situation, a man's mother was a dentist who paid constant attention to his teeth. He had repeated dreams in which someone was working on his teeth from behind. In his dreams his teeth were cleaned, drilled, scraped, inspected, and probed, fillings were made, impressions were taken, etc. There were constant references to the transference, with the analyst representing his mother as the dentist. The patient was convinced the analyst would be more interested in his teeth and in his oral hygiene than in him.

He recalled, apropos of one such dream, that one day he had come home from school and started to tell his mother about a quarrel he had had with a classmate. He remembered that his mother had said nothing about it, but looking at his teeth had said, "Your teeth are so dirty. Why don't you brush them more often? If you can't, then come to the office and I'll clean them for you." As his thoughts then led to his mother's interest in his hygiene and other personal habits, it became apparent that at this time the reference to his teeth in the dream had taken on an anal significance.

Punishment Dreams

Basing his explanation on his structural theory (1921, 1923b), Freud indicated that "punishment dreams [are] fulfilments of the wishes of the super-ego" (1900, p. 476n2) or that they "replace the forbidden wish-fulfilment by the appropriate punishment for it . . . they fulfil the wish of the sense of guilt which is the reaction to the repudiated impulse" (1920a, p. 32).

Frequently, punishment dreams are part of a pair of

dreams in which the "crime" is expressed in one part and the punishment in the other. Sometimes a split occurs so that the punishment appears in a dream one night and the wish or the "crime" in another the following night, or the previous night. Sometimes only the punishment appears in the dream and the patient's associations reveal the nature of the crime. According to the law of Talion, which the superego follows scrupulously, the punishment must in every instance fit the crime.

The form of these dreams generally expresses a causal relationship: "since I wished it therefore I must be punished," or "if . . . then. . . ." In one rather simple dream, a physician dreamed he was in traffic court and the referee suspended his driver's license for thirty days. The patient's associations led to his confession that he had falsified a bill to a third-party payer for a patient under his care. He felt very guilty about what he had done and was fearful that if he were caught his license to practice medicine would be suspended for a long period of time.

It is important to bear in mind, however, that punishment dreams do more than fulfill the demands of the superego. "They arise, rather," Freud writes, "in obedience to the compulsion to repeat, though it is true that in analysis that compulsion is supported by the wish (which is encouraged by 'suggestion') to conjure up what has been forgotten and repressed" (1920a, p. 32).

Inability to Overtake Someone in a Dream

Freud quotes Stekel, who "explains failing to catch up with a carriage as regret at a difference in age which cannot be caught up with" (1900, p. 358).

While children often have the fantasy that they can catch up with an older sibling or even a parent in age, quite frequently the idea of catching up refers to catching up in some accomplishment that is a part of the child's ambitious strivings. The accomplishments which the individual wants to achieve may be in various areas: physical appearance and maturation, attractiveness, breast or genital size, urinary or sexual potency, wealth, professional advancement, cultural achievements. Running after somebody may also be the expression of the wish to be loved in a way that the child felt an older sibling was loved and he was not. It may also be the expression of an oedipal wish, but with the feeling that the goal is unattainable.

Reconciliation Dreams

These dreams deal with "a reconciliation with people with whom friendly relations have long since ceased." In such cases, Freud writes, "analysis habitually reveals some occasion which might urge me to abandon the last remnant of consideration for these former friends and to treat them as strangers or enemies. The dream, however, prefers to depict the opposite relationship" (1900, p. 476). Reconciliation dreams occur most frequently after the breakup of a close relationship, as in a family, a partnership, or a friendship. They are likely to occur also after the breakup of an affair, whether heterosexual or homosexual. The dreamer wants to reestablish a relationship that has proven nonviable.

A man who had remarried after a long and difficult divorce found that he often dreamed of his first wife. In his dreams he met her in various resorts, restaurants, bars, and the like. The scene was of a joyful reunion. They would embrace and he would tell her how much he missed her and apprise her of the activities of their children, who were in his custody. He would often awaken from these dreams realizing what they meant, thinking over and over again that maybe he had made a mistake and that he should not have initiated the divorce. But then the bitter reality of the impossibility of the former marriage would hit him anew and he would cry as though all had turned to ashes.

Sometimes these dreams occur when an individual is confronted with giving up an impossible relationship with a parent or sibling. In one instance a woman who had been deeply attached to her older sister was forced to give her up. The sister had become a criminal, had been imprisoned, and had alienated herself totally from her family, refusing to have any contact with them. She returned their letters unopened, hung up when they phoned her, etc. Originally, the patient was worried and sad about this turn of events, but gradually she became angry and harbored bitter feelings toward her sister. She had repeated dreams in which she would meet her sister and they would be reconciled, only to awaken and find that this was not so at all.

There are situations in which a therapist loses a patient after a lengthy period of time because of irresolvable transference on the part of the patient. The therapist, who has invested a good deal of himself in working with the patient, feels alternately upset and angry with the patient for having abandoned him in this way. In the process of working through his own unresolved countertransference reactions, the therapist may have dreams in which he sees the patient again, discusses the problem with him, and they are reconciled.

In reconciliation dreams the individual struggles with all the elements of the separation and mourning. These dreams represent a working through of the termination of the relationship. Sometimes these dreams occur during the termination phase of an analysis or in the post-termination period. In such dreams the old relationship is rekindled and situations are conjured up in which the dreamer and his lost love object are reunited. But then, after the dream, the dreamer realizes that the relationship cannot be and eventually, as happens when the work of mourning is successful, the tie is effectively severed.

Recurrent and Traumatic Dreams

Concerning these dreams, Freud writes that "only the kernel of the dream has recurred each time" (1922a, p. 213). He explains: "Experience shows that people often assert that they have had the same dream, when as a matter of fact the separate appearances of the recurrent dream have differed from one another in numerous details and in other respects that were of no small importance" (1905a, pp. 92–93). Abraham (1909) elaborates:

> If the dream was based upon a complex of strong emotional significance, then that complex will reassert itself, during the same or subsequent night, in further dreams. Such further dreams tend to contain the same wish-fulfilment as the first. They merely incorporate new means of expression, other symbols and different associations. A powerful complex can manifest itself for many years in the shape of a recurring dream. [p. 189]

Dreams of this sort are not at all unusual, and at times seem almost banal. Sometimes the underlying wish in such dreams may be the wish to return to the dreamer's youth or to a happier period of his life (Freud, 1900, p. 476). In other instances these dreams refer to the individual's problems. One man, when confronted with a problem or a decision, invariably dreamed that he was adding up columns of figures and trying to get the sums to balance. He was suffering from a severe obsessional neurosis and in his recurrent dream he was actually expressing his need to balance things off, to go from one sum to another to equalize them. He could come to no decision in these dreams, just as he could not come to a decision in real life. These dreams varied in details, amounts, and setting, and it was to these details that the analytic exploration was directed.

With Freud's understanding of traumatic neurosis and the concept of repetition compulsion, he was able to provide a further explanation of these dreams. He writes:

> Now dreams occurring in traumatic neuroses have the characteristic of repeatedly bringing the patient back into the situation of his accident, a situation from which he wakes up in another fright. [1920a, p. 13]

We may assume . . . that [these] dreams are endeavouring to master the stimulus retrospectively, by developing the anxiety whose omission was the cause of the traumatic neurosis. [1920a, p. 32]

Frequently such dreams refer to some traumatic incident in childhood and repeat in great detail the circumstances of the event. At times details are added which were not present in the initial reporting of the dream, and these specific details are helpful in understanding the underlying nature of the traumatic event. A patient who had travel dreams had been taken to a distant city by his mother when he was a young child. She had temporarily separated from her husband, and the boy missed his father very much. The dreams of going from city to city alluded to that traumatic period in his life. The patient who had been masturbating in his mother's bed (see chapter 8), and whose father, razor in hand, had shouted "What are you doing?" had many dreams that alluded to that scene. What was impressive, however, and pertinent in this connection was that the detail that it was his mother's bed was not revealed for a long time, even though the material had appeared repeatedly. The patient had "not thought of it." Quite frequently, when the underlying reasons for the repetitive dreams are dealt with, they cease.

Unfortunately the mastery of a traumatic event is not always accomplished through its repetition in dreams. "The repetition in dreams while serving to bind the trauma may in and of itself by the very virtue of the repetition be traumatic" (Levitan, 1980b, p. 280).

A variant of recurrent traumatic dreams are the so-called "Catastrophic Dreams" reported by Kardiner (1932) and Levitan (1967, 1976–1977). These dreams are rare and represent a waking life trauma (e.g., a flare-up of chronic dermatomyositis, a grand mal seizure). The patient experiences the condition as a "body-shattering experience." The memory of the experience (e.g., a convulsion) is then represented in the manifest content of the dream (Levitan, 1980b, p. 274).

We may now consider in the category of typical dreams with a variety of meanings those that have a special significance with regard to the therapy itself. These dreams help the therapist judge the direction of his interpretations.

"Self-State" Dreams

Kohut (1977) describes a type of dream which attempts, "with the aid of verbalizable dream-imagery, to bind the nonverbal tensions of traumatic states (the dread of overstimulation, or of the disintegration of the self [psychosis])" (p. 109). He writes:

> Dreams of this . . . type portray the dreamer's dread vis-à-vis some uncontrollable tension-increase or his dread of the dissolution of the self. The very act of portraying these vicissitudes in the dream constitutes an attempt to deal with the psychological danger by covering frightening nameless processes with nameable visual imagery. . . . In [this] type of dream . . . free associations do not lead to unconscious hidden layers of the mind; at best they provide us with further imagery which remains on the same level as the manifest content of the dream. The scrutiny of the manifest content of the dream and of the associative elaborations of the manifest content will then allow us to recognize that the healthy sectors of the patient's psyche are reacting with anxiety to a disturbing change in the condition of the self—manic overstimulation or a serious depressive drop in self-esteem—or to the threat of the dissolution of the self. [p. 109]

Kohut indicates that while some elements of the dream are to be understood as a result of structural conflict and are "resolvable through the analysis of free associations that gradually lead toward formerly hidden wishes and impulses" (p. 111), others contain "elements (often the total setting of the dream, its atmosphere) [which] portray aspects of the archaic self that have emerged" (p. 110).

Socarides (1980) writes that "manifest perverse dreams are similar to the 'self-state' dreams" that Kohut described. He writes that these dreams do not express in visual imagery the content of drives or wishes in an attempted solution to a conflict represented by the manifest content, but helps the narcissist to reintegrate himself by pressing into service primitive modes of adaptation which have proven useful and necessary in the earliest years of life. Sexualization has played and continues to play a major role to this end. A sexualization of narcissistic needs promotes a discharge of narcissistic tension: seeking a penis; incorporating the body of the male partner in homosexuality; wearing the clothes of the opposite sex in transvestitism; the libidinization of aggression in a spanking perversion, etc., are all attempts at achieving internalization and structure formation. [p. 250]

Confirmatory or Corroborative Dreams

These dreams are the type that, "as it were, 'tag along behind' the analysis" (Freud, 1911, p. 96; 1923a, p. 115). They "merely present what the treatment has inferred during the last few days from the material of the daily associations" (1911, p. 96). These patients "reproduce the forgotten experiences of their childhood only after one has constructed them from their symptoms, associations and other signs and has propounded these constructions to them" (1923a, p. 115). The corroborative dreams then follow the analytic construction. "When this happens, it looks as though the patient has been amiable enough to bring us in dream-form exactly what we had been 'suggesting' to him immediately before" (1911, p. 96). Their "evidential value" must be questioned, however, "since they may have been imagined in compliance with the physician's words instead of having been brought to light from the dreamer's unconscious" (1923a, p. 115). Sometimes, in fact, the patient may comply with what he thinks the therapist may be thinking, even when the therapist has said nothing.

One form of confirmatory dreams are those that may be called "lying or obliging dreams." These serve the unconscious wish to please the therapist but at the same time may betray him. This need to betray may at times result from the repression of the wish to please (1920b, p. 166). These dreams often express the patient's ambivalence toward the therapist in the transference. It is important to understand, however, why the patient makes use of this particular defense.

Freud goes on to say that the analyst

> accepts such [corroboratory or confirmatory] dreams as hoped-for confirmations, and recognizes that they are only observed under certain conditions brought about by the influence of the treatment. The great majority of dreams forge ahead of the analysis; so that, after subtraction of everything in them which is already known and understood, there still remains a more or less clear hint at something which has hitherto been hidden. [1911, p. 96]

> with some patients these [confirmatory or corroborative dreams] are the only dreams that one obtains. . . . The patients who produce only corroborative dreams are the same patients in whom doubt plays the principal part in resistance. [1923a, p. 115]

Confirmatory or corroborative dreams are derived from the material of recent analytic sessions. Their specific content is important, but they must also be considered in conjunction with the entire therapeutic situation at the time. The clue to unraveling these dreams lies in understanding the patient's transference: his general attitude toward the analyst and to what is being expressed in the analytic situation. While some patients are obsessed with constant doubts, others find a way of expressing resistance by agreeing with everything the analyst says even before he says it. They say yes and shake their heads affirmatively even before the analyst has had a chance to make his interpretation or discuss what is involved. Glover (1955) writes that the rejection of an interpretation may be "masked by an immediate assent which is too good to be true" (p. 53).

These patients are prone to bring up confirmatory dreams which in their minds somehow fit in with the analyst's construction regarding their dynamics. Generally, they are more likely to do so when the analyst does not deal with their resistance and when, for various reasons, they have a need to please or placate the analyst so that he will like them and not reject them. In some analysands this attitude may hark back to an early educational situation in which they were taught to be singularly polite and well-mannered. One patient, a nurse by training, always stood until her analyst was seated, and always responded to his remarks with, "Yes, doctor." She had been taught that this was proper etiquette and decorum when speaking to a physician. There were other early determinants as well. When she was a child, her family had employed a black nursemaid who was very polite and softspoken. She inculcated in the patient an almost servile code of etiquette.

It is my impression that confirmatory dreams occur less often when the analyst deals with characterological problems in the analysis as well as with specific resistances.

When corroborative dreams occur, it is important that the therapist pick out for discussion those elements that do *not* confirm his constructions, i.e., the nonconfirmatory elements in confirmatory dreams, those that "forge ahead of the analysis." In all dreams one observes material that has not been heard before. It is therefore insufficient to accept a corroborating dream at face value without exploring all possibilities that could further the treatment. The therapist may then offer an interpretation of the new material to which the patient responds by associations and/or by a dream. The new material will then reveal to the therapist whether he is on the right track or has missed the mark.

In one instance, a patient's erotic attachment to his highly seductive, possessive mother was discussed as being a major factor in his obsessive homosexual thoughts. The following night the patient had a short dream consisting of two words: "no—sister." This dream neatly modified and corrected the analyst's constructions.

Sometimes the patient responds to an interpretation by

providing the therapist a "confirmatory dream," one that he has had recently but has not mentioned, or one that he had prior to going into therapy, as for example a dream from childhood. In these instances the confirmatory dream is in the nature of another association that truly corroborates the analyst's interpretations.

A variant of confirmatory dreams are "review dreams," "some of the manifest content of which can be readily interpreted as an assessment of the patient's progress in overcoming his difficulties" (Glover, 1955, pp. 157–158).

Freud gives another variant of what may be regarded as confirmatory or corroborative material. It concerns oedipal dreams in analysis:

> When I insist to one of my patients on the frequency of Oedipus dreams, in which the dreamer has sexual intercourse with his own mother, he often replies: 'I have no recollection of having had any such dream.' Immediately afterwards, however, a memory will emerge of some other inconspicuous and indifferent dream, which the patient has dreamt repeatedly. Analysis then shows that this is in fact a dream with the same content—once more an Oedipus dream. I can say with certainty that *disguised* dreams of sexual intercourse with the dreamer's mother are many times more frequent than straightforward ones. [1900, pp. 397–398]

In clinical practice, such dreams may occur in analysis when the patient is involved in dealing with the general theme of his oedipal feelings. Old dreams may be spontaneously recalled or the patient will have new ones which are disguised representations of the childhood wishes. At times the material may be divided so that one part of the Oedipus complex is dreamt one night, the other part another night; alternatively, there may be pairs of dreams, each part of the pair representing a part of the Oedipus complex.

In such instances the manifest content of one dream may represent a conflict situation or aggression toward an authority figure, while the other dream represents a sexual scene. Usually these dreams contain many references to the patient's defenses. It is therefore necessary to attend to the defensive resistance aspects of the material before the patient is able to deal meaningfully with his oedipal strivings.

Recovery Dreams

A variant of confirmatory or corroborative dreams are dreams of recovery. In dreams of this kind, the patient "seems to abandon the restrictions of his neurosis." Freud writes:

> We are inclined to think that he has made a great step forward, that he is ready to take his place in a new state of life, that he has begun to reckon on his recovery, etc. This may often be true, but quite as often such dreams of recovery only have the value of dreams of convenience: they signify a wish to be well at last, in order to avoid another portion of the work of analysis which is felt to lie ahead. In this sense, dreams of recovery very frequently occur, for instance, when the patient is about to enter upon a new and disagreeable phase of the transference. He is behaving in this just like some neurotics who after a few hours of analysis declare they have been cured—because they want to escape all the unpleasantness that is bound to come up for discussion in the analysis. [1923a, pp. 112–113]

Sometimes such dreams occur after analytic work has helped the patient deal with some of his symptoms, albeit not with all their complex overdeterminants. At other times they indicate a wish to be treated by another therapist, one who would not pursue the analytic investigation into dangerous areas or who would understand the patient and his problems better. The latter instance may have a transference basis or may occur when the analyst has in fact *not* picked up on certain material.

Freud indicates that recovery dreams may occur early in treatment, even before there has been any possibility of improvement. In dealing with these dreams, it is important to keep in mind the manner in which the patient is expressing his wish to be out of treatment and his reasons for it.

A homosexual patient who was referred for treatment by a judge because he had been molesting small boys had a dream in which he was in a vehicle (the treatment) with a young woman. The dream occurred very early in treatment and expressed the wish that he was heterosexual and going out with women so that he would not need treatment. This patient's dream also contained the wish that he could be heterosexual, as his homosexuality troubled him. The fact that this man could have such a dream, even though it was a defense, suggested that on a deeper level he had once attained a heterosexual position.

Dreams of recovery may refer not only to the dreamer's recovery but to that of someone else. A woman who was in analysis for a washing compulsion, who spent many hours scrubbing herself and her bathroom, dreamed that she was completely well and free from her symptoms. In the dream she told her analyst, a man who "is dressed in a long white coat, like a regular doctor," that she is well and does not need to come to see him any more. The dream expressed her wish that she was now well and did not need to deal with further material. The painful material she wished to avoid dealt with the death of her son from an acute illness a few years earlier. She had often verbalized the thought that if her son were alive (i.e., had recovered) she would not need to be in treatment. The dream element of the "regular doctor" in the long white coat referred to one of her son's physicians and her wish that she had been told that her son was well.

Termination Dreams

In their manifest content these dreams allude to the patient's thoughts of ending the therapeutic relationship and becoming independent. The metaphors used in these dreams to represent the therapy are often similar to those the patient has used previously. The difference is that now some reference to an ending is added. Thus, when the analytic process has been represented as a journey, a trip, or a voyage, the typical termination dream will indicate that the journey is coming to an end. The patient may dream, for example, of a train coming into the station, a plane coming in for a landing, or a boat coming into port. He may dream of having come through a stormy voyage and now finding himself in calm waters, or that he has reached the top of the mountain, sees a peaceful plain below him, and begins to climb down. Sometimes the metaphor is quite simple: "I dreamed I was coming out of the woods into a clearing." "I dreamed that I was reborn."

Where the analogy has been to an educational process or to professional training, the metaphors may now deal with graduation, with the completion of courses or training, with certification, with licensure and the like. In those instances where the patient's problems have dealt with instinctual control, the termination phase may be heralded by imagery dealing with the taming of wild animals, with keeping them in check or on a leash. Where there has been a problem of inhibition, the patient may now dream of being able to perform various tasks and activities freely and easily: "I dreamed I was playing golf better than I had ever played before." In another instance, a man who had suffered from premature ejaculation now dreamed of being a better lover. Sometimes changes are represented in dreams by a new car, motorcycle, etc. that drives better than the old one, by new clothing that fits better, or by the person's improved appearance.

True terminations dreams, as distinguished from so-called "recovery dreams" that express the patient's resistance to therapy, occur only after a great deal of analytic work has been accomplished. When the origins of a patient's symptoms have been accessible to genuine understanding associated with clinical improvement, the termination phase is in earnest. Sometimes termination dreams occur in response to a discussion of the patient's therapeutic achievements, when there has been a diminution of anxiety, a decrease in crippling and inhibiting effects of an overly strict superego, and a general characterological improvement. At times such dreams may occur spontaneously, announcing the patient's own awareness of the changes he has achieved. Sometimes his dreams present his feeling that he has had enough, in rather gross or crude imagery. In their manifest content the patient's dreams may deal with regurgitation, vomiting, defecation, the vomiting of fecal matter (Fenichel, 1945), or the dumping of garbage. In these dreams the patient metaphorically expresses his wish and his readiness to give up all the filth and garbage of his neurosis and/or his dissatisfaction with the therapy or the therapist. The general characteristics of dreams during the termination phase of an analysis are that they are shorter, less complicated, and easier to understand (Sharpe, 1937). Nor are they characterized, in the main, by any persistent anxiety or terror (Glover, 1940). Whatever feelings of depression or sadness emerge are not experienced with a feeling of desperation, "no exit," or "dead end."

Even when the patient's dreams clearly refer to his wish to terminate, however, one frequently finds allusions to his ambivalence to do so. The therapist must judge in every instance whether the intent of such dreams is to indicate improvement or to express the wish to flee from new and disturbing material. In a dream in which the patient reported that he was now climbing down off a steep mountain, he said, "The rest was easy. It was downhill all the way." The latter metaphor alluded, however, to the dangers and difficulties of the descent as well as to the idea of "going downhill," signifying destruction and demise. In the example of the termination dream that referred to a plane coming in on the "runway," the reference not only signified the patient's wished-for arrival to his therapeutic destination but also contained a reference to his wish to "run away."

The anticipation of termination often brings about dreams and fantasies about terminal illness and death. People who have died appear in the manifest content of the patient's dreams, and his associations lead to thoughts of long or permanent separations, expressing a fear that either he or his therapist will die. Quite often such dreams lead to the patient's profound fear of abandonment or rejection being uncovered. With these ideas there often emerges in the patient a good deal of aggression against the therapist for abandoning him, for not really curing him, for not giving him what he really wanted. Frequently dreams with a primal scene content occur at this time. (Izner, 1959).

It is sometimes quite difficult to evaluate, from a clinical standpoint, how much reliability one can place on typical termination dreams: whether one is to take the patient's expression at face value, that he is ready to terminate in the imminently near future, or that the dream is to be regarded as a wish referable to the distant future.

Some termination dreams clearly indicate the work ahead. One patient dreamed that he had gone to the National Archives in Washington, D.C., to look at the Declaration of Independence. After telling the dream, which he immediately recognized as having to do with his readiness to become independent and to free himself from his parents and his analyst, he then added, "After that came the Revolutionary War." Thus he recognized that his battle for independence had still to be fought.

In practice, since the process of working through termination brings up many issues which must be dealt with, there is ample opportunity to ascertain the status of the patient's progress. There is therefore no need to base any definitive assessment of the patient's readiness to terminate on a single dream or even a group of dreams. Therapist and patient can together evaluate whether the patient is really ready to give up the therapeutic relationship or whether there are unresolved dependency needs or other problems that have yet to be settled.

In one instance a patient dreamed that he wanted to get off at an exit on a limited access highway, but as he started to get off, he got stuck on the shoulder and could not move.

The patient was very ambivalent about termination; when he considered it seriously, he found that he was stuck and could not bring himself to leave (exit). For him leaving meant being on his own, and this was very frightening to him.

Another patient, by contrast, approached the last session of his highly successful analysis by dreaming that he was in heaven looking at a clock, the hands of which pointed to seven o'clock. He knew he was in Seventh Heaven.

Bibliography

Abel, K. (1884), *Uber den Gegensinn der Urworte*. Leipzig.

Abraham, K. (1907), The experiencing of sexual traumas as a form of sexual activity. In: *Selected Papers of Karl Abraham, M.D.* London: Hogarth Press, 1927, pp. 47–63.

———— (1909), Dreams and myths: A study in folk-psychology. In: *Clinical Papers and Essays on Psycho-Analysis*, ed. H. Abraham. New York: Brünner/Mazel, 1955, pp. 153–209.

———— (1911), Giovanni Segantini: A psycho-analytic study. In: *Clinical Papers and Essays on Psycho-Analysis*, ed. H. Abraham. New York: Brunner/Mazel, 1955, pp. 210–261.

———— (1913), Should patients write down their dreams? In: *The Psychoanalytic Reader*, ed. R. Fliess. New York: International Universities Press, 1948, pp. 326–328.

———— (1920), The cultural significance of psycho-analysis. In: *Clinical Papers and Essays on Psycho-Analysis*, ed. H. Abraham. New York: Brunner/Mazel, 1979, pp. 116–136.

———— (1921), Contributions to the theory of the anal character. In: *Selected Papers of Karl Abraham, M.D.* London: Hogarth Press, 1927, pp. 370–392.

———— (1922), The spider as a dream symbol. In: *Selected Papers of Karl Abraham, M.D.* London: Hogarth Press, 1927, pp. 326–332.

Adelson, J. (1960), Creativity and the dream. *Merill-Palmer Quart.*, 6:92–97.

Alexander, F. (1925), Dreams in pairs. In: *The Psychoanalytic Reader*, ed. R. Fliess. New York: International Universities Press, 1948, pp. 371–377.

———— (1930), About dreams with unpleasant content. In: *The Scope of Psychoanalysis: Selected Papers of Franz Alexander, 1921–1961*. New York: Basic Books, 1961, pp. 50–55.

———— (1941), The voice of the intellect is soft. . . . In: *The Scope of Psychoanalysis: Selected Papers of Franz Alexander, 1921–1961*. New York: Basic Books, 1961, pp. 244–260.

Altman, L.L. (1959), West as a symbol of death. *Psychoanal. Quart.*, 28:236–241.

——— (1969), *The Dream in Psychoanalysis*. New York: International Universities Press.

Arlow, J.A. (1951), A psychoanalytic study of a religious initiation rite: Bar mitzvah. *The Psychoanalytic Study of the Child*, 6:353–374. New York: International Universities Press.

——— (1955), Notes on oral symbolism. *Psychoanal. Quart.*, 24:1–63.

——— (1961a), Ego psychology and the study of mythology. *J. Amer. Psychoanal. Assn.*, 9:371–393.

——— (1961b), A typical dream. *J. Hillside Hosp.*, 10:54–58.

——— & Brenner, C. (1964), Psychoanalytic Concepts and the Structural Theory. *J. Amer. Psychoanal. Assn.*, Monogr. 3. New York: International Universities Press.

Babcock, C. (1966), Reporter: Panel on "manifest content of the dream." *J. Amer. Psychoanal. Assn.*, 14:154–171.

Bach, R. (1970), *Jonathan Livingston Seagull*. New York: Macmillan.

Barchilon, J. (1973), Pleasure, mockery and creative integrations: Their relationship to childhood knowledge, a learning defect and the literature of the absurd. *Internat. J. Psycho-Anal.*, 54:19–34.

Bartemeier, L.H. (1941a), A counting compulsion: A contribution to the unconscious meaning of time. *Internat. J. Psycho-Anal.*, 22:301–309.

——— (1941b), Micropsia. *Psychoanal. Quart.*, 10:573–582.

——— (1950), Illness following dreams. *Internat. J. Psycho-Anal.*, 31:8–11.

Beck, A.T., & Ward, C.H. (1961), Dreams of depressed patients. *Arch. Gen. Psychiat.*, 5:462–467.

Beck, D.H. (1977), Dream analysis in family therapy. *Clin. Soc. Work J.*, 5:53–57.

Bell, A.I. (1961), Some observations on the role of the scrotal sac and testicles. *J. Amer. Psychoanal. Assn.*, 9:261–286.

——— (1965), The significance of scrotal sac and testicles for the prepuberty male. *Psychoanal. Quart.*, 34:182–206.

Benedek, T., & Rubenstein, B. (1939), The correlations between ovarian activity and psychodynamic processes: I. The ovulative phase; II. The menstrual phase. *Psychosom. Med.*, 1: 245–270; 461–485.

Bergler, E. (1943), A third function of the "day residue" in dreams. In: *Selected Papers of Edmund Bergler, M.D.: 1931–1961*. New York: Grune & Stratton, 1969, pp. 81–93.

Bergmann, M.S. (1966), The intrapsychic and communicative aspects of the dream. *Internat. J. Psycho-Anal.*, 47:356–363.

Bernstein, I., & Fine, B.C. (1969), The Manifest Content of the Dream. *Kris Study Group Monogr.* 3, New York: International Universities Press, pp. 59–113.

Bibliography

Blank, H.R. (1958), Dreams of the blind. *Psychoanal. Quart.*, 27:158–174.

Blaustein, A.B. (1975), A dream resembling the Isakower phenomenon: A brief clinical contribution. *Internat. J. Psycho-Anal.*, 56:207–208.

Blitzsten, N.L., Eissler, R.S., & Eissler, K.R. (1950), Emergence of hidden ego tendencies during dream analysis. *Internat. J. Psycho-Anal.*, 31:12–17.

Blum, H.P. (1968), Notes on the written dream. *J. Hillside Hosp.*, 17:67–78.

——— (1973), The concept of erotized transference. *J. Amer. Psychoanal. Assn.*, 21:61–76.

——— (1976), The changing use of dreams in psychoanalytic practice. *Internat. J. Psycho-Anal.*, 57:315–324.

Bond, D.D. (1952), *The Love and the Fear of Flying*. New York: International Universities Press.

Bonime, W., & Bonime, F. (1962), *The Clinical Use of Dreams*. New York: Basic Books.

——— (1980), The dream in the depressive personality. In: *The Dream in Clinical Practice*, ed. J.M. Natterson. New York: Jason Aronson, pp. 131–147.

Bourke, J.G. (1891), *Scatologic Rites of All Nations*. New York: American Anthropological Society, 1934.

Bradlow, P.A. (1971), Murder in the initial dream in psychoanalysis. *Bull. Phila. Assn. Psychoanal.*, 21:70–81.

——— (1973), On reporting an initial dream in psychoanalysis of undisguised sexual activity between family members. Abs. *Bull. Assn. Psychoanal. Med. N.Y.*, 12:18–22.

——— & Coen, S.J. (1975), The analyst undisguised in the initial dream in psychoanalysis. *Internat. J. Psycho-Anal.*, 56:415–425.

Breger, L. (1967), Function of dreams. *J. Abnorm. Psychol.*, Monogr. 641, 72(Suppl.):1–28.

——— (1980), The manifest dream and its latent meaning. In: *The Dream in Clinical Practice*, ed. J.M. Natterson. New York: Jason Aronson, pp. 3–27.

Brenneis, C.B. (1970), Male and female ego modalities in manifest dream content. *J. Abnorm. Psychol.*, 76:434–442.

——— (1975), Theoretical notes on the manifest dream. *Internat. J. Psycho-Anal.*, 56:197–206.

——— & Ross, S. (1975), Ego modalities in the manifest dreams of male and female Chicanos. *Psychiatry*, 38(2): 172–185.

Brenner, C. (1969), Dreams in clinical psychoanalytic practice. *J. Nerv. Ment. Dis.*, 149:122–132.

——— (1976), *Psychoanalytic Technique and Psychic Conflict*. New York: International Universities Press.

Breuer, J., & Freud, S. (1893–1895), Studies on Hysteria. *Standard Edition*, 2. London: Hogarth Press, 1955.

Broughton, R.J. (1968), Sleep disorders: Disorders of arousal. *Science*, 159:1070–1078.

———— (1970), The incubus attack. In: *Sleep and Dreaming*, ed. E. Hartmann. Boston: Little, Brown, pp. 188–192.

Calef, V. (1954), Color in dreams. *J. Amer. Psychoanal. Assn.*, 2: 453–461.

Cavenar, J.O., Jr., & Nash, M.L. (1976), The dream as a signal for termination. *J. Amer. Psychoanal. Assn.*, 24:425–436.

Colby, K.M. (1951), *A Primer for Psychotherapists*. New York: Ronald Press.

Coriat, H.I. (1913), Zwei sexualsymbolische Beispiele von Zahnarzttraumen. *Zbl. Psychoan.*, 3:440.

Curtis, H.C., & Sachs, D.M. (1976), Dialogue on "The changing use of dreams in psychoanalytic practice." *Internat. J. Psycho-Anal.*, 57:343–354.

Darlington, H.S. (1942), The tooth-losing dream. *Psychoanal. Rev.*, 12: 71–79.

———— (1944), The fear of false teeth. *Psychoanal. Rev.* 31:181–194.

DeMartino, M., ed. (1959), *Dreams and Personality Dynamics*. Springfield, Ill.: Charles C Thomas.

Dement, W.C., & Fisher, C. (1960a), The effect of dream deprivation and excess: An experimental demonstration of the necessity for dreaming. Read at New York Psychoanalytic Society, March 1960. Abs. *Psychoanal. Quart.*, 29:607–608.

———— (1960b), Studies in dream deprivation and satiation: An experimental demonstration of the necessity for dreaming. Read at Philadelphia Association for Psychoanalysis, January 1960. Abs. *Bull. Phila. Assn. Psychoanal.*, 10:30–33.

De Saussure, J. (1971), Some complications in self-esteem regulation caused by using an archaic image of the self as an ideal. *Internat. J. Psycho-Anal.*, 52:87–97.

Dunbar, H.F. (1947), *Mind and Body: Psychosomatic Medicine*. New York: Random House.

———— (1954), *Emotions and Bodily Changes: A Survey of Literature on Psychosomatic Interrelationships, 1910–1953*. 4th ed. New York: Columbia University Press.

Eder, M.D. (1930), Dreams as resistance. *Internat. J. Psycho-Anal.*, 11:40–47.

Bibliography

Edward, J. (1978), The use of dreams in the promotion of ego development. *Clin. Soc. Work J.*, 6:261–273.

Eggan, D. (1952), The manifest content of dreams. *Amer. Anthropol.*, 54:469–484.

Eisenbud, J. (1965), The hand and the breast with special reference to obsessional neurosis. *Psychoanal. Quart.*, 34:219–248.

Eisenstein, S. (1980), The dream in psychoanalysis. In: *The Dream in Clinical Practice*, ed. J.M. Natterson. New York: Jason Aronson, pp. 319–331.

Eisenstein, V. W. (1949), Dreams after intercourse. *Psychoanal. Quart.*, 18:154–172.

Eisnitz, A.J. (1961), Mirror dreams. *J. Amer. Psychoanal. Assn.*, 19:461–479.

———— (1980), The organization of the self-representation and its influence on pathology. *Psychoanal. Quart.*, 49:361–392.

Eissler, K. (1958), Notes on the problems of technique in the psychoanalytic treatment of adolescents: With some remarks on perversion. *The Psychoanalytic Study of the Child*, 13:223–254. New York: International Universities Press.

Erikson, E. (1954), The dream specimen of psychoanalysis. *J. Amer. Psychoanal. Assn.*, 2:5–56.

———— (1964), Inner and outer space: Reflections on womanhood. *Daedalus*, 93:582–606.

Faraday, A. (1972), *Dream Power*. New York: Coward.

Federn, P. (1913), Beispiel von Libidoverschiebung wahrend der Kur. *Internat. Z. arztliche Psychoanal.*, 1: 303–306.

———— (1914), The infantile roots of masochism. *N.Y. Med. J.*, 100:351–355.

———— (1922), Scheme der Libidoaufname zur Begutachtung und Indikationsstellung. Abs. *Internat. Z. Psychoanal.*, 8:486–487.

Feldman, S. (1945), Interpretation of a typical and stereotyped dream met with only during psychoanalysis. *Psychoanal. Quart.*, 14:511–515.

Fenichel, O. (1927), Examples of dream analysis. In: *The Collected Papers of Otto Fenichel: Series One*, ed. H. Fenichel & D. Rapaport. New York: Norton, 1953, pp. 123–127.

———— (1928), Some infantile sexual theories not hitherto described. *Internat. J. Psycho-Anal.*, 9:346–352.

———— (1929), Analysis of a dream. In: *The Collected Papers of Otto Fenichel: Series One*, ed. H. Fenichel & D. Rapaport. New York: Norton, 1953, pp. 160–166.

———— (1945), *The Psychoanalytic Theory of Neurosis*. New York: Norton.

Ferenczi, S. (1912a), Dirigible dreams. In: *Final Contributions to the*

283

Problems and Methods of Psycho-Analysis, ed. M. Balint. New York: Basic Books, 1955, pp. 313–315.

——— (1912b), To whom does one relate one's dreams? In: *Further Contributions to the Theory and Technique of Psycho-Analysis.* New York: Boni & Liveright, 1927, p. 349.

——— (1913), The kite as a symbol of erection. In: *Further Contributions to the Theory and Techniques of Psycho-Analysis.* New York: Boni & Liveright, 1927, pp. 359–360.

——— (1915), Two typical faecal and anal symbols. In: *Further Contributions to the Theory and Technique of Psycho-Analysis.* New York: Boni & Liveright, 1927, pp. 327–328.

——— (1916), *Sex in Psycho-Analysis.* Boston: Gorham Press.

——— (1921), The symbolism of the bridge. In: *Further Contributions to the Theory and Technique of Psycho-Analysis.* New York: Boni & Liveright, 1927, pp. 352–356.

——— (1922), Bridge symbolism and the Don Juan legend. In: *Further Contributions to the Theory and Technique of Psycho-Analysis.* New York: Boni & Liveright, 1927, pp. 356–358.

——— (1923a), The dream of the 'clever baby'. In: *Further Contributions to the Theory and Technique of Psycho-Analysis.* New York: Boni & Liveright, 1927, p. 349.

——— (1923b), On the symbolism of the head of Medusa. In: *Further Contributions to the Theory and Technique of Psycho-Analysis.* New York: Boni & Liveright, 1927, p. 360.

——— (1926), Gulliver fantasies. In: *Final Contributions to the Problems and Methods of Psycho-Analysis,* ed. M. Balint. New York: Basic Books, 1955, pp. 41–60.

——— (1930), Notes and fragments. In: *Final Contributions to the Problems and Methods of Psycho-Analysis,* ed. M. Balint. New York: Basic Books, 1955, p. 219–231.

Fine, B. (1969), The Manifest Content of the Dream. *Kris Study Group Monogr.* 3. New York: International Universities Press.

Fisher, C. (1964), A cycle of penile erection synchronous with dreaming sleep. Abs. *Psychoanal. Quart.,* 33:614–617.

——— (1974), A psychophysiological study of nightmares and night terrors: II. Mental content and recall of stage 4 night terrors. *J. Nerv. Ment. Dis.,* 158:174–188.

Fleming, J. (1972), Early object deprivation and transference phenomena: The working alliance. *Psychoanal. Quart.,* 41:23–49.

Fliess, R. (1953), *The Revival of Interest in the Dream: A Critical Study of Post-Freudian Psychoanalytic Contributions.* New York: International Universities Press.

Bibliography

Foulkes, D. (1978), *A Grammar of Dreams*. New York: Basic Books.

Foulkes, D., Larson, J., Swanson, E., & Rardin, M. (1969), Two studies of childhood dreaming. *Amer. J. Orthopsychiat.*, 39:627–643.

French, T.M. (1937), Reality testing in dreams. *Psychoanal. Quart.*, 6:62–77.

—— (1958), The art and science of psychoanalysis. *J. Amer. Psychoanal. Assn.*, 6:197–214.

—— & Fromm, E. (1964), *Dream Interpretation: A New Approach*. New York: Basic Books.

Freud, S. (1899), Screen memories. *Standard Edition*, 3:303–322. London: Hogarth Press, 1962.

—— (1900), The Interpretation of Dreams. *Standard Edition*, 4 & 5. London: Hogarth Press, 1953.

—— (1901a), On dreams. *Standard Edition*, 5:633–686. London: Hogarth Press, 1953.

—— (1901b), The Psychopathology of Everyday Life. *Standard Edition*, 6. London: Hogarth Press, 1960.

—— (1905a[1901]), Fragment of an analysis of a case of hysteria. *Standard Edition*, 7:7–122. London: Hogarth Press, 1953.

—— (1905b), Jokes and Their Relation to the Unconscious. *Standard Edition*, 8. London: Hogarth Press, 1960.

—— (1906), Psycho-analysis and the establishment of the facts in legal proceedings. *Standard Edition*, 9:103–114. London: Hogarth Press, 1959.

—— (1907[1906]), Delusions and dreams in Jensen's *Gradiva*. *Standard Edition*, 9:7–95. London: Hogarth Press, 1959.

—— (1909a), Analysis of a phobia in a five-year-old boy. *Standard Edition*, 10:5–149. London: Hogarth Press, 1955.

—— (1909b), Notes upon a case of obsessional neurosis. *Standard Edition*, 10:155–318. London: Hogarth Press, 1955.

—— (1910a), The antithetical meaning of primal words. *Standard Edition*, 11:155–161. London: Hogarth Press, 1957.

—— (1910b), The future prospects of psycho-analytic therapy. *Standard Edition*, 11:141–151. London: Hogarth Press, 1957.

—— (1910c), Leonardo da Vinci and a memory of his childhood. *Standard Edition*, 11:63–137. London: Hogarth Press, 1957.

—— (1910d), A special type of choice of object made by men (Contributions to the psychology of love I). *Standard Edition*, 11:165–175. London: Hogarth Press, 1957.

—— (1911), The handling of dream interpretation in psycho-analysis. *Standard Edition*, 12:91–96. London: Hogarth Press, 1958.

—— (1913a), An evidential dream. *Standard Edition*, 12:269–277. London: Hogarth Press, 1958.

———— (1913b), Observations and examples from analytic practice. *Standard Edition*, 13:193–198. London: Hogarth Press, 1955.

———— (1913c), The occurrence in dreams of material from fairy tales. *Standard Edition*, 12:281–287. London: Hogarth Press, 1958.

———— (1913d), The theme of the three caskets. *Standard Edition*, 12:291–301. London: Hogarth Press, 1958.

———— (1914), Remembering, repeating and working-through (Further recommendations on the technique of psycho-analysis II). *Standard Edition*, 12:147–156. London: Hogarth Press, 1958.

———— (1915a), A case of paranoia running counter to the psycho-analytic theory of the disease. *Standard Edition*, 14:263–272. London: Hogarth Press, 1957.

———— (1915b), Thoughts for the times on war and death. *Standard Edition*, 14:275–300. London: Hogarth Press, 1957.

———— (1916), A connection between a symbol and a symptom. *Standard Edition*, 14:339–340. London: Hogarth Press, 1957.

———— (1916–1917[1915–1917]), Introductory Lectures on Psycho-Analysis: Part I, "Parapraxes," (1916[1915]); Part II, "Dreams" (1916[1915–1916]), *Standard Edition*, 15. Part III, "General Theory of the Neuroses," (1917[1916–1917]), *Standard Edition*, 16. London: Hogarth Press, 1963.

———— (1917a), A childhood recollection from *Dichtung und Wahrheit*. *Standard Edition*, 17:147–156. London: Hogarth Press, 1955.

———— (1917b[1915]), A metapsychological supplement to the theory of dreams. *Standard Edition*, 14:222–235. London: Hogarth Press, 1957.

———— (1917c), On transformations of instinct as exemplified in anal erotism. *Standard Edition*, 17:127–133. London: Hogarth Press, 1955.

———— (1918[1914]), From a history of infantile neurosis. *Standard Edition*, 17:7–122. London: Hogarth Press, 1955.

———— (1919a), 'A child is being beaten': A contribution to the study of the origin of sexual perversions. *Standard Edition*, 17:179–204. London: Hogarth Press, 1955.

———— (1919b), The 'uncanny'. *Standard Edition*, 17:219–252. London: Hogarth Press, 1955.

———— (1920a), Beyond the pleasure principle. *Standard Edition*, 18:7–64. London: Hogarth Press, 1955.

———— (1920b), The psychogenesis of a case of homosexuality in a woman. *Standard Edition*, 18:147–182. London: Hogarth Press, 1955.

———— (1921), Group psychology and the analysis of the ego. *Standard Edition*, 18:68–143. London: Hogarth Press, 1955.

———— (1922a), Dreams and telepathy. *Standard Edition*, 18:197–220. London: Hogarth Press, 1955.

Bibliography

—— (1922b), Some neurotic mechanisms in jealousy, paranoia and homosexuality. *Standard Edition,* 18:223–232. London: Hogarth Press, 1955.

—— (1923a[1922]), Remarks on the theory and practice of dream-interpretation. *Standard Edition,* 19:109–121. London: Hogarth Press, 1961.

—— (1923b[1921]), A seventeenth century demonological neurosis. *Standard Edition,* 19:72–105. London: Hogarth Press, 1961.

—— (1925a), Negation. *Standard Edition,* 19:235–239. London: Hogarth Press, 1961.

—— (1925b), Some additional notes on dream-interpretation as a whole. *Standard Edition,* 19:127–138. London: Hogarth Press, 1961.

—— (1926[1925]), Inhibitions, Symptoms and Anxiety. *Standard Edition,* 20:87–172. London: Hogarth Press, 1959.

—— (1929), Some dreams of Descartes': A letter to Maxime Leroy. *Standard Edition,* 21:203–204. London: Hogarth Press, 1961.

—— (1932), The acquisition and control of fire. *Standard Edition,* 22:187–193. London: Hogarth Press, 1964.

—— (1933[1932]), New Introductory Lectures on Psycho-Analysis. *Standard Edition,* 22:5–183. London: Hogarth Press, 1964.

—— & Oppenheim, D. E. (1911), Dreams in folklore. *Standard Edition,* 12:180–203. London: Hogarth Press, 1958.

Friedman, P. (1952), The bridge: A study in symbolism. *Psychoanal. Quart.,* 21:49–80.

Friedmann, C.T.H. (1980), Nightmares. In: *The Dream in Clinical Practice,* ed. J.M. Natterson. New York: Jason Aronson, pp. 301–315.

Fromm-Reichmann, F. (1950), *Principles of Intensive Psychotherapy.* Chicago: University of Chicago Press.

Frosch, J. (1967), Severe regressive states during analysis. *J. Amer. Psychoanal. Assn.,* 15:491–507;606–625.

—— (1969), Reporter: Panel on "Dreams and psychosis." *J. Amer. Psychoanal. Assn.,* 17:206–221.

Furman, E. (1974), *A Child's Parent Dies: Studies in Childhood Bereavement.* New Haven: Yale University Press.

Garma, A. (1966), *The Psychoanalysis of Dreams.* Chicago: Quadrangle.

Gedo, J.E. (1975), Forms of idealization in the analytic transference. *J. Amer. Psychoanal. Assn.,* 23:485–505.

—— (1977), Notes on the psychoanalytic management of archaic transferences. *J. Amer. Psychoanal. Assn.,* 25:787–803.

—— (1980), The dream in regressed states. In: *The Dream in Clinical Practice,* ed. J.M. Natterson. New York: Jason Aronson, pp. 193–207.

Gill, M.M. (1963), Topography and systems in psychoanalytic theory. *Psychol. Issues*, 3(2), monogr. 10.

Gillman, R.D. (1980), Dreams in which the analyst appears as himself. In: *The Dream in Clinical Practice*, ed. J.M. Natterson. New York: Jason Aronson, pp. 29–44.

Giovacchini, P.L. (1966), Dreams and the creative process. *Brit. J. Med. Psychol.*, 39:105–115.

Gitelson, M. (1952), The emotional position of the analyst in the psychoanalytic situation. *Internat. J. Psycho-Anal.*, 33:1–10.

Glover, E. (1939), *Psycho-Analysis: A Handbook for Medical Practitioners and Students of Comparative Psychology*. London: Staples Press, 1949.

——— (1940), *An Investigation of the Technique of Psycho-Analysis*, ed. E. Glover & M. Brierley. London: Bailliere, Tindall & Cox.

——— (1955). *The Technique of Psycho-Analysis*. New York: International Universities Press.

Gold, V. (1973), Dreams in group therapy: A review of the literature. *Internat. J. Group Psychother.*, 23:394–407.

Goldberg, E.L., et al., eds. (1956), *The Boundaries of Casework*. London: Association of Psychiatric Social Workers.

Greenacre, P. (1950), General problems of acting out. *Psychoanal. Quart.*, 19:455–467.

Greenberg, R., & Pearlman, C. (1978), If Freud only knew: A reconstruction of psychoanalytic dream theory. *Internat. J. Psycho-Anal.*, 5:71–75.

——— ——— (1980), The private language of the dream. In: *The Dream in Clinical Practice*, ed. J.M. Natterson. New York: Jason Aronson, pp. 85–96.

Greenson, R.R. (1959), Phobia, anxiety and depression. *J. Amer. Psychoanal. Assn.*, 7:668–674.

——— (1967), *The Technique and Practice of Psychoanalysis*, Vol. I. New York: International Universities Press.

——— (1970), The exceptional position of the dream in psychoanalytic practice. *Psychoanal. Quart.*, 39:519–549.

Grinberg, L. (1962), On a specific aspect of counter-transference due to the patient's projective identification. *Internat. J. Psycho-Anal.*, 43:436–440.

Grinstein, A. (1951), Stages in the development of control over fire. *Internat. J. Psycho-Anal.*, 33:416–420.

——— (1954), The convertible as a symbol in dreams. *J. Amer. Psychoanal. Assn.*, 2:466–472.

——— (1962), Some comments on breast envy in women. *J. Hillside Hosp.*, 11:171–177.

Bibliography

———— (1980), *Sigmund Freud's Dreams*. New York: International Universities Press.

Grotjahn, M. (1945), Laughter in dreams. *Psychoanal. Quart.*, 14:221–227.

———— (1972), *The Voice of the Symbol*. Los Angeles: Mara Books.

———— (1977), *The Art and Technique of Analytic Group Therapy*. New York: Jason Aronson.

———— (1980), The dream in analytic group therapy. In: *The Dream in Clinical Practice*, ed. J.M. Natterson. New York: Jason Aronson, pp. 427–434.

Gutheil, E.A. (1939), *The Language of the Dream*. New York: Macmillan.

———— (1948), Dreams and suicide. *Amer. J. Psychotherapy*, 2:283–294.

———— (1951), *The Handbook of Dream Analysis*. New York: Liveright.

Hall, C.S. (1947), Diagnosing personality by the analysis of dreams. In: *Dreams and Personality Dynamics*, ed. M.F. DeMartino. Springfield, Ill.: Charles C Thomas, 1959.

———— (1951), What people dream about. In: *Dreams and Personality Dynamics*, ed. M.F. DeMartino. Springfield, Ill.: Charles C Thomas, 1959.

———— (1953), *The Meaning of Dreams*. New York: Harper & Row.

———— (1963), Strangers in the dream. *J. Personality*, 31:335–345.

———— (1964), A modest confirmation of Freud's theory of a distinction between the superego of men and women. *J. Abnorm. Soc. Psychol.*, 69:440–442.

———— & Van de Castle, R.L., (1966), *The Content Analysis of Dreams*. New York: Appleton-Century-Crofts.

Harris, I.D. (1960), Typical anxiety dreams and object relations. *Internat. J. Psycho-Anal.*, 41:604–611.

———— (1962), Dreams about the analyst. *Internat. J. Psycho-Anal.*, 43:151–158.

Hart-Davis, R., ed. (1962), *The Letters of Oscar Wilde*. New York: Harcourt, Brace & World.

Hartmann, E. (1976), Discussion of 'The changing use of dreams in psychoanalytic practice': The dream as a 'royal road' to the biology of the mental apparatus. *Internat. J. Psycho-Anal.*, 57:331–334.

Hauri, P. (1975), Dream content in patients remitted from neurotic depression. *Sleep Research*, 4:185.

Hendrick, I. (1958), Dream resistance and schizophrenia. *J. Amer. Psychoanal. Assn.*, 6:672–690.

Howard, S. (1927), *Silver Cord: A Comedy in 3 Acts*. New York: Scribner (Theatre Guild Library).

Isakower, O. (1938), On the pathopsychology of falling asleep. *Internat. J. Psycho-Anal.*, 19:331–345.

——— (1954), Spoken words in dreams. *Psychoanal. Quart.*, 23:1–6.

Izner, S. (1959), On the appearance of primal scene content in dreams. *J. Amer. Psychoanal. Assn.*, 7:317–328.

Jones, E. (1910), On the nightmare. *Amer. J. Insanity*, 66:383–417.

—— (1911), The Relationship between dreams and psychoneurotic symptoms. In: *Papers on Psycho-Analysis*. 5th ed. Baltimore: Williams & Wilkins, 1948, pp. 251–272.

——— (1914), Zahnziehen und Geburt. *Internat. Z. Psychoanal.*, 2:380–381.

——— (1916), The theory of symbolism. In: *Papers on Psycho-Analysis*. 5th ed. Baltimore: Williams & Wilkins, 1948, pp. 87–144.

——— (1923), *Essays in Applied Psycho-Analysis*. London/Vienna: International Psycho-Analytical Press.

——— (1927), The mantle symbol. *Internat. J. Psycho-Anal.*, 8:63–65.

Jones, R.M. (1962), *Ego Synthesis in Dreams*. Cambridge, Mass.: Schenkman.

——— (1965), Dream interpretation and the psychology of dreaming. *J. Amer. Psychoanal. Assn.*, 13:304–319.

——— (1969), An epigenetic analysis of dreams. In: *Dream Psychology and the New Biology of Dreaming*, ed. M. Kramer. Springfield, Ill.: Charles C Thomas.

——— (1970), *The New Psychology of Dreaming*. New York: Grune & Stratton.

Jong, E. (1973), *Fear of Flying*. New York: Holt, Rinehart & Winston.

Jung, C. (1911), On the significance of number dreams. In: *Collected Papers on Analytical Psychology*, ed. C. Long. New York: Moffat, Yard, 1917, pp. 191–199.

Kafka, J.S. (1980), The dream in schizophrenia. In: *The Dream in Clinical Practice*, ed. J.M. Natterson. New York: Jason Aronson, pp. 99–100.

Kant, O. (1942), Technique of dream analysis. In: *Dreams and Personality Dynamics*, ed. M.F. DeMartino. Springfield, Ill.: Charles C Thomas, 1959.

Kanzer, M. (1955), The communicative function of the dream. *Internat. J. Psycho-Anal.*, 36:260–266.

——— (1958), Image formation during free association. *Psychoanal. Quart.*, 27:465–484.

Kardiner, A. (1932), The bio-analysis of the epileptic reaction. *Psychoanal. Quart.*, 1:375–483.

Bibliography

Katan, M. (1960), Dreams and psychosis. *Internat. J. Psycho-Anal.*, 41:341–351.

Kavka, J. (1979), On examination dreams. *Psychoanal. Quart.*, 48:426–427.

Kelman, H. (1975), The 'day precipitate' of dreams: The Morris hypothesis. *Internat. J. Psycho-Anal.*, 56:209–281.

Kepecs, J.G. (1952), A waking screen analogous to the dream screen. *Psychoanal. Quart.*, 21:167–171.

Kernberg, O. (1975), *Borderline Conditions and Pathological Narcissism*. New York: Jason Aronson.

——— (1976), Technical considerations in the treatment of borderline personality organization. *J. Amer. Psychoanal. Assn.*, 24:795–830.

Kestenberg, J.L. (1968), Outside and inside, male and female. *J. Amer. Psychoanal. Assn.*, 16:457–520.

——— (1975), *Children and Parents: Psychoanalytic Studies in Development*. New York: Jason Aronson.

Khan, M.M.R. (1962), Dream psychology and the evolution of the psychoanalytic situation. *Internat. J. Psycho-Anal.*, 43:21–31.

——— (1974), *The Privacy of the Self*. London: Hogarth Press.

——— (1976), The changing use of dreams in psychoanalytic practice: In search of the dreaming experience. *Internat. J. Psycho-Anal.*, 57:325.

King, P. (1975–1976), The dream as dream stimulus. *Psychoanal. Rev.*, 62:659–661.

Klauber, J. (1967), On the significance of reporting dreams in psychoanalysis. *Internat. J. Psycho-Anal.*, 48:424–432.

Klein, M. (1923), The role of the school in the libidinal development of the child. In: *Contributions to Psycho-Analysis 1921–1945*. London: Hogarth Press & The Institute of Psycho-Analysis. 1948, pp. 68–86.

Kline, F.M. (1980), The dream in the treatment of the disadvantaged. In: *The Dream in Clinical Practice*, ed. J.M. Natterson. New York: Jason Aronson, pp. 259–270.

Knapp, P.H. (1956), Sensory impressions in dreams. *Psychoanal. Quart.*, 25:325–347.

Kohut, H. (1971), *The Analysis of the Self: A Systematic Approach to the Psychoanalytic Treatment of Narcissistic Personality Disorders*. New York: International Universities Press.

——— (1977), *The Restoration of the Self*. New York: International Universities Press.

——— (1979), Two analyses of Mr. Z. *Internat. J. Psycho-Anal.*, 60:2–27.

Kramer, M. (1969), Manifest dream content in psychopathologic states. In: *Dream Psychology and the New Biology of Dreaming*, ed. M. Kramer. Springfield, Ill.: Charles C Thomas.

——— Baldridge, B., Whitman, R., Ornstein, P., & Smith, P. (1969),

An exploration of the manifest dream in schizophrenia and depressed patients. *Diseases of the Nervous System,* 30:126–140.

———— Whitman, R.M., Ornstein, P.H., & Baldridge, B.J., eds. (1969), *Dream Psychology and the New Biology of Dreaming.* Springfield, Ill.: Charles C Thomas.

———— & Roth, T. (1973), A comparison of dream content in laboratory dream reports of schizophrenic and depressive patient groups. *Comprehensive Psychiatry,* 14:325–329.

Kris, E. (1954), New contributions to the study of Freud's *Interpretation of Dreams. J. Amer. Psychoanal. Assn.,* 2:180–191.

———— (1956), On some vicissitudes of insight in psycho-analysis. *Internat. J. Psycho-Anal.,* 37:445–455.

———— (1975), *Selected Papers of Ernst Kris,* ed. L.M. Newman. New Haven: Yale University Press.

Langs, R.J. (1966), Manifest dreams from three clinical groups. *Archiv. Gen. Psychiat.,* 14:634–643.

———— (1971), Day residues, recall residues and dreams: Reality and the psyche. *J. Amer. Psychoanal. Assn.,* 19:499–523.

———— (1973–1974), *The Technique of Psychoanalytic Psychotherapy,* 2 vols. New York: Jason Aronson.

———— (1980), The dream in psychotherapy. In: *The Dream in Clinical Practice,* ed. J.M. Natterson. New York: Jason Aronson, pp. 333–368.

Lebe, D. (1980), The dream in acting out disturbances. In: *The Dream in Clinical Practice,* ed. J.M. Natterson. New York: Jason Aronson, pp. 209–223.

Leveton, A.F. (1961), The night residue. *Internat. J. Psycho-Anal.,* 42:506–516.

Levitan, H. (1967), Depersonalization and the dream. *Psychoanal. Quart.,* 36:157–171.

———— (1972), Dreams preceding hypomania. *Internat. J. Psychoanal. Psychother.,* 1:50–61.

———— (1974), The dream of a phobic patient. *Internat. Rev. Psycho-Anal.,* 1:313–323.

———— (1976–1977), The significance of certain catastrophic dreams. *Psychotherapy and Psychosomatics,* 27:1–7.

———— (1980a), The dream in psychosomatic states. In: *The Dream in Clinical Practice,* ed: J.M. Natterson. New York: Jason Aronson, pp. 225–236.

———— (1980b), The dream in traumatic states. In: *The Dream in Clinical Practice,* ed. J.M. Natterson. New York: Jason Aronson, pp. 271–281.

Lewin, B.D. (1946), Sleep, the mouth and the dream screen. *Psychoanal. Quart.,* 15:419–434.

Bibliography

—— (1948a), Inferences from the dream screen. *Internat. J. Psycho-Anal.*, 29:224–231.

—— (1948b). The nature of reality, the meaning of nothing, with an addendum on concentration. *Psychoanal. Quart.*, 17:524–526.

—— (1949), Mania and sleep. *Psychoanal. Quart.*, 18:419–433.

—— (1950), *The Psychoanalysis of Elation*. New York: Norton.

—— (1952), Phobic symptoms and dream interpretation. *Psychoanal. Quart.*, 21:295–322.

—— (1953a), The forgetting of dreams. In: *Drives, Affects, Behavior*, vol. 1, ed. R.M. Loewenstein. New York: International Universities Press, pp. 191–202.

—— (1953b), Reconsiderations of the dream screen. *Psychoanal. Quart.*, 22:174–199.

—— (1954), Sleep, narcissistic neurosis and the analytic situation. *Psychoanal. Quart.*, 23:487–510.

—— (1955a), Clinical hints from dream studies. *Bull. Menninger Clin.*, 19:78–85.

—— (1955b), Dream psychology and the analytic situation. *Psychoanal. Quart.*, 24:163–199.

—— (1958), *Dreams and the Uses of Regression*. New York: International Universities Press.

Linn, L. (1954), Color in dreams. *J. Amer. Psychoanal. Assn.*, 2:462–465.

Lipschutz, L.S. (1954), The written dream. *J. Amer. Psychoanal. Assn.*, 2:473–478.

Lipton, S. (1967), Later developments in Freud's technique. In: *Psychoanalytic Techniques*, ed. B. Wolman. New York: Basic Books, pp. 51–92.

Litman, R. E. (1980), The dream in the suicidal situation, In: *The Dream in Clinical Practice*, ed. J. M. Natterson. New York: Jason Aronson, pp. 283–299.

Little, R.B. (1971), A self-dissecting dream. *Internat. J. Psycho-Anal.*, 52:503.

Loomis, E.A., Jr. (1956), A rare detail in the dreams of two patients. *J. Amer. Psychoanal. Assn.*, 4:53–55.

Lorand, S. (1946), *Technique of Psychoanalytic Therapy*. New York: International Universities Press.

—— (1950), *Clinical Studies in Psychoanalysis*. New York: International Universities Press.

—— (1956), Panel report: The dream in the practice of psychoanalysis. Reported by L. Rangell. *J. Amer. Psychoanal. Assn.*, 4:122–137.

—— & Feldman, S. (1955), The symbolism of teeth in dreams. *Internat. J. Psycho-Anal.*, 36:145–161.

Mahler, M., Pine, F., & Bergman, A. (1975), *The Psychological Birth of the Human Infant: Symbiosis and Individuation*. New York: Basic Books.

Margolis, M., & Parker, P. (1972), The stork fable: Some psychodynamic considerations. *J. Amer. Psychoanal. Assn.*, 20:494–511.

Martin, J. (1982), The analyst in the dream: A reappraisal. *J. Advancement Psychoanal. Education*, 2:43–47.

Michaels, J.J. (1941), Parallels between persistent enuresis and delinquency. *Amer. J. Orthopsychiat.*, 11:260–274.

——— (1955), *Disorders of Character: Persistent Enuresis, Juvenile Delinquency and Psychopathic Personality*. Springfield, Ill.: Charles C Thomas.

Miller, J.B. (1969), Dreams during varying stages of depression. *Arch. Gen. Psychiat.*, 20:560–565.

Miller, M.L. (1948), Ego functioning in two types of dreams. *Psychoanal. Quart.*, 17:346–355.

Mintz, R.S. (1968), Psychotherapy of the suicidal patient. In: *Suicidal Behaviors*, ed. H. Resnik. Boston: Little, Brown, pp. 271–296.

Murphy, G. (1959), The dreamer. In: *Dreams and Personality Dynamics*, ed. M.F. DeMartino. Springfield, Ill.: Charles C Thomas.

Nagera, H. (1969), The imaginary companion: Its significance for ego development and conflict solution. *The Psychoanalytic Study of the Child*, 24:165–196. New York: International Universities Press.

Natterson, J.M., & Gordon, B. (1977), *The Sexual Dream*. New York: Crown.

Niederland, W.G. (1957), River symbolism. *Psychoanal. Quart.*, 25:469–504; 26:50–72.

Noble, D. (1951), The study of dreams in schizophrenia and allied states. *Amer. J. Psychiat.*, 107:612–616.

Nunberg, H. (1931), The synthetic function of the ego. *Internat. J. Psycho-Anal.*, 12:123–140.

——— (1932), *Principles of Psychoanalysis: Their Application to the Neuroses*, trans. M. Kahr & S. Kahr. New York: International Universities Press, 1955.

——— & Federn, E., eds. (1962–1974), *Minutes of the Vienna Psychoanalytic Society*, 4 vols. New York: International Universities Press.

Oremland, H.D. (1973), A specific dream during the termination phase of successful psychoanalysis. *J. Amer. Psychoanal. Assn.*, 21:285–302.

Bibliography

Palombo, S. R. (1978a), The adaptive function of dreams. *Psychoanalysis & Contemporary Thought*, 1:443–447.

——— (1978b), *Dreaming and Memory: A New Information Processing Model*. New York: Basic Books.

Pao, P. (1980), The dream in manic-depressive psychosis. In: *The Dream in Clinical Practice*, ed. J.M. Natterson. New York: Jason Aronson, pp. 111–130.

Plata-Mujica, C. (1976), Discussion of "The changing use of dreams in psychoanalytic practice." *Internat. J. Psycho-Anal.*, 57:335–341.

Pomer, S.L., & Shain, R.A. (1980), The dream in phobic states. In: *The Dream in Clinical Practice*, ed. J.M. Natterson. New York: Jason Aronson, pp. 177–191.

Pontalis, J.-B. (1974), Dream as an object. *Int. Rev. Psycho-Anal.*, 1:125–133.

Pulver, S.E. (1978), On dreams. *J. Amer. Psychoanal. Assn.*, 26:673–683.

Rangell, L. (1956), Reporter: Panel on "The dream in the practice of psychoanalysis." *J. Amer. Psychoanal. Assn.*, 4:122–137.

Rank, O. (1912), Die Symbolschichtung im Wecktraum und ihre Wiederkehr im mythischen Denken. *Jb. psychoan. psychopath. Forsch.* 4:51–115.

Raphling, D.L. (1970), Dreams and suicide attempts. *J. Nerv. Ment. Dis.*, 151(6):404–410.

Rappaport, E.A. (1959), The first dream in an erotized transference. *Internat. J. Psycho-Anal.*, 40:240–245.

Reik. T. (1949), *Listening with the Third Ear*. New York: Farrar, Straus.

Renik, O. (1981), Typical examination dreams, "superego dreams," and traumatic dreams. *Psychoanal. Quart.*, 50:159–189.

Renneker, R. (1952), Dream timing. *Psychoanal. Quart.*, 21:81–91.

Rhan, A. (1932), Erklarungsversuch des Zahnreitztraumes. *Internat. Z. arztliche Psychoanal.*, 18:19–20.

Richardson, G.A., & Moore, R.A. (1963), On the manifest dream in schizophrenia. *J. Amer. Psychoanal. Assn.*, 11:281–302.

Roland, A. (1971), The context and unique function of dreams in psychoanalytic therapy: Clinical approach. *Internat. J. Psycho-Anal.*, 52:431–439.

Rosenbaum, M. (1965), Dreams in which the analyst appears undisguised: A clinical and statistical study. *Internat. J. Psycho-Anal.*, 46:429–437.

Roth, N. (1958), Manifest dream content and acting out. *Psychoanal. Quart.*, 27:547–554.

Rothstein, A. (1978), Towards a place for 'the analyst undisguised' in the psychoanalytic theory of dream analysis. Presented at the midwinter meeting of the American Psychoanalytic Association. New York, December 14.

Rycroft, C. (1951), A contribution to the study of the dream screen. *Internat. J. Psycho-Anal.*, 32:178–184.

Sachs, H. (1914), Das Zimmer als Traumdarstellung des Weibes, *Internat. Z. Psychoanal.* 2:35–36.

Sackheim, G. (1974), Dream analysis and casework technique. *Clin. Soc. Work J.*, 2:29–35.

Saul, L.J. (1947), *Emotional Maturity: Development and Dynamics of Personality*. Philadelphia: Lippincott.

——— (1953), The ego in a dream. *Psychoanal. Quart.*, 22:257–258.

——— (1956), Panel on "The dream in the practice of psychoanalysis." *J. Amer. Psychoanal. Assn.*, 4:122–137.

——— (1958), *Technique and Practice of Psychoanalysis*. Philadelphia: Lippincott.

——— (1966), Embarrassment dreams of nakedness. *Internat. J. Psycho-Anal.*, 47:552–558.

——— (1967), Dream form and strength of impulse in dreams of falling and other dreams of descent. *Internat. J. Psycho-Anal.*, 48:281–287.

Savitt, R.A. (1969), Transference, somatization and symbiotic need. *J. Amer. Psychoanal. Assn.*, 17:1030–1054.

Schoenberger, S. (1939), A dream of Descartes: Reflections on the unconscious determinants of the sciences. *Internat. J. Psycho-Anal.*, 20:43–57.

Segal, H. (1977), The function of dreams. In: *The Work of Hanna Segal*. New York: Jason Aronson, 1981, pp. 89–97.

Seguin, C.A. (1981), *Introduction to Psychosomatic Medicine*. New York: International Universities Press.

Sheppard, E., & Saul, L.L. (1958), An approach to a systematic study of ego function. *Psychoanal. Quart.*, 27:237–245.

Sharpe, E.F. (1937), *Dream Analysis*. London: Hogarth Press, 1949.

Silber, A. (1973), Secondary revision, secondary elaboration and ego synthesis. *Internat. J. Psycho-Anal.*, 54:161–168.

Simenauer, E. (1978), A double helix: Some determinants of the self-perpetuation of Nazism. In: *The Psychoanalytic Study of the Child*. New Haven: Yale University Press, pp. 411–425.

Sloane, P. (1975), The significance of the manifest dream: Its use and misuse. *J. Phil. Assn. Psychoanal.*, 2:57–78.

——— (1979), *Psychoanalytic Understanding of the Dream*. New York: Jason Aronson.

Socarides. C.W. (1980), Perverse symptoms and the manifest dream of perversion. In: *The Dream in Clinical Practice*, ed. J.M. Natterson. New York: Jason Aronson, pp. 237–256.

Spanjaard, J. (1969), The manifest dream content and its significance for the interpretation of dreams. *Internat. J. Psycho-Anal.*, 50:221–235.

Sperling, M. (1958), Pavor nocturnus. *J. Amer. Psychoanal. Assn.*, 6:79–94.

Steiner, M. (1937), The dream symbolism of the analytic situation. *Internat. J. Psycho-Anal.*, 18:294–305.

Stekel, W. (1909), Beiträge zur Traumdeutung. *Jb. psychoanal. psychopath. Forsch.*, 1:458–512.

———— (1922), *Die Sprache des Traumes*. Munchen/Weisbaden: J.F. Bergmann.

———— (1943), *The Interpretation of Dreams: New Developments and Technique*, 2 vols. New York: Liveright.

Sterba, E. (1941), Homesickness and the mother's breast. *Psychiat. Quart.*, 14:701–708.

Sterba, R. (1928), An examination dream. *Internat. J. Psycho-Anal.*, 9:353–354.

———— (1940), Aggression and the rescue fantasy. *Psychoanal. Quart.*, 9:505–508.

———— (1946a), Report on some emotional reactions to President Roosevelt's death. *Psychoanal. Rev.*, 33:393–398.

———— (1946b), Dreams and acting out. *Psychoanal. Quart.*, 15:175–179.

———— (1950), On spiders, hanging and oral sadism. *American Imago*, 7:21–28.

Stern, A. (1915), Night terrors: Etiology and therapy. *N. Y. Med. J.*, 101:951–952.

Stewart, H. (1973), The experiencing of the dream and the transference. *Internat. J. Psycho-Anal.*, 54:345–347.

Stewart, W. (1967), Comments on the manifest content of certain types of unusual dreams. *Psychoanal. Quart.*, 36:329–341.

Stolorow, R. D. (1978), Themes in dreams: A brief contribution to therapeutic technique. *Internat. J. Psycho-Anal.*, 53:473–475.

Tarachow, S. (1963), *An Introduction to Psychotherapy*. New York: International Universities Press.

Tausk, V. (1913), A contribution to the psychology of child-sexuality. *Internat. J. Psycho-Anal.*, 5(1924): 343.

Thompson, V. (1932), Toothache and masturbation. *Internat. J. Psycho-Anal.*, 13:374.

Waelder, R. (1949), Panel on "Dream theory and interpretation." *Bull. Amer. Psychoanal. Assn.*, 5:36–40.

Waldhorn, H. (1967), Report on "The place of the dream in clinical psychoanalysis." In: *Kris Study Group Monogr. 2.* New York: International Universities Press, pp. 52–106.

────── (1971), Dreams, technique, and insight. In: *Currents in Psycho-Analysis,* ed. I. Marcus. New York: International Universities Press.

Warren, M. (1976), On suicide. *J. Amer. Psychoanal. Assn.,* 24:199–234.

Weigert, E. (1956), Panel on "The dream in the practice of psychoanalysis." *J. Amer. Psychoanal. Assn.,* 4:122–137.

Weiss, E. (1952), Introduction to P. Federn, *Ego Psychology and the Psychoses.* New York: Basic Books.

Whitman, R.M. (1963), Remembering and forgetting dreams in psychoanalysis. *J. Amer. Psychoanal. Assn.,* 11:752–774.

────── (1969), Dreams about the patient: An approach to the problem of countertransference. *J. Amer. Psychoanal. Assn.,* 17:702–727.

────── (1980), The dream in sexual dysfunction therapy. In: *The Dream in Clinical Practice,* ed. J.M. Natterson. New York: Jason Aronson, pp. 463–476.

────── Kramer, M., Ornstein, P. H., & Baldridge, B. J. (1967), The physiology, psychology and utilization of dreams. *Amer. J. Psychiat.,* 124(3):287–302.

────── ────── ────── ────── (1970), The varying uses of the dream in clinical psychiatry. In: *The Psychodynamic Implications of the Physiological Studies on Dreams,* ed. L. Madow & L.H. Snow. Springfield, Ill.: Charles C Thomas.

Winget, C., Kramer, M., & Whitman, R. (1972), Dreams and demography. *Can. Psychiat. Assn. J.,* 17(2):203–208.

Winnicott, D.W. (1971), Dreaming, fantasying and living. In: *Playing and Reality.* London: Tavistock.

Winterstein, A. (1954), A typical dream sensation and its meaning. *Internat. J. Psycho-Anal.,* 35:229–233.

Yazmajian, R.V. (1964), First dreams directly representing the analyst. *Psychoanal. Quart.,* 33:536–551.

────── (1968), Dreams completely in color, *J. Amer. Psychoanal. Assn.,* 16:32–47.

Zullinger, H. (1934), Prophetic dreams. *Internat. J. Psycho-Anal.,* 15:191–208.

AUTHOR INDEX

299

Author Index

SUBJECT INDEX

Subject Index

Characterological manifestations and associations to dream, 58-59

Childhood, representation of, in dreams, 167-169

Childhood games, symbolized in flying dreams, 249

Children, symbolized in dreams, 83, 84, 111, 112, 123, 259-260

Chimney sweep, symbolized in dreams, 120, 121

Chronological approach to beginning work with dreams, 5

Cinderella, 59

Clarity or sensory intensity of dream elements, 7-8, 189-191

Clever baby, dream of, 259-260

Cloaca theory, 102

Clothing as symbol in dreams, 93

Color in dreams, 43, 191-192

Comments and glosses on a dream, 200-213, 220, 241

Common element between two persons, representation of, 178

Companions in dreams, 154-155

Composite figures in dreams, 176-178

"Composition" and parallels represented in dreams, 173-180

Condensation in dreams, 186-188

Confirmatory or corroborative dreams, 269-273

Conflicts expressed in dreams, 55-56

Confusion, vagueness, vividness and lucidity in dreams, 3, 7-9, 180-181, 188-191, 214-215

Conjunctions (if, because, as, though, etc.) in dreams, 215-216

Content in dreams, representation of, 167-199

Contradiction in dreams, 50, 215

Control, instinctual, and dreams of falling, 251-254

Corroborative or confirmatory dreams, 269-273

Contraries and contrasts in dreams, 178-180

Countertransference, 2-3, 25, 28

Creativity and dream production, 29-30

Criminals in dreams, 80

Day residues in dreams, 9-11, 12-13, 54, 57
and dreams from above, 32,
and interpretation, 57-58

Dead person, alternately alive and dead in dreams, 238

Death in dreams,
fear of, 245
of persons of whom dreamer is fond, 232-236
symbols of, 50, 138, 139-143, 244, 245

Decapitation in dreams, 131

Deceased persons in dreams, 236-240

Decision to tell dream to therapist, 208

Defecation dreams, 124

Degraded figures in dreams, 80

Déjà Vu in dreams, 129-130, 203

"Dental stimulus" dreams, 116, 260-262

Diagnostic value of dreams, 43-45

Diffuse and voluminous dreams, 27-29, 214

Diminutives as symbols in dreams, 111

Dinner at Eight, 169

Directions in dreams, 184-186

Dirigibles as symbols in dreams, 92, 104, 253

Displaced persons, dreams of, 130

Displacement in dreams, 132, 133

Doubts and uncertainties about dream elements, 205-207

Dreams *from above* and dreams *from below*, 32

Dream within a dream, 222-225

Dreamer, symbolized, 83-84

Earl of Gloucester, 132

Early and initial dreams, 12, 36-47

Ego,
fragmentation and dreams, 43-44, 212-213
in dreams, 87, 150-156, 214-215
or self, pathological aspects of, 153-154
source of resistance in, 34
structure and voluminous dreams, 29

"Either-or" in dreams, 180-181

Elements of dream,
antithetical consideration of, 46-54
eliciting specific information about, 54, 55
specific considerations of, 3, 46-72
transformation of one into another, 220

Embarrassing dreams of being naked, 228-232

Emission dreams, 162-164, 219

Erection, symbolized in dreams, 91, 92, 249

Examination dreams, 240-244

Exhibition in dreams, 229-231

Fairy tales and dreams, 59

Falling dreams, 251-254

Subject Index

Familiarity, feeling of about dream element, 203

Family, symbolized in dreams, 79-84

Father, symbolized in dreams, 81-82

Fear of Flying, 250

Feces, symbolic equivalents of in dreams, 123, 124

Fee, representation of in dreams, 123, 149, 194

Female genitals, symbols of in dreams, 97-102
    external, 98-100
    internal, 100-102

Fire as symbol in dreams, 127-129 *See also* Urination

Flying dreams, 249-251

Form of a dream, 214-225

Fruit as symbol in dreams, 110-111

Gardens as symbols in dreams, 110

General considerations about dreams, 21-35

Ghosts in dreams, 80, 81

Gift, dream as a, 19, 123

Guilt and punishment in dreams, 262-263

Guilt feelings in dreams of death of persons of whom the dreamer is fond, 233-236

Hair as symbol in dreams, 130-131

Hat as symbol in dreams, 109

Hansel and Gretel, 255

Heights and dreams of falling, 251-254

Hindenberg, 253

Historical standpoint, consideration of dream elements from, 54-60, 217-219

Homosexual impulses in dreams, 50
    and reversal, 183

House or building in dreams,
    as symbol of body or person, 84-86, 130
    as symbol of marriage, 79

Human figure as a whole, symbols of in dream, 84-88, 112

Id, source of resistance in, 34

"Identification" and similarity represented in dreams, 171-173, 179-180

Illness, physical and dreams, 63-66

Inability to overtake someone in a dream, 263-264

Infection or infestation symbols in dreams, 133, 134

Inhibited movement, sensation of, in dreams, 164-166, 228-232

Initial and early dreams, 12, 36-47

Interpolated dream fragment, 220

Interruptions in therapy, dreams during, 31

Intrauterine life, birth and parturition in dreams, symbols of, 135-139

Inversion in dreams, 181-184
    temporal, 183-184

"It's only a dream," 208-210

Jonathan Livingston Seagull, 251

Journeys and trips as symbols of death in dreams, 139, 140, 244-247, 276-277

Judgments about a dream or part of it, 200, 208-210, 241

King Lear, 81, 132

Lactation, symbols of in dreams, 134-135

Landscapes as symbols in dreams, 98

Language, therapist's, in explanations, 27

Latent dream thoughts and associations, 3, 57, 58

Left and right in dreams, 185-186

Lengthy or voluminous dreams, 27-29, 214

Levels of interpretation of a dream, 1, 24-27

Locale or setting of a dream, 6-7

Localities represented in dreams, 174-175

Logical connections, representation of in dreams, 170, 215-216

Lucidity, vividness, vagueness and confusion in dreams, 3, 7-9, 180-181, 188-191, 214-215

Luggage as symbol in dream, 113

Machinery as symbol in dreams, 91

Male genitals,
    and psychic equivalents, 123
    symbols of in dreams, 89-97

Manner of speech and characterological attitude in dreams, 58-59

Marriage, symbols of in dreams, 78-79

Masturbation, symbols of in dreams, 113-116

Matura and examination dreams, 240-244

Means of representation in dreams, 144-166

Medusa's head as symbol in dreams, 98

Menstruation, symbols of in dreams, 103

Metaphors and symbols, 73, 76-78

Metathesis and antithesis, 46-53, 181

Mirror dreams, 153

Missing a train (boat, bus, etc.), dreams of, 244-247

Money, symbolic equivalents of in dreams, 123

Subject Index

Mother, symbolized in dreams, 79, 83
Movement, sensation of inhibited in dreams, 164-166
Multiple meanings of a dream, 24-27

Nakedness and embarrassment in dreams, 228-232
Narcissistic needs in perverse dreams, 268-269
Neurosis in dreams, 38, 152, 153, 212, 213, 218, 268, 269, 273-274
Night fantasies in dreams, 212
Number of dream fragments, 215
Numbers,
    and calculations in dreams, 149, 193-195
    and names as symbols in dreams, 99
Numerical repetition of object in dreams 170

Obscure sexual symbols in dreams, 107-113
Observation dreams, 256-260
Obsessional commands and speeches in dreams, 198-199
Oedipal dreams, 272
Oedipus Rex, 132
Omitted dream, or portion of dream added, 14-15
Opposites in dreams, 46-53, 181-183
Oral aggression in dreams, 44, 261

Pain and dreams, 64-66
Pairs and series of dreams, 218
Parallels, similarities and contrasts in dreams, 171-180
Parts of body as symbols in dream, 100
Parts of dreams, 13,
    relation of, 219-222
Parturition, birth and intrauterine life, symbols of in dreams, 135-139
Patients' sophistication about dreams, 4, 17, 76
Paucity of dreams, 30
    and characterological problems, 30
People and places in dreams, 67-68
Perseveration about a dream, 26-27
Persons as symbols in dreams, 95
Perverse dreams and "self-state" dreams, 268-269
Physical illness and dreams, 63-66
Pictorial representation in dreams, 66-72
Plants as symbols in dreams, 95
Plastic word representation in dreams, 68-72

Poisoning as symbol in dreams, 137
Polarities in dreams, 49
Pregnancy, symbols of in dreams, 133-134, 251
Pressure of resistance and dreams, 32-35
Preverbal fixation and acting out, 63
Primal scene content in dreams, 105, 106, 169, 256-260, 277
Primal words in dreams, 50-51
Prognostic value of dreams, 42-45
Psychic equivalents in the unconscious in dreams, 122-124
Psychosomatic disturbances and dreams, 64-66
Punishment dreams, 236, 262-263
Pursuit, dreams of, 248

Relatives as symbols in dreams, 111
Reality of dream images, belief in, 204-205
Reality situation and the dream, 22-23, 27, 34
Reconciliation dreams, 264-265
Recovery dreams, 273-274
Recurrent and traumatic dreams, 265-268
Repetition of account of dream as technique in beginning work on dream, 12-13
Repetition of an act in dreams, 170
Representation, means of, in dreams, 144-166
Reptiles and fish as symbols in dreams, 92
Rescue dreams, 137-138, 254-256
Resistance,
    pressure of, 32-35,
    sources of, 34,
    and transference manifestations in dreams, 7-8,
    to dream production, 23, 30
    to remembering dream, 208
Reversal in dreams, 46-53, 181-184,
    and homosexuality, 50
    and homosexual impulses, 183
Review dreams, 272
Right and left in dreams, 185, 186
Rooms in dreams, 101-102, 248
Royalty as symbol in dreams, 79-80

Scene of dream, 6, 7, 174-175, 220
    change of, 220
Scopophilia and exhibitionism in dreams, 49
Secondary elaboration in dreams, undoing, 4
Secret or secrecy in dreams, 47-48

Subject Index

Self or ego in dreams, 150-156
"Self-state" dreams, 268-269
Series of dreams, 31, 218
Sexual function in dreams, 97, 102, 162-164
Sexual intercourse, symbols of in dreams, 116-121
Sexual relations and primal scene observation represented in dreams, 256-260
Sexual symbols in dreams, 89-121
Shame in dreams, 228-232
Shoes and slippers as symbols in dreams, 109
Siblings, symbols of in dreams, 84
Similarities, parallels, and contrasts in dreams, 171-180
"Since-therefore" in dreams, 216-218
Single night, dreams during, 30-31
Sister, symbolized in dreams, 84
Size in dreams, 51-52, 53
Sleeping Beauty, 59
Snakes as symbols in dreams, 74, 92-93
Snow White and the Seven Dwarfs, 59
Sophistication about dreams, patients', 4, 17, 76
Spatial and temporal relations in dreams, 167-171
Special interest in dreams, dangers of, 23-24
Specific information about dream elements, 55
Specific use of dreams in therapy, 60
Speeches in dreams, 9, 195-199
Spiders as symbols in dreams, 125
Strangeness, feeling of, about dream element, 203
Strangers in dreams, 47-48, 229
Streetcar Named Desire, 146
Suicidal thoughts in dreams, 63, 141-143, 239
Super-ego,
  and punishment dreams, 262-263
  resistances from, 34
Swimming in dreams, 129
Symbolism and symbols in dreams,
  general discussion of, 73-78
  and typical dreams, 228
  miscellaneous symbols, 100, 122-143
  sexual symbols, 89-121
Symptoms and character traits in dreams, 38, 152, 153, 212-213, 218-220, 273-274

Tables in dreams, 87
Tape recording of dreams, 19, 20

Tears and urine as psychic equivalents in dreams, 122
Teeth in dreams, 116, 260-262
Temporal inversion in dreams, 183-184
Temporal and spatial relationship in dreams, 167-171
Termination dreams, 274-278
Therapeutic situation,
  and dreams, 212, 213
  represented in dreams, 147-149
Therapist,
  attention of, 2, 21
  in dreams, 11, 42-43, 144-145, 148-151
  interest in patient's dreams, 23-27
  own thoughts and associations to patient's dream, 2
  undisguised in dreams, 42-43
Therapy,
  interruption of, represented in dreams, 149-151
  representation of in dreams, 141, 145-148, 274-278
  sessions, previous, as day residues for dreams, 11, 12
Time and space in dreams, 170-171
Time of day in dreams, 169
Train, as switch word in dreams, 246-247
Transference,
  and repetition of account of dream, 13
  and therapist's suggestion about chronological approach to dealing with dream, 5, 6
  in dreams, 11
  in early dreams, 38-42
  resistance in initial dreams, 38-42
Transformation of one dream element into another in dreams, 220-221
Traumatic and recurrent dreams, 265-268
Travel dreams, 139, 140, 244-247, 267, 277
Treatment represented in dreams, 11-12, 22, 145-146
Treatment situation represented in dreams, 147-149
Typical dreams,
  with constant meaning, 226-247
  with a variety of meanings, 248-278

Uncertainty about dream element, 203
Unconscious, represented in dreams, 146-147
Underclothing as symbols in dreams, 107-109
Undisguised therapist in dreams, 42-43
Unsophisticated dreams, 36
Untranslatable dreams in an analysis, 17

305